WHORES

WHORES

An Oral Biography of
PERRY FARRELL
and **JANE'S ADDICTION**

Brendan Mullen

DA CAPO PRESS
A Member of the Perseus Books Group

Text design by Trish Wilkinson
Set in 11-point Berkeley by the Perseus Books Group

Library of Congress Cataloging-in-Publication Data
Mullen, Brendan.
    Whores : an oral biography of Perry Farrell and Jane's
Addiction / Brendan Mullen. — 1st Da Capo Press ed.
        p.   cm.
    Includes index.
    ISBN 0-306-81347-5 (hardcover : alk. paper)
    1. Jane's Addiction (Musical group)—Interviews. 2. Farrell,
Perry—Interviews. 3. Rock musicians—United States—Interviews.
I. Title.
ML421.J38M85 2005
781.66'092'2—dc22
                2005001582

First Da Capo Press edition 2005

Published by Da Capo Press
A Member of the Perseus Books Group
http://www.dacapopress.com

Da Capo Press books are available at special discounts for bulk purchases in the U.S. by corporations, institutions, and other organizations. For more information, please contact the Special Markets Department at the Perseus Books Group, 11 Cambridge Center, Cambridge, MA 02142, or call (800) 255-1514 or (617) 252-5298, or email special.markets@perseusbooks.com.

1 2 3 4 5 6 7 8 9—09 08 07 06 05

This book is dedicated to Perry Farrell, Eric Avery, Dave Navarro, and Stephen Perkins—with props to the late Chris Brinkman, Matt Chaikin, Ed from the Lovedogs, and everyone else who helped get the ball rolling.

I have nothing to add or subtract from any conclusions the reader may draw on hard narcotic usage as a lifestyle. . . . This book is for rock 'n' roll fans wherever ye may be.

Brendan Mullen
2005

INTRODUCTION

I first recall seeing Perry Farrell while he was carting his Echoplex box into the Anti-Club on eastern Melrose Avenue in Los Angeles late one afternoon around 1984 or '85, and watching him from the back of the empty room set up with one mic. He turned the delay and echo effects up to 11, outer-space deep dub stylee, somewhere between Prince Far-I and Robert Plant during the screamo orgasmic percussion break-down of Led Zep's "Whole Lotta Love." I cannot for the life of me remember what I was doing in the Anti-Club at that time of the day. Maybe the bar was open. Probably. Whatever. The scene now dissolves in my mind. However, this guy was such a striking figure that I remembered him clearly when he next popped up in my life.

At that time I was a booker-schmooker at the Club Lingerie in Holly-wood and the Variety Arts Center in downtown L.A.—as well as a small-concerts promoter, a free-drinks art slut, and an all-around voyeur-louche-participant. Eventually, I met Perry when I booked both bands he fronted—first Psi Com and then Jane's Addiction—into the Lingerie and the VAC. He was also a frequent guest at the home of a mutual friend, the late concert promoter Rick Van Santen, who invited business associates over to watch ball games and boxing matches. I found Perry to be an amusing and agreeable character, a strange metro cockatoo with a bizarre style and a superb eye for detail, notably for lighting and staging, as well as the flyers he designed himself, many of which are included in this book.

I hadn't thought much about Jane's since they broke up in 1992, al-though I'd become a major Porno for Pyros fan after the *Good God's Urge* album. But when Marc Spitz (my collaborator on *We Got the Neu-tron Bomb: The Untold Story of L.A. Punk*) called me in early 2003 after Jane's reunited—with a new bass player—to do an oral history on the band for *Spin* where he's a senior staffer and columnist, I couldn't re-sist delving headlong into the surreal, hair-twirling, tragi-comedy of Jane's Addiction.

The article made the cover in August 2003, after extensive interviews with all the band members, their families, friends, lovers, business associates, musical peers, promoters, journalists, and so forth. I was told that, at sixteen pages, it was the longest feature in the history of the magazine. It was the first and probably the last time I'll ever be told by editors not to worry about going over the word count—just keep it coming. I think it wound up about 10,000 words over the original assignment.

And that, I thought, was the end of Jane's for me. I was trying hard to land a book deal (for a novel—I was ready for a change after *Lexicon Devil*, an oral history of the Germs published in 2002) when I unexpectedly got an offer, not for the newest book proposal I was attempting to hawk, but to expand the article. The idea of documenting Jane's as well as the great "post-punk" arts and music renaissance of late '80s/early '90s L.A. proved too seductive to pass up.

However, as these things sometimes happen, the band, led by Perry, decided not to do any more interviews, a fortuitous decision as it turned out that ultimately gave the story a greater scope and depth. It forced me to dig deeper and to talk to more people than I might otherwise have done had the band dished the full story themselves. Because let's face it, we're all the heroes of our own narratives; it's the people around us who offer perspective. Or many different perspectives, those shifting nuances that create a more complex portrait.

I'd like to thank the following people, without whom this book would never have been completed: Marc Spitz, Jud Laghi of ICM Talent (for the vision and the kick-ass proposal), Kateri Butler (for keeping me alive and focussed), and Ben and Bella Vendetta (my secret assets for transcriptions). I owe eternal gratitude to my editors at Da Capo Press, Ben Schafer (for clarity and guidance), Erin Sprague (for putting up with me and the quirky monster an oral history can be), and Norman MacAfee (for making me comply with all those pesky copyediting rules). I'd also like to toast Trish Wilkinson for the design. And shout-outs to Eduardo Salamon, Tulsa Kinney, Mitch Handsone, Shelley Leopold, and Ryan Ward for their assistance in getting the photos scanned.

Finally, thanks to the photographers/artists whose compelling images make this book a striking visual record: Lynda Burdick, Karyn Cantor, Edward Colver, Fin Costello, Chris Cuffaro, John Eder, Heide Foley, David Hermon, Jerry Jung, Bruce Kalberg, Ian Tilton, and Valerie (whose last name we don't know—wherever you are, we tried to locate you).

Above all, to the musicians for creating the sounds and the legacy—especially Perry Farrell for giving so much of himself to his art, thanks for the inspiration; may you continue to make great music.

CAST OF CHARACTERS

Agent Ava: founder of Demolisten, a key college radio show at KXLU.

"Tupelo Joe" Altruda: musician, co-founder of Tupelo Chainsex, among the first local L.A. musicians Perry Farrell hung out with.

Jeff Ament: bassist for Pearl Jam, Mother Love Bone, Green River. Seattle rock icon.

Daniel Ash: musician-songwriter, member of Bauhaus, Love & Rockets, Tones on Tail; gigged locally, recorded and toured—both as a band and as individual session musicians—with Jane's and Porno for Pyros.

Ian Astbury: singer, the Cult, the Doors 21, founder-conceptualist of Gathering of the Tribes, the precursor to Lollapalooza.

Tom Atencio: manager New Order. Former manager of Jane's Addiction.

Eric Avery: bassist, songwriter, co-founder of Jane's Addiction. Wrote/co-wrote the most memorable songs.

Rebecca Avery: sister of Eric, girlfriend of Stephen, who hooks Navarro and Perkins up with Farrell and Avery to form Jane's Addiction.

Jane Bainter: former housemate of PF. She is the lyrical muse of the band's name and its most riveting song, "Jane Says."

Steven Baker: former Warner Bros. Records executive.

Xiola Blue: deceased, a member of the Love Troika, which included PF and Casey Niccoli depicted on *Ritual de lo Habitual* album cover artwork.

Carla Bozulich: musician, songwriter. Introduced PF to Eric Avery.

Jennifer Brannon: girlfriend of Xiola Blue.

Joseph Brooks: DJ/promoter of the Veil, the Fetish Club, TVC15, Cherry. Original co-owner Vinyl Fetish. Cathouse DJ.

Charley Brown: Jane's first manager. Co-founder Triple X Records, founder Triple X Management. Realtor. Agent.

Karyn Cantor: photographer, dancer, jeweler. Best early photography.

Chris Chaney: session bassist, member of Jane's Addiction, Panic Channel.

Chris Cornell: vocalist Soundgarden, Audioslave. Another Seattle rock icon gives props to pioneering Jane's.

Chris Cuffaro: photographer. Documented many Jane's tours.

Jonathan Dayton: filmmaker, video producer. Worked on *Gift* with Perry and Casey.

Alan di Perna: journalist who interviewed Navarro numerous times.

Peter di Stefano: musician-songwriter, member Porno for Pyros, surfing bud of Eric and P.

Willie Dread (aka Willie McNeil): musician, former roommate. Member of Tupelo Chainsex, among the first local L.A. musicians PF hung out with.

John Eder: photographer for Porno for Pyros, shot cover of *Good God's Urge*.

Bob Ezrin: rock producer from the '70s (Alice Cooper, Lou Reed, Pink Floyd, Peter Gabriel), tracks and mixes the 2003 reunion album *Strays*.

Valerie Faris: filmmaker, video producer. Worked on *Gift* with Perry and Casey.

Perry Farrell (PF): leader, lyricist, songwriter, co-founder of Jane's Addiction, Lollapalooza, Porno for Pyros. Aka DJ Peretz.

Kurt Fisher: owner, Club Lingerie, Razzberries.

Norwood Fisher: musician, member of Fishbone who occasionally recorded as individual session musicians and gigged with Jane's as a band. Card-carrying member of the mythical Best of the West Club.

Flea: Red Hot Chili Peppers bassist. Pal. Hires Navarro as the Peppers' guitarist to cover for John Frusciante to take four or five years off. Filled in for Avery on a reunion tour after failing to talk him into rejoining.

Bob Forrest: songwriter, leader Thelonious Monster. Peer. Played early shows together.

Modi Frank: Filmmaker. Directed Mountain Song and Live at John Anson Ford Theater. Taught P and C filmmaking basics.

John Frusciante: lead guitarist-songwriter-arranger for the Red Hot Chili Peppers. Disciple of PF.

Ted Gardner: Jane's Addiction tour manager, band manager, a co-founder of Lollapalooza.

Pleasant Gehman: West Coast punk legend. Author, poet, editor. Her band Screamin' Sirens played at one of Jane's first gigs.

Marc Geiger: William Morris booking agent; conceptualized and co-founded Lollapalooza with PF.

Rhian Ghittins: Navarro's ex-wife. PA to aristo-rockers.

Dayle Gloria: DJ, club booker-promoter. Scream booker during its heyday.

Kevin Haskins: musician-songwriter, member of Bauhaus, Love & Rockets.

David J: musician-songwriter, member of Bauhaus, Love & Rockets.

Dave Jerden: producer of Jane's two studio albums for Warner Bros.

Texacala Jones: lead vocalist, Tex & the Horseheads, legendary 80s goth-a-billy punk band.

Donusha Kibby: Walt's wife. Dancer for Jane's seven-night run at John Anson Ford Theater.

Walt Kibby, Jr.: former member Fishbone.

Anthony Kiedis: Singer, Red Hot Chili Peppers.

Martyn Le Noble: former bassist Thelonious Monster, Porno for Pyros, Jane's (post-Avery), The Cult, and others.

Mariska Leyssius: former keyboardist with Psi Com, P's first original club band. Organizer with Stuart Swezey of the Desolation Center shows in the Mojave Desert (beyond L.A. County). Video producer, filmmaker.

Inger Lorre: leader of Nymphs, a mid-80s glam-punk outfit; og riot grrl, predating the Washington shriek-babe scene, who inadvertently became a feminist icon for jumping on a big-time record exec's desk and urinating all over it and him after he'd allegedly made repeated unwanted sexual advances.

Dennis Martino: bar manager, Club Lingerie.

Patrick Mata: musician-songwriter. L.A. goth icon. Former leader of Kommunity FK. PF's first inspiration when he arrives in L.A.

Angelo Moore: musician, singer, dancer, poet. Member of Fishbone and the Best of the West Club.

Keith Morris: former singer with Black Flag and the Circle Jerks. A&R rep, V–2 Records.

Bob Moss: performance artist, mime, comic actor, friend of Jane Bainter.

Dan Navarro: first cousin of Dave. Early inspiration. Musician, songwriter (Lowen & Navarro).

Dave Navarro: guitarist with Jane's Addiction. Later plays with Red Hot Chili Peppers.

Johnny Navarro: first cousin of Dave's, journalist, ad copy writer.

Dean Naleway: partners in Triple X Records. Helped finance the classic *Live at the Roxy* record.

Casey Niccoli: PF's girlfriend, collaborator, filmmaker.

Erica Paige: well-known doorperson at numerous underground clubs, including Scream. Now a TV producer.

Matt Paladino: musician, software writer. Former neighbor of the Navarro family in Bel-Air.

Stephen Perkins: drummer, percussionist. High school bud of Navarro. Member of Dizastre, a pre-Jane's metal band with Navarro.

Bryan Rabin: club promoter, party planner.

Twiggy Ramirez: bassist for A Perfect Circle and Marilyn Manson. Friend of Dave's.

Lee Ranaldo: musician, Sonic Youth member.

Heidi Richman: designer, promoter/marketer.

Josh Richman: club promoter, party planner, amusing hypeman/raconteur.

Henry Rollins: former singer with SOA, Black Flag. Leader Rollins Band. Actor, publisher, author. Toured with Jane's during Lolla '91.

Adam Schneider: former manager Jane's Addiction; former agent Jane's Addiction, Porno for Pyros. Producer Lollapalooza.

Jon Sidel: co-promoter of Power Tools. Major player in L.A.'s proto-rave downtown dance club scene. Director, West Coast A&R, V–2 Records.

Slash: musician, member of Guns N' Roses, Slash's Snakepit, Velvet Revolver.

Mike Stewart: DJ, club owner, original promoter of Scream.

Stuart Swezey: promoter of the proto-rave "Desert Shows" with Meat Puppets, Psi Com, Redd Kross, and Sonic Youth. Lived with PF in the house with Jane Bainter, Karyn Cantor, etc.

Paul V.: former promotions person at Warner Bros. Records, former co-manager, Porno for Pyros; DJ, club promoter.

Allan Wachs: producer of *Gift*.

Don Waller: veteran rock journalist.

Brian Warner: former rock writer becomes showman known as Marilyn Manson.

Mike Watt: former member of Minutemen, firehose. Toured and recorded with Porno for Pyros while Martyn Le Noble recovering.

Pete Weiss: member of Thelonious Monster, chartered "Best of the West" band.

Michael Zimmerman: musician. Former high school mate of Navarro.

Eric Zumbrunnen: editor of *Gift*.

"I'm a pretty good-looking fellow. Verily, I end up fucking a lot."

"If anybody wants to talk trash about me, I'll guarantee it's probably seventy percent true."

"What's up, sluts? I like your drinkin' and your attitude . . . "

"Jane's Addiction was definitely degraded. . . . Oh man, we were definitely wasted and deluded."

"I wanna fuckin' take my clothes off!!"

"Name something degrading and I've done it . . . "

"I'm bored shitless! I want something weird to happen!"

"Sometimes I want to be serious, sometimes an idiot."

            🌺 PERRY FARRELL

"HAD A DAD" (1959–76)

PERRY FARRELL (né BERNSTEIN, co-founder, leader of Jane's Addiction, Porno for Pyros, Lollapalooza): I was a Queens kid. I lived in Flushing for a few years, then moved to Woodmere, Long Island. But in the 70s and 80s everybody thought Miami was the spot and *Scarface* was reigning. So my family moved down there when I was about 15—ninth grade—the first year I ever gotten head—and got into a better life. We had a lake in our backyard and a little sailboat. It was fun, swimming and surfing. (I had older brothers and sisters, and the best times I remember are when they'd crank up the radio or play records out on the balcony where we lived in Queens. I'd hang out with them, and I could dance pretty good. In high school [in Florida], I was into David Bowie and Lou Reed, but I didn't know they were punk rock. It wasn't labeled yet, but these guys were fucking out there. When I got to California, I saw it firsthand. Pretty awesome.)[1]

JANE BAINTER (former housemate of Perry Farrell, the lyrical muse of the band's name and the song "Jane Says"): Perry's dad, Al Bernstein, was a jeweler, a goldsmith from New York City. The Bernsteins were the type of New York Jews who moved to Florida. His sister wore white-fringe leather jackets.

PERRY FARRELL: My dad was a real character, a fun guy. Sharp, with a ton of style. Cared about his hair. Always had a Corvette.

STUART SWEZEY (promoter, film producer, book publisher): I'd heard his dad was some Jewish mobster guy, so I asked Perry about it. He told me stories, like *Sopranos, Goodfellas* stuff. Some guy would be found in a trunk with his dick cut off, stuffed in his mouth. I couldn't tell you if he was pulling my leg or not.

PERRY FARRELL: Celebrities and regular people gravitated toward him. The wise guys knew my dad, too. Everybody knew Al Bernstein. He was one of those guys walking around Miami Beach in the 70s with a Fila headband and a bikini bathing suit with gold around his neck. You didn't want to get in a car with him because he would hit ninety if he didn't see a car in front of him.

CASEY NICCOLI (former girlfriend, creative collaborator, stylist for Jane's Addiction, co-director of Soul Kiss and Gift): Perry's mother committed suicide when he was a young boy. I met Al Bernstein when he was a little more mellowed-out. Family legend has it that he was pretty hardcore in his youth. Perry blamed him for his mother's death. Al was bringing a lot of women into the house and doing drugs and stuff when he was younger.

PERRY FARRELL: I was a rebellious kid who just didn't like what I saw.

CASEY NICCOLI: The Al I met was an old man who was very sweet.

PERRY FARRELL: My father was an old 47th Street kind of jeweler. I got a lot of creativity from him. He was a hardworking designer and repairman who'd cut you a good deal, the kind whose thumb is jet black with hundreds of saw marks, who'd come home with his nostrils black from sucking up buffing and polishing rouge all day. We didn't go to Temple that much. But my father sent me to Hebrew school so that I could sing before the congregation.[2] Every weekend we'd go in from Queens. He'd grab me by the hand and drag me through these people up the street and on the subways. I would be the salesman. All the Yentas thought I was adorable. He'd put me up on a tall chair with a little display box. They'd say, "Can I see this ring over there?" And I'd pull the rings out. My mother was a fine artist. She loved to take throwaway things and make art out of them, or refinish them.

I barely made it out of high school. Surfing was very high on the totem pole, more important to me than school. Surfing just became *it*. You didn't have to pay a lot of money—you could buy a second-hand surfboard and just go. But the thing I appreciate most was that it balanced me out as a human being.[3] I just wanted to get out of there. I was seventeen. What did I have to lose? My surfing buddy [the late] Jimmy Mulali was this big Samoan dude who also played football and was living in San Jacinto about six hours from the beach. He told me if I wanted to come out to California he was on the coast. I looked at a map of California and San Jacinto looked like it was very close to the beach, but actually it was like a six-hour drive down to Tressels which is the first place I surfed out West. I just jumped on a bus and took off. I started my affair with California in a Greyhound bus station with all my belongings—a surfboard, some art supplies, an ounce of weed, one phone number—and no place to go. The first place I lived was the Californian high desert, a place called Hemet. And I lived there for about a year or so working construction. I was a rough carpenter. Then I moved down to the beach and I was going to school. I did everything from driving trucks and I was a liquor deliveryman. I was a graphic artist. I designed jewelry. But I also waited tables, bussed tables, washed dishes . . . you name it, just to keep going . . .

"UP THE BEACH" (1976–83)

PERRY FARRELL: I was living in my car in Newport Beach, an old, red Buick Regal big enough for two people to live in. If you park down by the beach, you can always shower or go surfing in the morning to stay clean. And you get yourself a banana or an orange for breakfast. You keep your clothes in the trunk folded neatly so you've always got nice clean threads to go looking for work in. I was a dishwasher and a bus-boy for about a year, moved up to waiter. I was living at the beach for six or seven years before I got in my first band, Psi Com.

CASEY NICCOLI: Perry's family weren't poor by far. They had a nice house and stuff. But his father did not give him money or support him when he moved to L.A.

PERRY FARRELL: Two years later [circa '78] my father found out where I was in California. Time makes things soften up—water under the bridge—and you feel like you want to talk to your family again. I was cleaning myself up. I was thinking my dad is going to get me off the street. And he did help me. He called a friend who had a liquor distri-bution company. He says it's a good business. Says it's got a good fu-ture. Eventually I could be a district manager or something like that. But it was one of those asshole schmooze jobs where you're going to have to wear a tie and shake somebody's hand and ask them, "Hey, how about putting the Midori ad up front by the cash register this month?"

For like three weeks or a month I worked for my dad's buddy. I went to these condos that have brooks running through them and maybe some ducks and tennis courts and a pool. I thought, "Man I want to live in one of these . . ." I'm a crafty guy. When you're left to your own de-vices you've got to figure out how to move ahead into better situations in life. Everybody was dancing and modeling down there [in Newport Beach]. Their aspirations were to be a bigger model, a bigger dancer, a bigger actor, a bigger actress, right? One day I was making a drop at one of those swanky Newport places—this private club—when this lady asked me, "Do you model?" And I said, "Oh yeah, I'm a model. I'm an actor. I'm a singer. I'm a dancer. Sure." So she said, "Do you want to au-dition for our Friday night show?' I went in there and said, "Look, I'll help you organize your show." Within a few weeks I was impersonating people like Bowie and Jagger.

CASEY NICCOLI: He'd do Sinatra for them, too. Perry loved Frank Sinatra.

PERRY FARRELL: I thought, "Man, I've got a great future." When I did these impersonations I got a reaction. People wanted to sit me down for a drink. Girls wanted to get their picture taken with me. I had made my beginning in show business. I had never thought I was going to be a musician. I didn't start singing until I was twenty-one. Now I wanted to really practice because I could tell innately that I could sing. I quit my job and my girlfriend started selling bud. I put fliers up in the laundry areas of these fancy condos and this divorcée guy let me move in. Two weeks later I moved my girlfriend in. It quickly became a nightmare. We'd have these battles and be breaking things so this guy booted us and so I was living in my car with her in Newport. There was no real income and we had no backup plan other than, "Let's head to L.A. . . . there's gotta be some work up there." Sometimes we'd all go up to the Odyssey disco [West Hollywood], and get up on the risers, to try and take the place over. We were just dancing like maniacs and goofballs, taking our shirts off and swinging them around. These talent agents would chat us up. One weekend one of them said, "Look, I need a roommate. Come up here for good and I'll get you into show business. I'll get you on a soap and we'll move from there." So this guy took me in. That's when I moved from the beach to the city.

PF IS TAKEN BY THE HOLLYWOOD GOTH SCENE (1983–85)

PERRY FARRELL: When I reached L.A., I started hanging out with the underground, subversive people that worked at the trendy clothing stores, and the best up-and-coming bands, like X, the Minutemen, Black Flag, Saccharine Trust, Savage Republic, Redd Kross, even the Bangs who became the Bangles, and the Go-Gos. The English stuff from Factory and 4AD was coming at us—the Cocteau Twins—and it was very anti-rock 'n' roll: you don't do anything similar to the Old Wave.[4] I became a waiter at Oscar's Restaurant at the base of Laurel Canyon [Boulevard] and Sunset. I'd drive my motorcycle up into the Canyon. I had a place in the basement with no windows. I saved up my money and got myself a P.A.

WILLIE DREAD (aka WILLIE McNEIL, musician, co-founder Tupelo Chainsex, Jump with Joey): I did my first gig with Tupelo Chainsex in September '82. We used to headline the Lingerie. That was a big deal at the time. We also played the Sunday Club at the Cathay de Grande [restaurant], the Music Machine, Al's Bar, the Anti-Club, the O.N. Klub, Blackie's, the Lhasa . . . anywhere we could get in . . .

PERRY FARRELL: I started hanging out with Willie Dread and Tupelo Joe. They were outsiders. People who were having fun. Every night they're going to the smallest, darkest little club to see germinating music. They're going out Monday. They're going out Tuesday. I'm tired, but they're still going out Wednesday. Those guys became my initial circle and introduction to many of the local musicians.

WILLIE McNEIL: I was playing in two bands, Tupelo Chainsex and Animal Dance, and working part-time at Flip [iconic used clothing emporium on Melrose Avenue]. Perry used to just come along to our shows to hang out.

PERRY FARRELL: The kids in the city were trying to come up with new things. Punk rock had given them new fuel to be different. You had new indie labels [SST, Dischord, Alternative Tentacles, TwinTone, Subpop, Epitaph, Touch & Go] hatching all around the country. Suddenly college radio mattered to the record industry. R.E.M. helped to propel the notion of indie rock across the country. Los Angeles was just a great place to germinate as a musician at that particular moment in time.

L.A. PUNK IDEOLOGY (VERY FAR FROM DEAD IN THE 80S)

"TUPELO JOE" ALTRUDA (musician, co-founder, Tupelo Chainsex, Jump with Joey): The local club scene was very thriving. It was the 70s' punk dream come alive: anything goes, just be yourself. It was a really good time for live music. The entire scene evolved around it. Every club had at least three or four cool bands a night, unlike these posey little DJ cigarette lounges of today. We were always looking for a party or a gig or any other reason to throw down. Every night there would be like a phone call, "Hey, what's goin' on tonight?"

WALT KIBBY, JR. (musician, vocalist, Fishbone): As far as clubs go, if you compared the club scene now to the club scene then, then it was a party which started with the bands and the people that hung out with them before they even got to the club, and then it just continued on in the band room . . . and then it finished up on the stage, a special show

for everybody, for the other people they brought in from the street.
Now it's all business.

NORWOOD FISHER (musician, vocalist, Fishbone): Everybody was up to
the same shit all the time. We were all looking for the same thing. Trying to end up at the Zero Zero after the Lingerie and the other regular
clubs closed. Always trying to end up at the same places . . . Disgraceland; The Rhythm Lounge when Matt Dike was DJ'ing, the same spot
where the Chili Peppers got started. Go see Psi Com at the Anti-Club,
Tex and the Horseheads at the Cathay de Grande. The Untouchables
and the Skanksters at The O.N. Klub with the Box Boys and the Baby-
lon Warriors. . . .

WALT KIBBY, JR.: All the bands were like real raw at the beginning.
There weren't many real slick performers. The more punk rock that
you would appear, the better off you were for that scene at that time.

WILLIE McNEIL: I was living in a house with a bunch of young party
people off Melrose sometime around '82–'83 near the Grandia Room,
where the Rhythm Lounge was held. . . . Matt Dike DJ'd there on
Thursdays. So this girl moved out who was a hairstylist known for doing crazy haircuts and dye jobs. Perry was a friend of hers who took
over her room. We each paid like $180. When Perry first moved in he
worked at Oscar's [now the Union]. Oscar's was a too hip English
restaurant/bar at the time. Perry was a waiter there. He always paid his
rent on time, which made him very cool in a sharing situation like ours.

JOEY ALTRUDA: Tupelo Chainsex was a mad, free-for-all thing. We did a
spin-off jam session downstairs at the Cathay de Grande called the
Slap and Rampant Trio. It was like me and Willie, Limey Dave and Flea
and Anthony. I played upright bass, Flea played electric. Just one of
these throw-together things for laughs and free beer. Upstairs you had
Modi or Bob Forrest DJ'ing Grandmaster Flash. Somehow it all went
together. . . .

WILLIE McNEIL: Eventually Perry jammed with us a few times on tim-
bales. Once he came out onstage with us in a pink Mohawk [*sic*] with
pink and black checked mod pants and a sleeveless greaser T-shirt
with Beatle boots on. We were total shameless "Melrose People" back
then. Melrose Flip where I worked had all kinds of looks. People

would just cut and paste their own crazy patchwork image. Perry definitely needed to stand out, to be noticed. . . .

PATRICK MATA (musician, songwriter, Kommunity FK): Thrift-shop scavenging had become an artform and Melrose Avenue was getting famous over the world as this Holy Mecca for freaky-deaky postmodern fashion . . . anything went, any era, all styles, all deliberately crossed and mismatched. . . .

HEIDI RICHMAN (designer/promoter): Fiorucci in Beverly Hills, where Patrick worked, predated Flip [first mega thrift store on Melrose Avenue] in the way all the coolest musicians and artsy folk worked there. Patrick Mata was like one of their star employees, their in-house master of style. . . .

PERRY FARRELL: I thought Kommunity FK's lead singer, Patrick Mata, was the most beautiful, coolest-looking, most talented musician I saw when I first came to the city.

Patrick Mata, "the coolest, most beautiful musician in L.A. . . ." (David Hermon)

PATRICK MATA: I'm astonished and flattered to hear this . . . all these years later. . . . He never said anything to me at the time. . . . I can't think of a time when either of us were properly introduced. . . .

HEIDI RICHMAN: Patrick had the voice of an angel. No matter how extreme his music was or the other dissonance going on, here would rise this vocal that was amazing.

WILLIE McNEIL: From '81 to '85, if you showed up at Lingerie, or some cool club, there's a good chance that if you were in one of the bands, some guy would come backstage and say, "Wanna do a bump of coke?" Kind of like a musician's perk. I remember wild parties at Disgraceland [notorious crash pad/party house] and at Limey Dave's house, where people would be lining up for hours to go to the bathroom. There was nearly always piles of coke on the table. We all used to do mushrooms, Perry too. Of course we also smoked weed, dropped acid once in awhile. It was still fashionable to do blow in the mid-80s. It hadn't got to crack yet. Just snorting. We were all doing a fair amount.

JOEY ALTRUDA: But it wasn't like we were doing anything more than anyone else.

WILLIE McNEIL: I had gotten all this weird face paint because it was around Halloween. One morning I got up and saw Perry had been up all night on acid or speed, or whatever . . . painting his face in the mirror! It was fantastic looking! He was just gazing at his face in the mirror without moving for hours on end. His face was all these crazy colors, all blotched and dripping down. It made me laugh so hard, even though I was a little pissed he'd used up all the paint I was planning for my Halloween drag. . . .

PERRY FARRELL: I badly wanted to get into a band because I wanted to have fun. The Paisley Underground scene was happening, so I'd see lots of ads for psychedelic bands: "Must like The Blues Magoos." I was in a Paisley Underground band for a minute. I got a Paisley shirt and combed my hair down into bangs, and then I thought, "Shit, this is pretty short-sighted." Then I'd see other ads in (local classifieds paper) *The Recycler.* Looking for a singer. Influences: Siouxsie and the Banshees. Joy Division. Bauhaus. Psychedelic Furs. The Cure.

PATRICK MATA: There was no term goth yet. When KFK opened for Killing Joke, [*L.A. Times* reviewer] Terry Atkinson called us "gloom and doom" because the songs were like really slow deliberately, but we also had some angry, superfast punk songs because it was fitting for what I was saying in the lyrics. One of the angry songs was "Fuck the Community" which means fuck the community before it fucks you.

PERRY FARRELL: Bands like Kommunity FK were doing great on the local "death rock" scene.

JOSEPH BROOKS (promoter-DJ, co-founder of Vinyl Fetish, the Veil): Before the Veil was even over [April '81–August '83] the scene was already beginning to morph into this death rock club. It wasn't called goth yet.

PATRICK MATA: The Veil started the "Blitz Kids" West Coast in Los Angeles . . . [iconic early 80s predominantly gay club kids from London who regularly adorned *The Face*, a now-defunct internationally influential music and style magazine] . . . although Henry [Peck] and Joseph [Brooks] added their own spice to the Blitz playlist. The biggest highlight of that scene was when Steve Strange showed up at Club Lingerie in an Edwardian era horse-drawn carriage on one of the Veil theme nights [sometime in early '81]. Even when the Veil was in full flight, Kommunity FK were NEVER "New Romantic." Please. I've always been into fashion and my own way of looking. I wasn't copping anybody's look, but I will say I was inspired by the energy and the attitude of the original Blitz kids to step out all dolled up. . . .

PERRY FARRELL: I had the same admiration for Rozz Williams from the original Christian Death as I did for Patrick. Rozz was an amazing performer. He was so twisted that it was compelling. But I didn't want to be like him because Rozz was so effeminate and I'm the kind of doof who can tumble down the stairs and have a laugh about it . . . and I wasn't past a good dive off the stage. Rozz had style, but it was all so delicate, so precious. I thought he's that way because he wasn't accepted in high school. And now look what he's made himself into, a for-real death rock icon. I don't want to say that hanging yourself is stylish, but in his case. . . .

The late Rozz Williams, dear to the goth crowd. (Edward Colver)

Psi Com live at Club Lingerie,
circa 1984. (David Hermon)

Perry Farrell already dancing
to a different drummer.
(David Hermon)

HOOKING UP WITH PSI COM

"Psi Com [is] a new combo that label makers will file under post-punk or neo-psychedelic, but for now, let's just say they are one of the most promising new modern music combos in town. . . ."

L.A. WEEKLY, NOVEMBER 1983

STUART SWEZEY: Mariska [Leyssius] and Rich [Robinson] were two artist friends who had this band Psi Com which had a bit of a gloomy goth vibe to it. They found Perry through the local classified paper, *The Recycler,* and he became their lead singer.

PERRY FARRELL: They were in a band prior to that called After Image that played at the Anti-Club and the Theoretical parties put on by Jim Van Tyne and Jack Marquette. I was so impressed by how the Psi Com people were living out their creative life. They loved music.

They loved art. They put their own band together. They put their own press together, their own artwork, their own flyers.

JOSEPH BROOKS: Mariska [Leyssius] had this magazine *Contagion*, which we carried at the [Vinyl Fetish] record store. She played keyboards in Psi Com and we carried that record, too. She'd bring copies herself. That's how we knew Perry. Perry would also come around. We immediately noticed that he had great clothing sense, as much as the musicality; we liked his look.

PERRY FARRELL: When I started out [as a singer] nobody liked me. They thought I was too flipped out. In fact, Psi Com almost didn't pick me up because at the first rehearsal I just started jumping around. They would look at one another like, this guy is fucking nuts! It's not like I'd never sung before and just got up there. I'd been practicing in my room with headphones for four years while looking for a band that I could relate to, with people that I thought were great people.[5]

MARISKA LEYSSIUS (musician, member of Psi Com, promoter, film-maker): My then-husband Rich and I had, like, 3,000 albums. We'd just sit around and play music all day. We turned him on to Joy Division. . . .

PERRY FARRELL: The music of Joy Division hit me. The story behind it was so compelling. I only found out about them after Ian Curtis died. This fellow was so saddened by love. His heart was broken. I couldn't stop playing the music. Stuart [Swezey] started a business contracting work for commercial art companies. I was in the dark room developing images and listening to Joy Division and KXLU all day. I began doing my own artwork-flyers for my shows. Eventually he fired me after he figured out why no work was getting done.

JOSH RICHMAN (club promoter, character actor): Psi Com performed at the Lhasa Club, the Lingerie, and Al's Bar; they were like an art rock band who used to open up for Kommunity FK. . . .

PERRY FARRELL: Rich was a great commercial artist . . . Mariska, too. How good you did with your artwork really mattered. You could get people to come if you had some really funny or bizarre twisted flyer. Everybody was into making 8 × 10's. You'd Xerox them at Kinko's and hand them out in front of the Lingerie when people were leaving.

PATRICK MATA: KFK and Psi Com played on the same bill at the Lingerie one night, probably around '84. At soundcheck I was very wary of him because he was dressed down, very down, and then he pulls out a Gucci wallet! I remember thinking that's not very alternative, punk, or post-punk, whatever you want to call it. When you grow up with nothing that

14

"How good you did with your flyer artwork really mattered." Psi Com flyers designed by Perry Farrell.

PSI COM WITH SHADOW MINSTRELS & EYES OF MIND WEDNESDAY FEBRUARY 29 FM STATION 11700 VICTORY (AT LANKERSHIM) NORTH HOLLYWOOD

PSI COM

WITH

THE WEB
DIE
SCHLAFLOSEN

FRIDAY
APRIL 13

ON KLUB

10 PM

反者道之動弱者道之用
天下萬物生於有有生於無

THURSDAY
JULY 5th
LINGERIE

PSI ◆ COM

WITH
TEST
DEPT.

kind of thing rubs against you. I'd never be seen dead with a Gucci wallet! I was quite shy. Maybe he was, too. We never approached each other.

HEIDI RICHMAN: Psi Com gigs were small with ten to fifteen people there to see them. Mostly the same fifteen people.

PERRY FARRELL: Psi Com opened for Southern Death Cult [who eventually shortened their name, first to Death Cult and finally to The Cult) when Ian Astbury was still wearing that Indian hat with the feather in it. We opened up for Sex Gang Children, Gene Loves Jezebel . . . all these glammy, goth-type bands from across the pond who came out about the same time as the "positive punk" movement from London; but it was the goth scene that moved in and took over L.A.

PATRICK MATA: This audience had no use for the rockabilly and American roots music revival led by the Blasters, Top Jimmy and X . . . that was a whole other branch of the old '77 punk scene . . . although Tex was kinda goth-looking and her band was sorta like Gun Club goth-a-billy. . . .

NORWOOD FISHER: We [Fishbone] were big Psi Com fans. We just loved watching Perry's kooky stage moves. We first saw them play in front of this hot dog stand near Hollywood Boulevard, and that's where we first met Perry. After that we'd go see him all the time. He was real entertaining to watch. We loved him. We just thought Perry was the shit.

ANGELO MOORE (lead vocalist, horn player, Fishbone): They were playin' in this parking lot, right? They had the drums, bass and guitars, maybe keyboards, and a little PA and everything. My boys thought they were real cool. It was like rock/new wave, like Bauhaus type of shit.

WALT KIBBY, JR.: Psi Com was real artsy, but it was still a rockin' band. Perry was so funny when he opened his mouth, a real strange lookin' cat. You could see him slowly becoming a great frontman. . . .

MIKE WATT (musician, co-founder, the Minutemen): Psi Com was on the scene probably at the end days of the Minutemen, around '85, playing the same circuit, Lingerie, Al's Bar, Anti-Club, Lhasa, and stuff. We played with them on top of a hot dog stand or something. It was like synthesizer music. It wasn't like Jane's Addiction.

Texacala Jones, singer with Tex & the Horseheads.
(Edward Colver)

PERRY FARRELL: Tex and the Horseheads would be on the same bill
with Psi Com at the Lingerie. Or Kommunity FK. We're bottom of the
bill, but I can't wait to see the Minutemen at the top. None of our
bands look or sound anything like each other. This Mohican punker
dude's walking by with this whacked-out rockabilly cat from the Zero
Zero Club with his hair slicked back in a duck's ass; Mike Martt [guitar
player-songwriter for the Horseheads] is coming over to have a beer
with us and the Chili Peppers, too; they're crazy, they've got coffee
mugs on their shoulders like epaulets . . . and there's a Fishbone or two

. . . oh, hi . . . there's Mr. Thelonious Monster himself, Bob Forrest . . . and we're all having fun.

TEXACALA JONES (lead vocalist, songwriter, Tex & the Horseheads): There'd be like rockabilly acts with the punk acts and the psychedelic bands, the goth bands and there was the ska mod groups out of the O.N. Klub; they just kind of all mingled . . . at the Underwear is what we called the Lingerie. I started there as a waitress before I got in a band. Connie Clark did like really neat rockabilly hairdos and she was part of the original punker community.

WALT KIBBY, JR.: [There was] a goth scene, hip-hop, a reggae, ska scene. It had a little of everything, a punk-rock scene, rockabilly. It was just full of everything and it was all good. One time Fishbone, the Dickies, Run-DMC, and Social Distortion, I think it was, played on the same bill at the Stardust Ballroom and there was somebody else, too. Like Cathedral of Tears, this gothic group with the TSOL guy. Back then you could mix it up like that.

PERRY FARRELL: There were a lot of different niches to fit into. You weren't just cornered into being a hair band. The Chili Peppers had a funk angle on their thing, Psi Com had an art angle on our thing. . . .

WALT KIBBY, JR.: There was a lot more unity in the fact that everybody was trying to do something artistic and different. Today's mentality, that don't work.

PATRICK MATA: I liked the sound of Psi Com. Perry was singing very differently back then. Not as high in the registers. And, like us, the music was very tribal.

ANGELO MOORE: Time for props, man. Perry became a great showman.

"Psi Com . . . are quickly becoming one of the best of the young, post-punk new music bands in L.A., possibly because this rhythmically propulsive combo is more concerned with music than fashion."

L.A. WEEKLY, APRIL 1984

AGENT AVA (aka SOLANA REHNE, college radio pioneer, radio DJ): There was a riot at the L.A. Street Scene [September 27, 1985]. Legal Weapon and Fear had played and there was tear gas . . . me and my pal Buzz were running for our lives from these out-of-control mounted cops. We were trying to find our friends in the chaos when suddenly the smoke cleared and there was the lead singer from Psi Com sitting coolly on a curb in a purple suit with a yellow hat holding an ornate cane with these elegant white silk gloves, like this trippy clockwork statue in white pancake. He stood up and said, "Agent Ava, I have a brand new recording, would you please, please play it on Demolisten?" I held onto that tape through thick and thin for the rest of the ordeal of getting away from the riot. Later when I listened I thought, "This is amazing." It was Psi Com. I called Perry immediately and said, "I have a bulletin board at the station, when and where are you guys going to be playing next?"

PERRY FARRELL: The cool thing about KXLU's Demolisten show was if you were a local band you could just call in, request your song and if you went down there, they would interview you. Was the world smaller then?

AGENT AVA: I was out in the clubs every night before I even started working at KXLU (Loyola Marymount University, Los Angeles). That's how I first started developing the Demolisten show. There were so many great bands without record deals. People would give me tapes and I would mark up songs I thought would do well. Those I wanted to put into rotation I would cart up on the old eight-track and give to the music director who would add the songs for the week. Record company people would call and want details on the bands. Bands were getting signed off the show.

PETE WEISS (member, Thelonious Monster): Whatever was on KXLU, back in those days that was the big time—if you got played on KXLU woo-hoo! KROQ was out to lunch, completely out of touch with the ground. Had been for years, but if you got played on KXLU that was the shit. . . .

AGENT AVA: Demolisten featured songs that would play throughout the weekdays for the sake of people who maybe didn't tune into my show on Sunday nights because I only had an hour, 6:00–7:00. It was the only way for unsigned bands, or any kind of new band, to get any exposure.

PERRY FARRELL: I'd be listening to KLXU all day long because that's where all the good music was. The rest of the world was out of it. This was before KROQ really went into the alternative.

PAUL V. (promoter, DJ): There really was a true meaning to the term "alternative" at first before it degenerated into a bad joke. It was just a sound and a style that was not being played on commercial FM radio. It was an alternative to the mainstream.

AGENT AVA: The term "alternative" really came from FM radio in the 70s, I believe. It was an alternative to Top 40 rock 'n' roll. The songs were much longer so they called it alternative rock because there was more to it; a little more creativity, the songs were longer, and that basically was what FM rock radio focused on. My old KXLU shirt from '82 says, "The only rock really left . . . alternative radio."

CHARLEY BROWN (first manager, Jane's Addiction): They had college markets in the early 80s and they called it "college music," but it wasn't termed alternative yet. Jane's broke the ground on all of that in L.A.

PAUL V.: It used to be called "album rock" . . . or "album-oriented rock." The FM stations that were progressive played album rock in the 70s rather than focusing exclusively on singles and playing that one song to death. The DJ could say, "Here's the new whatever record . . ." and say, "I like the tracks X, Y, and Z" . . . and just like pick out personal favorites. That just doesn't happen anymore. Somehow this term "alternative" got rediscovered and heisted by college radio people during the 80s who applied it to new post-punk, indie, or underground-whatever music. . . .

BECOMING AN OVERNIGHT *SCRATCH* CELEB

TEXACALA JONES: Everybody was Goth, rockabilly, or doing the Johnny Thunders-Pistols-Hanoi Rocks revival. . . . Fishbone was going the same way, but with ska in their mix. All of those old *Scratch* magazines are full of it.

SCRATCH
MAGAZINE

Vol. 10
Aug. 25, 1983.

DAVE NAVARRO: The scene [covered by *Scratch* magazine] was exciting and decadent, it was also a little dangerous. We didn't get like A-list Hollywood celebrities back then. We got like C-list. When someone like Angelyne came to a club she was the big name. Everybody else was a local band or a band that was touring through, not like today where Christina Aguilera is gonna walk in. C-list celebs became the really exciting ones. Like if Gene Hackman or Jack Nicholson was there I wouldn't care, but if Tex [of Tex & the Horseheads] walked in I'd be very excited. It was great. Celebrities your parents had never heard of. (Designed by Donna Bates)

JOEY ALTRUDA: *Scratch* magazine documented that period really well.

PERRY FARRELL: Ruben Blue did *Scratch* magazine, which became the *Rock City News*, which is still around today. Here was another person showing up at Kinko's, writing about his friends and taking their picture . . . and publishing this weekly 'zine. . . .

JOSH RICHMAN: Ruben documented the explosion of Faster Pussycat and Guns N' Roses at the Cathouse . . . he also covered Matt Dike and the artsy downtown dance club scene at Power Tools where Jane's played.

PERRY FARRELL: Ruben had this perennial smile and a cheap camera, and you waited and hoped that he'd come up and say, "Can I take your picture?" Then you'd make it into *Scratch*. He could make you an overnight celebrity. Heck, yeah!

RUBEN BLUE (founder-proprietor *Scratch* fanzine, *Rock City News*): *Scratch* started ['83–'85] as a reaction against in-crowd snobbishness at the *L.A. Weekly*. I thought there was a whole bunch of other interesting people and bands doing great things, but they were getting ignored in the *Weekly*'s La Di Dah column because Craig Lee and his circle didn't consider them cool enough. *Scratch* was never trying to be cool. Everybody is a star was my basic thing; that meant anybody bold and loud enough to add to what was going on with the after-hours clubs and parties, creatively . . . just swelling the numbers of new local celebs was enough for *Scratch*.

TEXACALA JONES: Sometimes Ruben would let me go around with him to different places. When I think about Hollywood at that time, even though it's like Hollywood and it's a world-famous place, really, to me it was just like this teensy-weensy village where this little Xerox fanzine came out every week, always about these same people. Who the hell would care about these gnarly ole critters 'cept for us? The La Dee Dah column in the *L.A. Weekly*. Same thing. It was all about the same people who hung out together, which wouldn't have mattered to anyone if they hadn't been written up all the time. It was like our little scene but I guess it looked so attractive to some folks, and then everybody tried to get in on it.

BRIT-GOTH TAKES OVER L.A.

BOB FORREST (leader, singer-songwriter, Thelonious Monster): [By '84–'85] most of the cool bands from the original goth era had broken up or morphed into pop groups—Joy Division had become New Order and Bauhaus became Love & Rockets.

JOSEPH BROOKS: Precursor goth bands like the Banshees and the Damned were still around but they were more identified as old-school punk at the time and the Cure was becoming like a KROQ pop band. The original goth scene kicked in here locally [from around '83 to '86], but it was so unlike the dumbed-down farce today's goth dance clubs have become—where you'll see people from the outer burbs traipsing around in *pirate* outfits. Nowadays goth clubs have become scary Halloween office and frat parties! Poor Rozz Williams would turn over in his sepulchre. . . .

BOB FORREST: All these second-generation bands—Sisters of Mercy, Specimen, Southern Death Cult, Flesh for Lulu—started playing around. I found out later that those bands were only popular in Los Angeles! They'd play L.A. and cause a big stir, but then they went home to play small pubs and bars.

KEVIN HASKINS (musician, Bauhaus, Love & Rockets, Tones on Tail): Bauhaus was told by the British rock press that we were "goth." We never coined the term or particularly tried to align ourselves with it. We were just amused at first. We thought, "Hmmm . . . so *that's* what we are!"

DAVID J (musician, Bauhaus, Love & Rockets): Why did Los Angeles become probably the biggest goth market in the world? It's something that's bred in dark, dank corners. You don't have as many of these in L.A. and the whole look of it and the tone of it is something that is otherly, there's always a big appeal in that. There's a romantic element to it in its pull to California.

DANIEL ASH (musician, Bauhaus, Love & Rockets, Tones on Tail): It was very grey in the U.K. in those times, mid-70s to mid-80s. It was a grey, grey time, especially where we came from . . . Northampton . . . It must

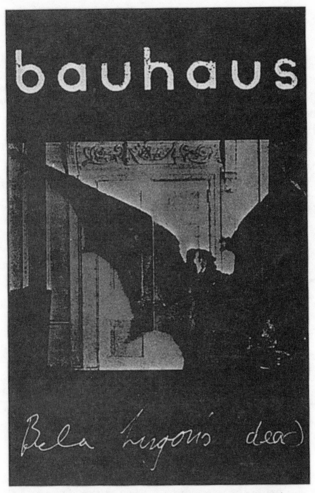

Bauhaus takes L.A. after dark. (Designer unknown)

have something to do with the extreme contrast of where we came from and the Los Angeles environment of sunshine and the beaches. . . .

DAVID J: It's coming from somewhere strange, not a sunny place in the same way that prior to punk, California was very appealing to English kids because it was so exotic, so different.

DANIEL ASH: We just thought of ourselves as a new English rock band. The only radio show you'd hear "Bela Lugosi's Dead" on in the U.K. would be the John Peel Show. It was a cult hit, a real underground thing.

Bauhaus was one of the most musically adventurous post-punk English bands of the 80s whose influence and inspiration on the U.S. "alternative" scene is largely unsung. (Fin Costello, courtesy David J. collection)

DAVID J: In England, Bauhaus were initially known as "post-punk" and then it became "goth" later on. When we became Love & Rockets, the record label marketed us in the United States as "alternative." So was Peter's [Peter Murphy] solo career.

KEVIN HASKINS: We arrived at the Tropicana Motel—it's been pulled down now—during the first Bauhaus tour of the U.S.—and this coked-up metal band was having a wild do with Kiss music blasting out across the courtyard. I can still picture us as these four skinny, pasty English guys all in black who'd never even been to California before, just looking in amazement with our bags still in our hands, at these topless blond girls with perfect tans prancing around all these guys with shaggy hairdos jumping off the balcony into the pool. It was like a bad Motley Crue video . . . come to think of it now, it probably *was* Motley Crue!

JANE BAINTER: In the L.A. goth scene we wore the white pancake and the black lipstick for a reason. We were fighting so many things that it was almost like we were already dead. We were seen as the walking dead, we were perceived as something that was not a vital part of society. We were fighting the police state, fighting the establishment, fighting creepy frat-boy rock, fighting any kind of repressive social behavior. We were young and willing to fight those battles to be creative.

PERRY FARRELL: There's a goth link for sure. I liked the style and the music of goth right away. These [goth] kids were rejects. They were people who had been discarded by society, discarded by their family or their school. Any sort of social structure they just sort of threw their hands up, ran away. They were castigated because they were odd or awkward. And those were the people that I wanted to hang out with and sing for.

THE WILTON HOUSE

STUART SWEZEY: Perry was getting a group of people together to take over this older building on Wilton. It was going to be this whole arts collective thing.

A typical unplugged campfire singalong jam at the Wilton House, something that developed into one of the audience-interaction highlights of the Jane's Addiction live show even after they graduated from the Scream to big-league rock stages. Pre-show backstage acoustic jamming also became a staple of touring. (Karyn Cantor)

PERRY FARRELL: I found this place that has come to be known as the Wilton House. I told the landlords—these twin motorcycle cops—that I would love to put curtains here, do the walls a certain color. I got them to believe I was this quiet, shy, gay interior decorator who'd be no trouble. They ended up getting twelve musicians, photographers, artists, their girlfriends, dogs, snakes, loud music, and round-the-clock junkie shenanigans. Cops were crawling around band rehearsals all the time.

STUART SWEZEY: Perry would spend Sunday nights talking to his dad, pacing around while he was on the phone. He'd get really upset that the old man was putting so much pressure on him to succeed. Afterwards he'd say, "My dad doesn't understand what I'm trying to do, man. He says stuff to me like, 'You gotta be a singer like Manilow, Perry. Manilow don't answer to *nobody!*'"

JANE BAINTER, FIRST LADY OF THE WILTON HOUSE

Circa January 1985

JANE BAINTER: "Jane Says" was written while I was there.

KARYN CANTOR (Jane's first official photographer): One of our roommates was Jane Bainter who'd come out of some big Ivy League school [Smith], who had a really bad drug problem.

JANE BAINTER: I put feelers out and I heard about this room for rent in this huge house on Wilton. It was at 369 N. Wilton, between Melrose and Beverly. I called up and talked to Perry and he said, "Yeah, c'mon over." I took over Stuart Swezey's room, who was promoting bizarre industrial shows in the desert.

STUART SWEZEY: Before Jane moved in, one of Perry's house rules was no girls and no junkies.

JANE BAINTER: It was a gorgeous old house, a Craftsman built in the 20s with wide halls and other nice touches. The landlords were these

Jane Bainter finds the wig in time for this shoot.
(Karyn Cantor)

cops and we were all really paranoid to deal with them since it was still quite bad between cops and punks at that time. But Perry was like, "I'll deal with them."

PERRY FARRELL: Around the clock you've got bongos and your bass set up and your guitar in your living room and you're trying to sleep even though the people downstairs are having a jam because they're all coked out. That was L.A. for me.

JANE BAINTER: When I moved into Perry's house, Carla Bozulich had moved in with D. D. Troit a few blocks away. We were within walking distance and we were still hanging out quite a bit.

CARLA BOZULICH (musician, songwriter, solo artist, member Deathride 69, Ethyl Meatplow, Geraldine Fibbers): Jane and I were very close companions who liked to dress up in funny clothes and do drugs.

HEIDI RICHMAN: I went to many of the parties on Wilton. Sometimes it was very mellow, other times it was drug-filled craziness. People would come and go. Depending on where they were in their cycle of things, you could have a great time or you could be walking into a bunch of zombied people, all of them jonesing.

DANUSHA KIBBY (former dancer with Jane's Addiction): The house was never locked. I don't think I used my key once. It was like a party house and everyone's bedroom was like their individual apartment.

STUART SWEZEY: Perry was very kind of hippie during the Psi Com days at the Wilton House . . . but I don't remember him smoking pot or heroin, or crack cocaine. Or getting high in any way. That all seemed to come later. . . .

Connoisseur of the senses Perry smells the flowers at the Wilton House. (Karyn Cantor)

DANUSHA KIBBY: Perry really liked the idea of the Talking Heads and the way David Byrne had just taken his friends and created this whole kind of art band, this whole scene around them. He would talk about how he wanted to be kind of like David Byrne and make us all famous, too.

JANE BAINTER: There were two rooms available and, coincidentally, the other person moving in at the same time as me happened to be Chris Pederson [the original *Suburbia* movie kid from the Penelope Spheeris film of 1983] who I'd hung around with in Europe, but now we were at odds over drugs. I'd done my first drugs in London with Rude Boy Ray, the roadie guy in the Clash movie, when Chris was my traveling companion and he'd been dead against it. When we saw each other again a year later we were still at odds. Chris was very against drugs. He's like, "I'm not gonna live upstairs around Perry Farrell because I hear he does drugs." And I was like, "OK, I'll live up there. No problem."

KARYN CANTOR: We were constantly doing things like making films or doing photography. We were always trying to think of creative things to do.

DANUSHA KIBBY: We loved to stage our own little performances and make home movies for fun and love of art. Sometimes on a Sunday we would dive around L.A. with a video camera and make movies of Perry and Casey and me and Karyn doing crazy things.

KARYN CANTOR: I was really into making Super–8 films, and so I shot this movie, a mock wedding of Perry and Casey whose mom had just gotten remarried at this house for real, so there was all this leftover stuff. Her mom and her new dad took off for their honeymoon the same night as the wedding. Kelly and Karyn and Danusha came up and kinda took over the house. There were presents all over the place, and the tree outside had strings attached with little hearts.

DANUSHA KIBBY: There was leftover wedding cake and food and we all took acid and went inner tubing down the Kern River. We got back from that and went to Casey's mom's house where we made a video of Casey and Perry getting married in their underwear.

DESOLATION CENTER:
Psi Com Opens a Proto-Burning Man Desert Rave

Circa January 1985

Flyer for the Desolation
Center show.
(Bruce Licher)

STUART SWEZEY: I was putting on the Desolation Center shows . . .
which mixed live music and installations, like around '83–'85. The first
one was the Minutemen and Savage Republic. Mariska and I were also
organizing these events where we took people out in buses to the
desert to see experimental bands. Mariska was always great with these
absurd projects. Extreme industrial performers like Boyd Rice would
play and Mark Pauline [Survival Research Laboratories] would blow
things up. He'd detonate stacks of old refrigerators and stoves in the
middle of the desert.

LEE RANALDO (member, Sonic Youth): They put those shows together really well. You had to get directions out there and they didn't release the map until the day. We played one of them out in the Mojave Desert. Psi Com opened. It was one of Sonic Youth's very first Los Angeles area shows. A very trippy night, that's for sure. We hung out with Perry that week, Perry and all his pet snakes and tarantulas.[6]

AGENT AVA: We drove all over the backwoods of L.A. getting one ticket to get directions to get another ticket to get another map and so on. We drove this old '55 Chevy, some cool old hoodlum ride, cruising the desert looking for these old cafes to get maps, meeting characters left and right. Eventually, we scored the final map and made it to the jamboree.

PERRY FARRELL: Stuart and Ken Swezey and Mariska would put together these gigs mixing local SST bands like the Minutemen with bands on Bruce Licher's label [Independent Project Records] like Savage Republic. . . . They also hooked up with touring out-of-state bands like the Meat Puppets and Sonic Youth. They'd go out to the desert or take a boat trip around San Pedro Harbor. I was a volunteer ticket taker. People would bus out to see Mark Pauline blowing metal things up in the middle of the desert at sundown while this crazy German band [Einzurstende Neubaten] would be hammering away on concrete-splitting pneumatic drills.

STUART SWEZEY: Perry begged me to open one of the Desolation shows, and I was like, I don't need another band. And he was like, "We're just going to do this quick tribal drum thing, on and off, it's gonna be really cool." And I was like . . . oh, OK, sounds kinda fun, but when the time came it was basically all Perry . . . with guitars, and he was like a total stage hog, and a lot of people loved it, but a lot of people didn't because it caused everything to run late. Perry was saying, "I'm going to do my rock star thing, and I'm going to do it for an hour and you're going to have to drag me off."

AGENT AVA: Out in the middle of the desert, the freaks came out at night for mostly SST bands. The flyer was printed on cardboard. Psi Com, Redd Kross, the Meat Puppets, and The Minutemen. The sun started to set. It was so very beautiful. Redd Kross drove up covered with boa feathers in this battered old funky '50s convertible with fins. They were sitting up on the back dash with the lights on and everything, completely ripping people's peace, shredding our desert serenity. I remember thinking, "This is gonna be wild!" All of a sudden Psi Com took the stage and it was dark, no stage lighting yet. The moon and the stars were out. Perry looked gorgeous, like this slowly pirouetting reptile with a Pinocchio face, he was like a clockwork clown, a wind-up doll from a Fellini movie. . . .

PERRY FARRELL: We had a very fun, demented, and youthful view of how to put these shows on. That's where I cut my teeth watching how these guys did it. All sheer high-energy excitement from day to day waking up and it was your own campaign. We didn't expect to be signed by anybody. The closest prayer we had was Slash [Records].

ENTER: CASEY NICCOLI

CASEY NICCOLI: The first time I saw Perry was at a Psi Com show, and I immediately had this attraction. I said to my friend, "I want to have his babies." A year later, I had broken up with my boyfriend, and I heard through some mutual friends that he was attracted to me, too.

So I went to a Psi Com show and handed him a little note that said, "Instant Mashed Potatoes" and that was it. We started dating.

PERRY FARRELL: I thought Casey was a stunner the first time I saw her. She was like a punk Elizabeth Taylor. She stopped the show. She wore dresses and heels. Her hair was all chopped and dyed black. She was managing Rik L. Rik and going out with the drummer from Lions and Ghosts. I'm not a guy who steals girls, so I would look at her from afar and think, "Gosh, what a lovely girl." [Eventually] she sought me out and told me she was moving out and breaking off with this fellow and needed a place to live.

CASEY NICCOLI: I was born and raised in Bakersville. When I was sixteen, I traveled to the Whisky to see the Ramones. I [was] very much into the Hollywood punk-rock scene before I met Perry. I loved Iggy Pop, X, the Ramones, and a lot of bands that Perry had never really been into. He'd never heard T. Rex . . . or Iggy . . . all these bands that eventually became his biggest influences. I was a geek and the punkers at my first Ramones show made fun of my dress. Then I went to an X show and some punk-rock girls tried to beat me up in the bathroom.

After that, I very quickly wore bondage pants and totally dressed the part. I ended up moving to L.A. during '79, when I was eighteen.

CARLA BOZULICH: Perry got really into Iggy and the Stooges around this time. . . .

CASEY NICCOLI: Perry was living in the Wilton House the first night that I went out with him. We hung out there. I didn't move in right away. It took him a year to tell me he loved me. Sometimes I wouldn't talk to him for weeks. He would get involved in doing his music or whatever. He used to get up early in the morning and call all over the place to track the radio airplay of Psi Com.

✦

PERRY FARRELL: There were always a lot of people hanging out at the Wilton House. They'd come over looking for some fun, or to try and hook up. If someone was playing that night, that's where we were all going to go.

KARYN CANTOR: I had a darkroom there and a photography studio, and there were always people around. It felt maybe haunted, but it felt safe. It was a great house; huge, but very run-down. You could go up on the roof. The rent was inexpensive, $200 or less, for huge rooms. It was pretty dirty and messy, like the kitchen was just disgusting.

CASEY NICCOLI: Karyn used to make short films like *Rex Appeal* . . . a movie about what you could use a big tub of lard for. Me and Perry were in that. And then she made *Bakersfield Wedding,* which was filmed at my mom's house, outside, in the backyard.

JANE BAINTER: Perry and I became close because we had our little paradise upstairs. Our rooms were adjoining with a connecting porch.
We could go onto the roof. We had a really big space. It was organized. It was creative. It was clean. Perry's totally tidy. We had a nicer environment to talk in.

KARYN CANTOR: Once more women moved in we tried to get it more like a home. We arranged cleaning schedules and it gradually became a much nicer place. People were parking cars on the lawn, it was all dirt, and so we ended up planting grass. There was a nice garden in the back.

"The Bakersfield Wedding."
(Karyn Cantor)

DANUSHA KIBBY: It was a pigsty even when the girls were living there. Perry and Casey would cook once in a while but like the kitchen was definitely not one of those places where you would want to cook. It was more take-out containers everywhere.

JANE BAINTER: There were like seven guys living there at first. I was the first girl. There was this little pink room down by the kitchen and the guys were all like, "Well, Jane should have the pink room because she's a girl." We had three big rooms upstairs with like our own bathroom, and it was the other five or six guys downstairs. . . .

ON DRUGS

KARYN CANTOR: Drugs were recreational. It wasn't a big problem, it wasn't like, intervention time. It was not a household of people running around shooting heroin all day by any means. People did have jobs.

JANE BAINTER: At one point Casey was working in a medical clinic and supporting them while Perry was free to pursue his creative interest. . . .

STUART SWEZEY: Perry was a hardworking guy who always had different day jobs. My brother had this soda business and Perry was doing deliveries for him in Santa Monica.

JANE BAINTER: I got a job at a management consulting company in Century City. I was wearing these blue suits with white shirts and pumps and stockings although I didn't even have a car. Perry drove by Century City when he went to his day job as a typesetter-lithographer in Culver City, so he'd drop me off at work and it was just this real duality—the all-American girl showing up to work in the job that everybody wants, but she's an after-hours drug addict at home.

KARYN CANTOR: Perry's job was working on the band and he was very focused on that. Had he been a major drug addict, especially at that time, there's no way he could have gotten to the point that he did. He made this thing happen, it was not an overnight success story. It was a lot of work, and I saw him doing that work.

CARLA BOZULICH: Perry wasn't addicted to drugs—he seemed to still have so much spirit, whereas most of the people that I knew had slipped so far into addiction and being jaded that they had no enthusiasm, even for playing music.

KARYN CANTOR: I don't think Perry was doing [that many] drugs, really, at that time. It was Jane. The other people that lived there weren't necessarily involved in drugs either, and they just wanted to get rid of her because they felt that it was a problem, sort of like an intervention. It was very unfortunate for Jane that they pushed her out because she did have a very serious drug problem.

DANUSHA KIBBY: I didn't feel as if I didn't belong or fit in because I wasn't using heroin. There were people that were and people that weren't. There was a house across the street and there was another band that lived there. They came over a lot and they were all addicts. I remember Perry not liking those people very much.

JANE BAINTER: I lived there about a year and I ended up kicked out of the house, voted out because it was run by community and we had these house meetings . . . like that weird reality TV thing. It was three to four, with Perry on my side. Perry was very open and fair, but they were including Chris and some others from downstairs that voted me out. What sucked was the people that they let in after were much worse junkies than I ever was.

KARYN CANTOR: Perry was really upset because he didn't want her to leave. She and Perry were really close friends and he was the only one defending her. Jane was their scapegoat. It was like "As soon as we get rid of this Jane problem all our problems are gone. It's Jane's *problem*, it's all because of Jane's *addiction*. . . ." Perry said, "We all have one, you know, we all have an addiction, but we all sort of say, well it's her problem or it's his problem, but it's really all of us, we've all got one."

PERRY FARRELL: Jane is a very beautiful woman. She could also be called "Plain Jane"—thick glasses, very outcast, very insecure, a lot like us. I look at her like a tragic figure. She's a Smith graduate, she's extremely intelligent, which is very unappealing to most men. She still hasn't found love, pretty much like us. Every time I see Jane she's always hopeful that something great is about to happen. "I'm gonna kick tomorrow." Every time I see her, I just wanna cry. She'd give you her last apple if it was in her lunch sack, but no one appreciates her and she can't quite get herself together. Jane lives slightly out of linear time. She can talk to you and she can see you, but she's always slightly somewhere else. Maybe everybody feels like that and that's probably why people can relate to that song.[7]

DEAN NALEWAY (Triple X Records): Money was really tight. Everyone was broke. One of Perry's pet peeves was somebody stealing his food out of the refrigerator. They all had food stashed in separate compartments of the fridge. One time Perry was so pissed about it that he took this package of string cheese and he jacked off on to it and then closed the package back up, put it back in the fridge, and later on somebody ate it! At the next big house meeting, he told them what he did. He was trying to figure out who did it by whose face was going to turn sour. Nobody ate his food again after that.

PERRY FARRELL: Who else is going to move into my house but another artist or another musician? Not some nice sweet girl who's a bank teller with a steady paycheck. We scared the shit out of anybody else that we'd even consider. It was welcoming for musicians because there was a place in the back to rehearse and we'd always attend each other's parties.

KARYN CANTOR: Rick Parker [from Lions and Ghosts] moved out. He and Perry got into a fistfight.

CASEY NICCOLI: Perry found Rick's lyrics lying around and thought they were really cheesy. He went into Rick's room one night and thrashed it. When Rick came home the next morning you just heard this *r-r-r-roar* of anger. He came flying up the stairs and threw hot coffee at us. Perry jumped up from the bed and put Rick's head through a glass door window. I freaked out. I thought somebody was gonna die. I called the cops because I was so scared. I was really afraid for both of them. Cops came and everybody calmed down. Nobody got arrested. . . .

PERRY FARRELL: We were constantly looking for roommates because musicians are so flakey. Six times out of ten they don't have a job, or they're moving back to Colorado. Then it's like, "Sorry, Perry . . . can't pay rent . . . leaving next week." So we'd always have to get somebody in fast.

KARYN CANTOR: Eric Avery lived there, too, for a while—next door to Perry, upstairs.

ENTER: ERIC ADAM AVERY

Date of Birth: April 25, 1965
Place of Birth: Los Angeles, CA

Eric Avery as a
toddler at the beach.
(Courtesy Rebecca Avery)

ERIC AVERY (surfer, musician, songwriter, Jane's Addiction): I was born in downtown L.A. and grew up on the Westside. My father, Brian Avery, was an actor, and therefore, our family life was very feast or famine because he either had a part and was doing great, or he went for years without a job, and wound up selling perfume outside of Zody's. Then he'd get another job and we'd be living in a two-story house in Westwood and everything would be great again. Typical for an actor, or an artist in general. He was the guy in *The Graduate* who was the groom to Katharine Ross and he was in a bunch of stage productions of *Gigi* and things like that.

REBECCA AVERY (Avery's younger sister): I'm younger than Eric by three and a half years. We lived mostly on the Westside, including Santa Monica. We moved a lot when we were little. We lived in Westwood on many different streets, Camden, Veteran, Midvale. Santa Monica, Ashton, then again in Westwood. Brooks, Venice, and then Hancock Park. . . .

Pre-teen Eric Avery.
(Courtesy Rebecca Avery)

ERIC AVERY: I had a strict Italian-Irish Catholic upbringing, painfully so. I went to Catholic grammar school in West L.A. for the first eight grades. I was indoctrinated in all the usual ways. Fortunately, for me, I was in the far-left version of Catholicism. The priest was on *Falcon Crest,* this 70s TV soap, playing a priest. It fucked me up just the same, as it seems to everyone, although there wasn't a lot of caning or anything, it was psychological.

REBECCA AVERY: Eric and I both went to St. Paul The Apostle grade school, which is also where Dave Navarro went. I knew Dave vaguely but we didn't start dating until he left grade school, like into high school.

ERIC AVERY: I only sort of vaguely knew Dave Navarro as one of my sister's friends when we went to St Paul's. I had no interaction with him until later. He was also only there for a little while, too.

MATT PALADINO (musician, former neighbor of the Navarro family): St. Paul's was pretty strict. You had nuns who'd smack your hands with rulers. There was a uniform: blue pants, white shirts, sweater, or a blazer. We had to go to church every day. We had to study religion, and then a big mass at the end of the week, praying before school started. Dave was there when I was there.

DAVE NAVARRO: We had to wear uniforms and every kid was rich and got dropped off in a fancy car. Lisa Marie Presley was two grades under me, and there was a day when Elvis dropped her off with fucking cops on bikes protecting him.[8]

ERIC AVERY: Altar boying was my first humiliating performance. I was serving one of my first masses. My family were all there in the front pew. I knelt down on the side of the altar and unbeknownst to me, my gown got caught over my heels so when I went from kneeling down to standing up, I stood down on the back of my heels and it choked my throat with the front of my gown and I went careening back and flew across the floor!

MATT PALADINO: The goal of St. Paul's was preparation to transfer to a really good high school like Notre Dame, Crespi, Loyola, or Chaminade-Julienne, one of these upper-echelon private Catholic schools.

Teenage Eric. (Courtesy Rebecca Avery)

ERIC AVERY: I graduated from St. Paul's Elementary in '79–'80, which would have been eighth grade. Chris Brinkman was my best friend from grammar school. He went to St. Paul's with me. He was like a total mentor-hero figure. Artistically and musically, he was everything to me.

He was just one of those people that was really touched by something different. He was a really great painter and a really great sketch artist.

I connected with him over 50s Beat poetry. We wrote poems and read them at coffee houses. My personal creative adventures started with Chris and by his example. He became the first guitar player for Jane's Addiction.

REBECCA AVERY: In Westwood we lived right next door to this family group called The Weirz. They had a big influence on Eric. There were eight or ten of them, sisters and brothers, this whole family that was a band and they toured around. They used to practice in their garage. I think that might have been where the clarinet first came from. The guitar and bass came later. Same with the piano, he would just do it by ear. I was just amazed at this natural talent. He would just teach himself everything.

ERIC AVERY: The Weirz inspired me to play music because they had all these instruments lying around. I was twelve years old. It was like having a musical playground literally next door. There were three different horn players, a drummer, a bass player, guitar, vibes, any instrument you could think of all in this big house. I think I started on drums. One sister, Maria, was the bass player. I remember distinctly the way her amp looked. It was like the classic kind of Ampeg stack and I remember her plucking like an open E and it just rumbled to my core. I was astonished and inspired. Hooked on the idea of bass. Before that I'd sort of tinkered with my dad's out-of-tune guitar, getting picture diagrams of what to do with your fingers and stuff like that. I was this intensely uncomfortable unsocial kid who just needed something to do with myself, by myself, but it wasn't until I connected with the Weirz that the idea of plugging an instrument into an amp and it being loud became a reality. The Weirz would play the Troubadour and these weird church social type things and I would do the soundboard for them. I never took lessons. I started jamming in garages. I remember guys showing me Smoke on the Water . . . Zeppelin songs, Rush songs, stuff like that.

PETER DI STEFANO (musician, surfing bud of Avery, member Porno for Pyros): I went to St. Monica High School with Eric from tenth to twelfth grade. We used to play volleyball together and we'd ditch fourth and get two bottles of Olde English 800 and lay on our backs at this park just chuggin' away and laughin' our asses off during lunch. Then we'd go back and play volleyball. I don't remember him getting

expelled. I don't think he was a bad student. He was just an alcoholic
. . . having a good time until, just like me, he eventually just spun out.

REBECCA AVERY: Eric got kicked out of pretty much every high school
he went to. It was Loyola, gone. SMC, gone. He would get kicked out
and I don't remember exactly why. One time he was drunk like in the
middle of the day on a school day. I think he was at SMC at the time.
He was out on the street directing traffic and got arrested and I think
that was it. I forget what he did at Loyola.

Eric Avery with dark clouds hovering. Already a
troubled young man. (Courtesy Rebecca Avery)

ERIC AVERY: I was always in hot water over fighting or poor academics
and attitude . . . or never even showing up. I was truant all the time. My
high school career was a slow descent from an all-boys academic school
[Loyola High]. I got kicked out and went to St. Monica, which was still
private and OK; got booted again and went to Santa Monica High, same
thing . . . kicked out and then went to Uni [University] High where I
took the GED.

REBECCA AVERY: Eric was already a troubled youth. He'd started drinking at a young age, probably in eighth grade. He was angry, a bit out of
control. He was really rebellious, talking back to teachers who thought
he was "unfocused." Eric liked to refer to our parents as "the parental
units." They really didn't have a whole lot of control, and they'd get
really upset. They really didn't know what to do. There would be huge
fights if they'd come home and Eric would be drunk, but in the end,

Eric always did what he wanted to do. He'd much rather play music and listen to music—he listened to a lot of music—and he loved to party and surf.

PETER DI STEFANO: I remember going out with girls and playing in a garage band together. Eric played bass and I played guitar and this guy Sean Sullivan played drums. We never got further than the garage because Eric quit and I didn't see him for a while . . . then he joined the band with Perry, and the next thing I know he's on the cover of *L.A. Weekly*, the headline said, "Best New Band . . . Jane's Addiction."

ERIC AVERY: Peter and I were close friends. Surfing friends who played music together. There were like three or four of us. We played bad covers of Rolling Stones songs and stuff. We played some parties and barbecues and things. It wasn't until Flower Quartet that I started really listening to interesting music when Joy Division came out.

REBECCA AVERY: I used to hang out with Eric a lot and his friends. Pete was around during the St. Monica's time drinking and smoking pot and listening to music. And surfing. High school is when everybody started booming with their musical interests. Bands started forming and playing parties and stuff like that. Eric taught himself to play bass, the guitar, the piano, but I think he took lessons for clarinet, the very first instrument he took up with. Eric had a band in high school called Flower Quartet. Peter might have been in that band, too. Chris Brinkman was probably also in it, his closest friend who OD'd.

❦

REBECCA AVERY: The first time Eric went to rehab he was a high school senior. He did not want to go. It was a really big deal. Around that time, too, he found out that he had a different biological father. It's something my parents thought he was aware of. Eric is in my parents' wedding photos, which is really interesting, but none of us ever went like, "That's weird, why is Eric in mom and dad's wedding pictures?" He was like the ring bearer or something. It came out when one of my mom's sisters said, "Do you ever think about your biological dad?"

ERIC AVERY: I had repressed any memory of it. When my aunt asked me about it, it was sort of like a shock, but it wasn't really. This feeling was welling up in me. "What do you mean, my real father?" It was as if I were learning it for the first time. I wasn't really. I had seen my genetic father for the last time when I was like six or seven maybe so I should have had a memory of him. I had totally repressed it. When it came out it was very dramatic.

REBECCA AVERY: That sort of triggered a tailspin; he just went completely out of control. He was maybe seventeen, a really delicate age when I think he already had confused identity questions. It traumatized him, it sent him over the edge. That's when my parents finally said, we've got to do something.

ERIC AVERY: I had run away for maybe two or three weeks and the same night I came back, my parents had an interventionist come in. He was introduced as like a family friend but sort of convinced me that I had a problem and I went into rehab that night.

REBECCA AVERY: We did the whole thing with the interventionist and the entire family sitting in a big circle and we'd all talk about the situation individually. . . .

ERIC AVERY: I met my biological father as an adult. I was at a screening of *Lawrence of Arabia* with my present parents and he came up to me during the intermission because he recognized my mom and dad and he said, "Eric Avery?" And I said, "Yeah." I assumed he was a fan. That was around the time I started to get recognized on the street. Then he introduced himself as my genetic father. That was the last time I saw him.

⚜

CARLA BOZULICH: Eric and I were aged sixteen or seventeen; we were both in our first drug treatment programs when we met.

REBECCA AVERY: Carla was around a lot because she was dating Eric. Chris Brinkman, also hung out with us. We went dancing to the Odyssey all the time.

JANE BAINTER: Before I ever met Perry, I was living in this studio apartment on Fraternity Row in Westwood where Eric, Chris [Brinkman], and Carla [Bozulich] lived. I was a few years older. They were all like sixteen. Eric and Carla had just met in alcohol rehab. They were very close.

ERIC AVERY: It was such a bleak time. It was like one room with mattresses on the floor. Jane was working at the flower market where she had to be up by three A.M. to get there at four. She would shoot speed everyday to go to work. I was bussing tables and playing music and that's when I first started shooting drugs regularly. I got into speed because Jane was around. I'd been real squeamish about needles at first. Speed led me to doing heroin. The first time I shot drugs was when I was seventeen back east, and it was coke and it was a one-off thing. It had nothing to do with Jane. I was experimenting with heroin at that time, too.

PSI COM RECORDS AT RADIO TOKYO

Circa March 1985

AGENT AVA: It was probably Perry who dropped off the L.A. Mantra tapes or maybe it was Ethan James, the Radio Tokyo guy. It had some SST bands on it and Psi Com. I immediately carted the whole tape up and played it in its entirety on my next show [Demolisten KXLU.FM].

PERRY FARRELL: In Venice you might see a really nice restaurant, and the very next place is somebody's house and weeds are growing. And that might be Ethan James's house. He blocked the windows with mattresses; that's how you knew it was Ethan's place. You go in and it's a recording studio. Ethan's prices were negotiable if you were a first-time band with no money; but you had to do it in one or two takes. He was mostly doing porno movie soundtracks to subsidize all the avant-garde obscure shit he really liked to do.

FLEA (musician, member Red Hot Chili Peppers): I saw Psi Com at a private party on some ranch near Magic Mountain. The singer came out, and it was the craziest thing I'd ever seen. He was absolutely out of his mind on fire, shaking and quivering, every muscle in his body was doing a different dance. It was insane. I couldn't believe it. I was like "This guy is out of his mind, who is he?" And it was Perry.

PETE WEISS: The first time I saw Perry Farrell was at Jula Bell's—she had a barn painting party out in Apple Valley, two hours outside of Los Angeles. We painted half of a barn red. We were all on mushrooms—and Celebrity Skin played, an early incarnation with John Goodsall from

Brand X on guitar, and Cujo on drums. And then, this band we didn't know started playing. It was Psi Com. Perry with the hair and the braids, dancing like there was 10,000 people there. We were all just gawkin' at him, trippin' our brains out, wonderin' what's this guy gonna do next?

FLEA: I never knew that was him until years later [when I first saw Jane's Addiction]. I put two and two together, and when I became friends with Perry he said "Oh, yeah that was me. . . . I was on acid that night and had a blast."

PSI COM DISCONNECTS

PERRY FARRELL: I was breaking off with Psi Com. Casey had seen us a few times. She was working at a Stop Smoking place which gave her access to needles and things like that. . . .

CARLA BOZULICH: He was going through this furious change, like a caterpillar turning into a butterfly. It was that dramatic. He told me, "I'm changing my name!" And I was like OK, yeah. And he said I'm changing it to Perry Farrell. And I was like, huh? And he goes, get it— Peri Pheral, Perry Farrell—get it?

PERRY FARRELL: In Psi Com I had a Mohawk [*sic*] and three braids, one that was growing down the back of my neck, and I had two growing on the side of my head, right? My hair was braided for so long that the day that I broke up with Psi Com I said fuck this, I'm taking my braids out . . . they had this weird zig-zag dreadiness to them, and I just left them in like that.

CASEY NICCOLI: Eventually, he just outgrew Psi Com. He wanted something bigger. And more control.

CARLA BOZULICH: He felt like he had something to say that was meant to be said to large audiences and I think that what he has to say *is* meant to be heard by large audiences.

PERRY FARRELL: Psi Com was going through this weird phase. The band just got way too boxed in with the Krishna movement. One of the cats was a Krishna devotee, and he was an unbelievable guitarist. The Krishna issue was a personal thing, right? But it became overwhelming for me when it started to expand beyond the personal. Rich was trying to preach to us, amongst other things, no sex with women other than for the pleasure of Krishna.

JANE BAINTER: Psi Com were going in different directions. Some of them were becoming vegetarians, anti-sex, anti-drug.

STUART SWEZEY: Eventually Perry felt Psi Com lacked the level of intense hard-rock energy that the Red Hot Chili Peppers had. Psi Com were sort of like mid-period Cure, and he wanted to just get the hell on outta there. Everybody was looking to the Chili Peppers as the model for success. Perry was for sure. We used to read about them in the La-Di-Da column in the *L.A. Weekly* all the time. Perry would say, all you have to do in this town to make it, man, is pull down your pants onstage! And he was always really upset that that was what the Peppers did and people loved them for it.

PETE WEISS: Perry also became well known on the scene for droppin' trou and flashin' his schmecker in people's faces. . . .

PERRY FARRELL: One day, I just got this feeling that I'm going to out-grow my circumstances, like, "I think I'm gonna make it." But I had to get another band going, one that was happy, outrageous, and wild. I wanted to be able to sing truthfully. I didn't want to have to fake being in a bad mood. That's when I left Psi Com and started Jane's Addiction.

JANE BAINTER: I remember Perry saying one day when Psi Com was drifting apart: "Fuck those guys. I wanna *rock!*"

NORWOOD FISHER: When Psi Com broke up we were real sad. . . .

PERRY'S MUSE SOURCES

CARLA BOZULICH: Perry was a sponge. He was talking to everyone that he thought had any experience he might have missed. If something interested him or fascinated him he just soaked it right up. He's a genius like that. He can suck it out and make it his own like Bowie and Madonna, but I think Perry has better taste than Madonna. . . .

DAVE JERDEN (producer-engineer, produced Nothing's Shocking and Ritual de lo Habitual): Perry is like an antenna that picks up everything that's going on, and then he regurgitates it through his brain. That's his art.[9]

CARLA BOZULICH: Most people that I'd talk to, it seemed like there was a scam at the bottom of it somewhere so that they could eventually score some drugs. Not with Perry—Perry wanted to talk about art; he was interested in people's opinions. I wasn't really into his music, but I was taken by his style. . . . I'd never known anybody like Perry who was so determined, so focused . . . a different kind of musician than I'd ever played with up to that point.

"THANK YOU, BOYS" (1985–86)

CARLA BOZULICH: Perry told me he was starting a new band and that he was looking for players, and I think I told him about Eric and then he and Perry got together. I think I also told him about some guitarist, and maybe they got together and played but it didn't work out. And then Chris Brinkman, who was a best friend of Eric's and mine, tried out.

I only have eyes . . . (Courtesy Rebecca Avery)

ERIC AVERY: Carla introduced me to Perry. She asked if I'd seen Psi Com and I said, "Yeah." And she said, "What did you think?" And I said, "I think they blow." And she said, "Oh, OK, never mind." And then I said, "No, really . . . why?" Carla said, "They're looking for a bass player." I was on the verge of selling my amp and giving up music. What did I have to lose?

REBECCA AVERY: Eric came to me with this album by this band I'd never heard of called Psi Com. He played it for me and it was like nothing I had ever heard. I was like, hmmm. That's definitely different. He was like, "Yeah, what do you think of this music? I think I'm going to play with this guy."

CARLA BOZULICH: When Eric and Perry got together, Eric started playing those bass lines and Perry applied his lyrical and melodic ideas. That was the magical combination. As soon as Eric played them Perry really seemed to hear himself in there.

REBECCA AVERY: Eric technically never joined Psi Com because they were falling apart. He met them and maybe jammed with them once or twice, but it didn't get very far. Perry and Eric really connected. They both loved Bauhaus. Eric was enthralled by Joy Division.

ERIC AVERY: When we talked on the phone about me coming in and auditioning for Psi Com, it was Joy Division and the Velvets that we connected on.

PERRY FARRELL: Eric loved Joy Division and the punk band Flipper from San Francisco. Flipper's big thing was to stay in one groove without ever breaking it up. They weren't even trying to put together super well-arranged songs, but it *felt great*.

Eric the babe hunk with the grin.
(Karyn Cantor)

REBECCA AVERY: They were a couple of really creative guys, two sides of the same coin. Perry was more the charismatic, outgoing, magnetic type, while Eric was more internal, more intellectual, but really freaking creative, too.

PERRY FARRELL: He was the kind of guy I wanted to sit down and have a drink with and talk about music. Eric seemed like a wild kid, with this kind of half-cocked grin. I would look at his body language and I could tell what was going on in his head.

ERIC AVERY: I was a really shy, introverted guy. Perry was really energized, vivacious . . . extroverted. I was an outsider to the Hollywood underground band scene. I went to shows, but didn't know anybody, and I thought that maybe this [audition] would be a cool way to just meet interesting new people. But Perry told me, "I want to leave Psi Com. Let's start a whole new band." And I was down. I just thought Perry was great, an electric, creative guy.

WHO THE FUCK IS PERRY FARRELL ANYWAY?

NORWOOD FISHER: Between Psi Com and Jane's Addiction we were hanging with Perry and jamming on a few things; we did a Jimi Hendrix tribute at the Roxy. We rehearsed for Perry's portion of the show in my mom's living room. After that came the actual Jane's Addiction band. We were like, all psyched up . . . Jane's Addiction . . . wow . . . that's Perry's new band, let's get down there!

FLEA: I first heard the name Perry Farrell when I played a Jimi Hendrix tribute at The Roxy. Hillel [Slovak] and I got this Hendrix band together with the Fishbone guys and a bunch of different guests were set to jam on his birthday, I think it was, and I worked real hard on it. On the night of the gig I took acid and thought I played the greatest show of my life. The next day in the newspaper there's a big picture of Perry with the caption "Perry Farrell of Jane's Addiction Sings at Hendrix Tribute!" I was being a total brat. I didn't even see him play, and I was like "Who the fuck is Perry Farrell?" I was like "I worked so hard on this, I had the best show of my life, and now there's this picture of some guy who came up and blew a little harmonica! What's up with that?" Perry already had this magnetism; already people thought he was an important figure.

PERRY FARRELL: Between Psi Com and Jane's I'd go out there and improvise with just a drummer or with Eric on electric bass and I'd holler through my vocal effects box. I'd do off-the-top-of-my-head lyrics dressed in a see-thru unitard. It was a big hit at Lingerie, the Anti-Club, Charlie's Obsession. . . . I think we may have billed ourselves as the Illuminotics, or the Illuminati. . . .

ERIC AVERY: Once we played some hellhole bar on Skid Row, on the corner of 5th and Spring Street [downtown L.A.]. Charlie's Obsession was its name. The whole area outside the club was like *Dawn of the Dead*. Several thousand unchecked crackheads and mental patients wandering homeless around a two-mile radius. About five people inside, including us. I played bass. Perry sang and made noises with his effects unit. We played with Four Way Cross. They watched us play and then we finished and watched them play, there was nobody else there.

PERRY FARRELL: At the Anti-Club you could be very experimental, twisted, and weird. I was using delays, using one drummer and myself and then Eric. We'd do little pieces like that. It was all about art. We had nothing to lose, all to gain. We were having a good time. We could get booked in and have a party and that's it. It's a success.

CARLA BOZULICH: Perry and his spacey vocal effects, with the little Roland effects processor right on stage, that was pretty cute.

ERIC AVERY: There was a disco song playing while we were sound checking and I just started playing along with it. I just kept playing as they killed the houselights and we just started jamming and that's where "Pigs in Zen" got started. Another time I played on these chemical drums and Perry sang and that became "Trip Away." Perry is a master at improvising cool lyrics in jam situations. We did that for awhile and then we started playing with a guitar player and a drummer. We also tried to get grant money from some art college. None of us had any money. Perry and I used to go to Astro Burger all the time because you could get breakfast for like $1.99.

**NAMING OF JA
EARLY DAYS OF JA
BALLAD OF PF AND CASEY**

CASEY NICCOLI: We were trying to think of a name for Perry's new band with Eric. The other names just weren't doing it. I said, "Well, how about if we call the band Jane's Heroin Experience" like Jimi Hendrix Experience. . . . Perry said, "That's it, that's it . . . not Jane's Heroin Experience, that's too long . . . Jane's *Addiction!*" So that was it.

JANE BAINTER: They all came into my bedroom and they were like, "We have a great name for our new band!" I was like, "Uh, that's not so good."

BOB MOSS (performance artist, mime): She was really pissed at him over the name at first. This was before the lyrics to "Jane Says" were written, just the name of the band. I'm like, "Wait a minute, bro' . . . this is my best friend's secret, extremely personal habit!" I thought it was an outright invasion. Sure, there were a hell of a lot of junkies in Hollywood then but people weren't shouting it out with megaphones who's a big junkie. And that thing about relationships— "Jane's never been in love, all I know is if they want me"—she just had lots of little affairs.

CASEY NICCOLI: In the early days, Perry wanted me in the band. There was also another girl lined up who played saxophone. We were in the earliest Jane's Addiction band pictures. We even booked shows with me in the line-up. But Eric didn't like it, didn't want it. Perry put Eric in charge of teaching me the songs so he'd figure out the most intricate ways to play everything so I couldn't keep up . . . the fingering was so hard that I couldn't learn it.

JOSH RICHMAN: Perry and Casey were John and Yoko. They were an artistic couple. He looked to her for everything. Nobody was more instrumental than Casey and Perry in anything Jane's Addiction did.

ERIC AVERY: There was conversation about creativity between the two of them going on all the time. . . .

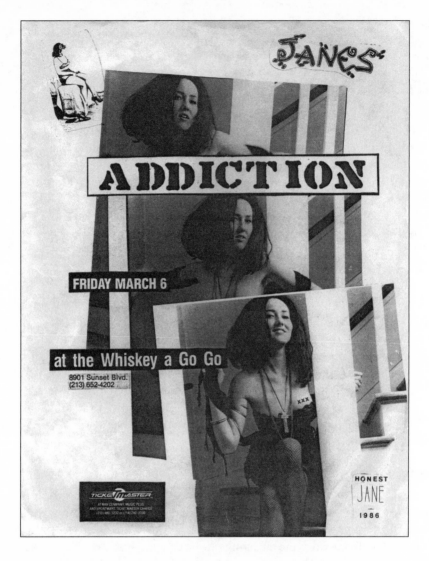

JON SIDEL (former club promoter, restaurateur, current A&R rep): Casey's on two album covers. She lived for Perry and Jane's Addiction. She became part of their art form. If you see candles and crazy artwork on the stage. That's Casey.

JANE BAINTER: Casey was artistically and lyrically a huge influence; also on stage design and all performance aspects. There could never have been a Jane's Addiction as we know it without her.

Perry Farrell and Casey Niccoli, first couple of the Wilton House and the Scream. (Bruce Kalberg)

JON SIDEL: She played the unsung Angie Bowie role . . . coming up with the staging, the styling, and the costuming of the Ziggy Stardust show to free up her spouse to focus on the music . . . so was Casey to Perry and the continually evolving Jane's Addiction's stage show. She was also his personal stylist who braided his hair before shows. . . .

CASEY NICCOLI: I was very in love with this man. When you're in a relationship with somebody, you share your life with them and a big part of that was my love for music. I was all for pushing the guy in my life and not pushing my own talent. All of my creative thoughts went into Perry and what Perry should do. Maybe I was too afraid to do it myself. Perry taught me that my art was really important and that what I did was good. Cause I didn't believe in myself. He made me comfortable to be an artist. I could write, I could paint, I could act, I could do anything when I was with him. He fulfilled a part of me that I couldn't fulfill myself.

ERIC AVERY: I don't remember who all exactly was in the band when the name Jane's Addiction came up. One guitar player we'd tried had a Ziggy Stardust vibe. He even had two different-color eyes. And then this other guy, Ed, had this nasty Les Paul classic rock guitar sound. Brinkman was another art fag like Perry and I. We opened for Gene Loves Jezebel at the Roxy [in early '86]. Chris played in his Jockey shorts. Matt Chaikin from Kommunity FK was the drummer. We went through three guitar players before Dave, but drum-wise I think we might have just played with Matt before Stephen.

HEIDI RICHMAN: Eric was very friendly with Matt's wife Stephanie. Both Matt and Stephanie got really strung out on dope during 1986. She used to call me all the time for money. Matt and Stephanie used to live in a really cute little house in the Valley. Eric used to spend a lot of time there.

JANE BAINTER: Chris Brinkman's father was a big business exec from Santa Barbara. His mom was Jeanne Crain, who was like this very cool movie actress from the 40s and 50s. His family was on the cover of *Life* magazine. He was very dynamic in the beginning, and I think he was never credited for his contributions to some of the songs on the first album. Soon Chris just spun out of control. He eventually OD'd, well it was a suicide, but it was like an OD after he'd been kicked out. He was so dysfunctional that he couldn't even show up. Perry is something of a relentless slave driver, he's pretty focused on what he wants and how to get it. . . .

ERIC TRICKS WITH BIANCA THE HOOKER . . .

ERIC AVERY: I was sleeping with this prostitute named Bianca. She was awful, but she was going to bankroll us.

PERRY FARRELL: It wasn't too hard to fall down with her. She was a very persuasive woman. Bianca was very sweet, if a little nutty. Nutty enough to want to manage us.

JANE BAINTER: Bianca helped launch Perry's career when he was still in Psi Com with money to make a record and now she was behind early Jane's Addiction with cash for him to rent venues to promote their own shows.

REBECCA AVERY: Eric kept from me that he was sleeping with Bianca. That's hilarious. I just thought, hmmm that's an interesting woman. I found out later that "Whores" was about her.

JANE BAINTER: Her clients were toupeed Hollywood B-Listers, like these wholesome married game-show hosts with awesome tans and big grinnin' teeth.

PERRY FARRELL: Bianca was our backer. After Psi Com broke up, Bianca put up the dough so we could put on our own shows. I started putting parties on.

JANE BAINTER: Bianca had lots of cash. She put him on songwriting retreats and paid for us all to go to Big Bear and Lake Arrowhead. She was a good businessperson.

THE BLACK RADIO EXPERIENCE: Jane's Addiction Begins to Gig as a Fourpiece

CASEY NICCOLI: We rented the Black Radio building on Hollywood Boulevard with Bianca's cash and that was a huge success. We promoted ourselves with Tex & the Horseheads and the Screamin' Sirens. The thinking was total DIY. It was, like, 101 punk-rock style. We served beer and stuff. There was no liquor license so we couldn't charge money. People bought a plastic trinket and traded it for a drink. It was a huge success. There was just money coming in everywhere.

PLEASANT GEHMAN (member Screamin' Sirens, former club-booker, author, journalist, belly-dancer): Hollywood Boulevard wasn't like it is now. These weren't real clubs with security. Police awareness was just about nil. They were only worried about bums or an occasional bar fight.[10]

PERRY FARRELL: It was jam-packed 'cause of Tex and the Sirens. We were bottom of the bill. Nobody knew who Jane's Addiction was.

PLEASANT GEHMAN: The [Black Radio] show with Tex and Jane's was beyond insane. Everyone was into making these underground parties

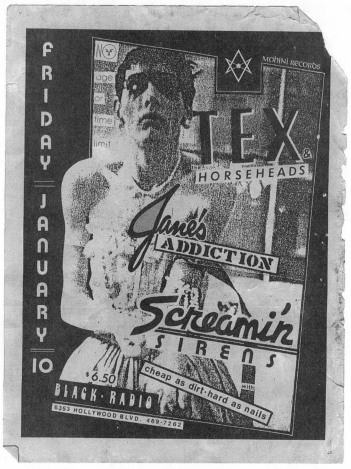

Tex & the Horseheads Black Radio flyer. (Courtesy Rebecca Avery)

into total events. You'd get dressed up. People were smuggling in booze, serving electric shots.[11]

TEXACALA JONES: It was right on Hollywood Boulevard. Kids were pourin' out onto the sidewalk at the front, hangin' out through the halls. They were doing their things in those alcoves there.

PLEASANT GEHMAN: Hitting up coke and slamming dope in the bathrooms and all over the stairs and the mezzanine.[12]

TEXACALA JONES: The crowd looked slightly different, some gothy types were showing up at my gigs, too. It was real gothy, punky, not mean-looking skinheady punky; more glam punky. It was the feel of like a weird Melrose fashion show.

PERRY FARRELL: We had this great guitar player, but he was a junkie who was ahead of me. He'd show up forty minutes late to rehearsal and he'd be tuning at top volume. I'd be saying, what the fuck is this guy doing? Something's wrong with him. He disappeared, we couldn't find him. Up until the minute we went on, we didn't have a guitar player.

PLEASANT GEHMAN: Tables and chairs [were] flying through the air. Broken glass all over the floor, like a throwback to the Masque days. People were hopping from tabletop to tabletop. The only way I can describe it is that blur some shows get when the entire crowd is completely whacked out of their mind on different substances, and it's like a swirling vortex and you're convinced that someone's gonna die.[13]

ENTER: DAVID MICHAEL NAVARRO

Date of Birth: June 7, 1967
Place of Birth: Santa Monica, CA

DAVE NAVARRO (musician, guitarist, Dizastre, Jane's Addiction, Deconstruction, Red Hot Chili Peppers, Camp Freddy, the Panic Channel): I was born in Santa Monica, California, the year of the Californian Summer of Love. My dad is in advertising. And my mom was an actress and a model. That's how they met. She was on *Truth or Consequences*. She would be the woman who'd twinkle and smile and point . . . to a new car! She was in some Doris Day films and a bunch of ads.

DAN NAVARRO (first cousin of Dave, musician, songwriter): Dave was an only child growing up. When I moved to Los Angeles he was two years old and I was seventeen. I lived with his father, Mike Navarro, for two years after he and Dave's mother divorced, sometime around '76–'77. Dave was over every other weekend and Wednesdays, the standard custody arrangement in those days. Mike and Connie were always

Dave Navarro's yearbook photo. St. Paul the
Apostle grammar school. Seventh grade.
(Courtesy Rebecca Avery)

very close, even after the divorce. I was around Dave a lot when he was
nine and ten. I wouldn't so much babysit—it was really more like he
would be over to just hang out.

DAVE NAVARRO: My mom has since died, but I talk to my dad regularly.
We're really close. I feel very fortunate. He's always been there for me
and has never been judgmental of anything that I do. And I've done
plenty to judge, believe me.

DAN NAVARRO: Dave's father Mike Navarro and my father are brothers.
Mexican-American.

**JOHNNY NAVARRO (brother of Dan, cousin to Dave, journalist, copy-
writer):** My branch of the family grew up in San Diego. We got Christmas cards every year from Mike with Dave's photo because Mike was
in advertising and he publicized his child's beauty as much as any dot-
ing father would.

DAVE NAVARRO: My grandfather [was] from the Basque country, the
Navarre region, a buffer between Spain and France. Everyone there
had a name that was a variation of Navarre.[14]

DAN NAVARRO: Our grandfather, Gabriel Navarro, was an illegal immi-
grant who came to Los Angeles, turn of last century, and eventually got
himself heavily ingrained into the local arts community. Gabriel
Navarro became a well-known creative icon in the Spanish-language
community who worked for the studios, sometimes synching Spanish

soundtracks with films. He had also worked as a publicist and owned a newspaper in Los Angeles in the 50s called *El Pueblo*. Dave's dad went to USC and became an advertising guy, starting out writing copy before becoming an account executive who ran his own company.

JOHNNY NAVARRO: Gabriel Navarro Senior was a very strong, charismatic, macho kind of guy with an incredible Valentino-esque type of look with the moustache and the eyebrows and this transfixing glare. He was extremely creative, a musician, an actor, a writer, but some of the stories I heard just made him sound like a flaming egomaniac and a prick. For example, my grandfather would walk into a room and time himself to see how long it would take to control everyone in it, but if you really think about it, there's a pathology behind that; it's so fucking egocentric and full of yourself, yet fearful and insecure at the same time. Not a person that I find appealing in any way . . .

DAN NAVARRO: It's a creative family that was inspired by this awesome, overwhelming guy, this towering figure in the background of all our family's lives.

JOHNNY NAVARRO: The seeds of rebellion and resentment were ingrained in me by my father, Gabriel Navarro Jr. who passed on to me and my brother the same message which had been drummed into him by his father, "You're a Navarro. So you're automatically different from everyone else. You're creative and you're artistic and you're a genius, and you just need to find the way to express this genius. Whatever it is it's going to excel, and it's going to be better than everyone else." This relentless drive is a double-edged sword. Yes, it is a good thing that Gabriel Navarro inspired in his children and grandchildren support and maintenance of a creative spirit, a drive to excel in the arts; but the quite drastic downside is that you can never achieve success in your mind. Perfection is unattainable. I know that exists in Dave, too. Whatever it is, it's just never going to be good enough.

DAN NAVARRO: Although he died before any of us grandkids were born, our grandfather set the tone for everything his sons and grandchildren would do with regards to the importance he placed on finding creative expression in life. He nurtured that in my father and my uncles. . . .

JOHNNY NAVARRO: Dan's closer to embracing the positive sides of that spirit because he is further up the tree, whereas Dave and I really had a hard time with it. Dave has the same feeling I do. We talked about it and decided, fuck all that "You're a Navarro" bit. You walk with it, but at the same time, you rebel. We're just like everybody else. We have fucked up and gone into sobriety and gone through some really dark shit because we were "Navarros." But of course you must know there are times when Dave *does* think he's better than anybody else.

⋘══✦══⋙

MATT PALADINO: I was born and raised in Bel Air, grew up in a house on Linda Flora Drive, near where the Navarros lived. They were about ten houses away. From age five to about age seven I lived in that area. There were three families on that block that hung out. There was the Tomichs, my mom and dad, and the Navarros. There was always a neighborly dinner party thing, that's probably how these families first got together.

DAN NAVARRO: Dave had gone to school at John Thomas Dye, then he went to school at St. Paul's. . . .

MATT PALADINO: I never really hung out with Dave like tight buds or anything—Dave's several years older than I am—but there were three brothers in the Tomich family. I was about the same age as the middle brother; the older brother, Steven, was Dave's age. At family get togethers Mike and Connie and Dave were always there. My mom and Connie Navarro, and subsequently, Mary Louise Tomich were three best of friends for years and years. . . .

REBECCA AVERY: Dave was like my first love. I started going out with him in junior high or high school. I was probably a freshman and he would have been a sophomore. Age-wise, I was probably fifteen and he was seventeen. I met Dave's dad, Mike, at the house several times, also when there were parties the cousins would be there. He and his dad just seem to genuinely like each other. His dad always seemed to treat him with respect.

MATT PALADINO: Dave was a boisterous, in-your-face bully, a rowdy kid, an only child, who was seen as the bad seed of the neighborhood in terms of pranks. He ran with Steven Tomich, who was also seen as a bit of a bad egg. Dave was always in trouble for something, mainly juvenile vandalism stuff, flower pots broken, shaving cream on cars, annoying petty nuisance shit, all of it ordinary for a growing kid. Authorities were never involved. This was old Bel-Air off of Roscomare, where it was never "Let's get the police involved." It was more like you called the family and said, "Your son did this, your son did that." I remember playing with the younger Tomich brother and Dave would just come in and fuck with us, take our toys away. We were just little kids so we'd get upset and go tell, but Dave never got in trouble for anything. We resented it that there was never any consequence for anything he did, because if we'd done those things we'd have been in deep shit with our parents or teachers, but when Dave pulled shit we were always told to just keep our mouths shut. Just go play with something else. Dave was a classic, compulsive exhibitionist who *had* to be the center of attention at all times. He was always showing off to us.

DAVE NAVARRO: My dad is suave: [a] tall, dark, and handsome James Bond type [who] could just pull women. He'd say, "twenty-four and out the door," meaning that when [a] girlfriend turned twenty-four, that was it.[15]

REBECCA AVERY: Mike Navarro had money, lived in a nice house. He got Dave nice things and cars. Dave would crash them one after the other. Dave was in many car accidents as a young lad. I think probably because of the divorce, maybe guilt, his dad gave Dave as much as he wanted. He was spoiled in the way that he could have parties all the time and never had to be concerned about working or money. He was drinking a lot.

DAVE NAVARRO: I'd hear yelling at night. I'd wake up and come into my parents' room and they would tell me that the dog was making a mess. I knew they'd been fighting.[16]

MATT PALADINO: Mike wasn't really around. He traveled a lot—he was a big-time ad exec. When he was around he overcompensated for his absence by spoiling Dave. He'd just buy him off with all kinds of stuff to make up for it. Whenever one of the families would throw one of these dinner party get-togethers, if Dave didn't like something or didn't want to do something, he'd throw a tantrum. Whether it was, "I don't want to eat that" or "I don't want to do this, I don't want to do that," Mike would always give Dave whatever he wanted, whatever it took to appease him, irrespective of the consequence it might have on the other people. Mike was kind of an asshole, really strict. I remember him like spanking the other kids, but with Dave it was always whatever Dave wanted, Dave got.

Dave with Rebecca Avery (center) and Kelly Wooldridge.
(Courtesy Rebecca Avery)

REBECCA AVERY: Dave's dad was great, a funny guy. His cousins, Dan and Johnny, too. Great people. Very creative, too. I met them at parties and coming to shows, all that kind of stuff.

MATT PALADINO: Connie was always really loving, really nice, really sweet, never much of a disciplinarian. Mike was the uptight over-controller, and Connie was very mellow, but in the long run, Mike providing Dave with whatever he needed, whatever he wanted . . . allowed him the complete freedom and the financial support to develop into this amazingly accomplished musician. . . .

DAN NAVARRO: Dave's family was affluent enough that he never had to fill out a job application in his life. He's never worked at the video store, never bagged groceries. He never did anything else but play and study music. He was eighteen when he really started playing out. At that age, maybe he would have had summer jobs like the other kids. He just never considered anything else as what to do with his life.

JOHNNY NAVARRO: Where is it written in stone that you have to come from the other side of the tracks to play great rock 'n' roll?

DAVE'S MUSICAL INFLUENCES

DAVE NAVARRO: My earliest influences when I first started playing rock were Hendrix, Page, The Who, The Doors. Cream. Not so much as a guitar player, just stuff I listened to. I went through this classic rock phase, a heavy metal phase, a punk-rock phase, a gothic-English phase. There was even a Grateful Dead phase. All of those phases helped develop the player I am. The jamming thing came from Hendrix. When I went to Dead shows I was too fucked up on acid to know that they were jamming! I didn't find out about that until ten years later.

DAN NAVARRO: Dave was first into Elton John, then it was Kiss. I remember the posters in his room. Like most young kids he blew through the Kiss phase pretty quickly. Soon he shifted to the Doors, The Who, and Hendrix. He picked his influences really well, the ones that caused him to really dive headfirst into what he was doing. The Doors, for sure, brought him to a darker viewpoint of the world.

JOHNNY NAVARRO: Dave was probably sixteen when he got the Les Paul. I said, "Dude, gimme a little Eddie [Van Halen]" and he goes, "Wanna hear 'Eruption'?" That was considered the most virtuoso piece of electronic rock guitar music there was in GIT geek circles at that time. I'm like, "Yeah . . . sure, man." He fuckin' played it note for note. That's how good his ear was. I said to myself, "This kid is going to be a rock star." You can't be that good of a mimic without having the ability to do your own thing. Jimmy Page was the same. A teenage musical prodigy who never did anything else. Dave could play absolutely anything you wanted to hear in classic rock. Wanna hear Zeppelin? Want some Jimi Hendrix? The Who? The Dead? Name it.

DAVE NAVARRO: I was twelve in my first band. We did really horrible Cream, Hendrix, and Zeppelin covers. Then I stopped listening to rock music altogether. All I listened to was classical music or talk radio.[17]

DAN NAVARRO: During the time I was living with Mike and Dave, I was beginning to play out in the clubs as a solo artist. There was always a piano in the house and I had guitars around all the time. Dave took guitar lessons to start around 1977. He learned really fast and outstripped his teacher in very short order. It was already evident to our family that we had a musically gifted child prodigy in our midst. Later, he told me in so many words that seeing me playing and writing and living that life made him think maybe he wanted to do that, too. I didn't teach him to play guitar, but I think I may have shown him his first three guitar chords, like A, E, and D or something.

MURDER OF CONNIE NAVARRO

DAVE NAVARRO: I had premonitions . . . for a whole month. I knew things were shit in the house.[18]

REBECCA AVERY: Dave and I would be together and then he'd break up, then we'd get back together again, and then he'd break up with me again. Dave would just get really drunk and call me up and want to get back together again. Of course I'd just be tickled pink and then he wouldn't remember the next morning. Or we would be together for a month or two and he'd break it up and then he'd get drunk again. He was getting so drunk all the time and dropping acid. It was a crazy time emotionally. It was during one of those periods that Dave's mom died.

DAN NAVARRO: Probably one of the watershed events in Dave's creative development was his mother's death. It led him to a kind of introspection where he began experimenting with the darker side of life and art, although taking such a big dive into the dark side musically and aesthetically is something I wouldn't have wished for him as someone who loves him. That he would go there with a vengeance again and again and again with the music of Jane's and what Jane's represented was a very frightening thing for me as a member of his family. It was extremely distressing for us. We were very worried for him.

DAVE NAVARRO: I come from a divorced household. I've gone through the murders of my mother and her best friend, Sue Jory, a woman I used to call my "aunt." I've gone through drug addiction. I spent a lot of time with the wrong people. I've seen that just about anybody will stab you in the back, given the opportunity. But at the same time, I feel that I have a good outlook and a realistic sense of humor about life. I feel very lucky. It's not like I walk around feeling as if I'm doomed in a world of doom, and that there's no hope in anything.[19]

DAN NAVARRO: He was fifteen when his mom died. It was as traumatic as you could imagine. It led him to a feeling that he's not able to trust anyone. It's led to a certain glibness when he's delving into some of the deeper parts of his psyche, although he is remarkably open about his biggest foibles, which I've always found to be an incredibly endearing quality.

REBECCA AVERY: When Dave's mom died, we knew he was either going to clean up and get on the straight and narrow and get his act together, or he was just going to spiral down, which is what ended up happening. It got much worse with the drinking and drugs.

DAN NAVARRO: We loved Connie, who loved Mike and Dave. She was still my aunt in my mind, although she and my Uncle Mike had split up. One day, Mike asked if I'd trade cars with Connie for a week because she had been threatened by her boyfriend, who she was trying to break up with. His real name was John Riccardi, but he went by the name of Dean.

DAVE NAVARRO: [Dean] broke in, held me up at gunpoint and made me promise not to tell anyone. And I didn't. A week later he killed my mother.[20]

DAN NAVARRO: [Dean] was a bodybuilder. Dave had grown pretty close with him. There was always some question as to how he made his income. I wasn't aware Connie had been trying to get a restraining order against him until later. When she didn't turn up for an appointment, which was not like her, a day or two after we traded cars back again, Mike went to her condo to check on her. Everybody was on edge because of these threats. Mike called demanding I get over there right now. He was virtually hysterical. When I arrived, he was in handcuffs. Cops were everywhere. My immediate thought was, "Oh, my god, he got into a fistfight with Dean." I yelled, "What happened?" The police just cut me off and Mike turned to me and said, "She's dead." I couldn't really comprehend it. Just couldn't process it. I said, "Who's dead?" "Connie's dead." The rest was surreal. Cops arrive on the scene and find dead bodies and a guy alive. Understandably, they're going to cuff the guy they find at the scene until they know what's going on. As soon as the cops let Mike out of the cuffs he collapsed in my arms. My first question was, "Does Dean know where you live?" He said, "Yes." I said, "Where's David?" "At my house." We immediately got a detective and rushed up to the house. I was there when Dave was told what happened and it was beyond comprehension. It was a scene I never want to see again. It's as devastating as anything could be.

REBECCA AVERY: Dave knew the guy really well. I remember him being scared but I think people around him were even more so. Mike and the cousins were worried about his well-being. I just remember them being scared not knowing where this lunatic is and that he could come again at any time. We found out that his mom had been killed through Lisa Rasmussen, who was a mutual friend who lived across the street.

DAN NAVARRO: Mike told me later he opened the door and entered the condo because he had keys and called out for her, but there was no reply. Her car was not there either. It turned out that Dean had tried to cover his tracks by moving the car a couple of blocks away so that people wouldn't drive by and decide to drop in. It took them several days to find it. Mike went upstairs and discovered the bodies.

DAVE NAVARRO: My mom's death was a major contributing factor to my drug problems. I went to therapy for a long, long time, and then to anonymous group meetings, and I'm okay with it now.[21]

DAN NAVARRO: It's beyond comprehension in terms of the impact on our extended family. It was a difficult period for Dave, where he was starting to act out, understandably, and he got into the kinds of things that would lead him to the person he is now. It was a very difficult time for the family for quite a few years. There is no such thing as "closure." You just get to the point where you learn how to say it out loud, without going to that place, and then it becomes this surreal event in your life that still exists. Facing that kind of horror at such a young age—Dave was fifteen going on sixteen—had unfathomable psychological consequence. . . .

DAVE NAVARRO: I discovered I didn't feel it as badly when I was loaded [on heroin].[22]

ERICA PAIGE (former club doorperson, friend of Dave's, TV producer): [The murder of his mother] definitely came up a lot when I was around him. Those are the feelings you want to make go away; try to drown it out with alcohol and drugs. You don't become a drug addict because you have a horrible thing happen, but if addiction is something you're already on the road to, it definitely gives you an even greater reason to pursue it.

JOHNNY NAVARRO: There was much darkness in Dave's life. He started doing even more drugs after his mom died. That was the shove he needed. Dave would have been an addict anwyay. He was going in that direction and that gave him a justification and motivation at the same time. He was doing acid, he was doing coke, and he was drinking crazy amounts, weed all the time, and a lot of mushrooms.

DAVE NAVARRO: I'm sad my mom is gone . . . and I'm grateful that I have such a wonderful father. I used to focus on the tragedy and how certain catastrophic negative things have defined my life. It took a long, long time to realize that I could just as easily be defined by the positive things.

REBECCA AVERY: I remember going to the funeral . . . open casket . . . it was so weird. She's buried in that cemetery in Westwood, the one where Marilyn Monroe is buried. The service was there. It was just really sad, one of those freakish things that you just can't believe. It really did fuck with him in a bad, bad way. None of us knew what to do. We were so young. I'd listen for hours, he just talked terrible thoughts and terrible things. We didn't have the wherewithal at that age to get together to say we need to approach someone. He needs some serious help. We thought we'll just listen and be supportive. What else can you do at that age?

ERICA PAIGE: They finally got the guy years later after they talked up the case on *America's Most Wanted*. . . .

DAVE NAVARRO: They finally caught him [August 1994]. He killed my aunt at the same time. I had to see him in court, and let me tell you, it was fucking heavy. (There were pictures from the scene on a fucking board. I had to ask for them to be covered.)[23] I could testify to a lot of stuff that had happened earlier. I was the only witness. I hadn't seen him for like twelve years, but he'd lived with us for five years before the murder. He was sentenced to death. I go back and forth about how I feel about it. I spent all these years wanting him to die. The way I look at the death penalty is that I don't have to feel any way about it; he did what he did and was judged that way, and not by me. He made his own destiny, and I'm not personally saying, "Kill him," and I'm not pulling the switch. The court thing was a nice closure to something that had been hanging over me [for twelve years].[24]

UNIVERSITY HIGH SCHOOL, WEST LOS ANGELES (PKA UNI)

Circa 1985

Dude, where's my bong?

MICHAEL ZIMMERMAN (musician, former neighbor, high school acquaintance of Dave Navarro): I grew up in Bel-Air near where the Navarro family lived. My circle was self-destructive, mostly rich kids mooching off our parents and stealing their drugs. I only knew Dave after his mother's death when we went to school together at Uni High. I'm a few years younger than him. Dave was always the shy guy who ran from me. People around campus at Uni knew what had happened to his mom and there was an unspoken boundary that said never to go there, never bring the subject up with Dave.

MATT PALADINO: Uni High was probably where Dave met Mike Ozair because Mike also went to Uni, so did Mike Zimmerman.

MICHAEL ZIMMERMAN: Uni High was very cool, the same school that Darby Crash and Pat Smear went to in the 70s. Attached to Uni was Indian Hills continuation school, where you could smoke cigarettes at the time. They gave you your own curriculum. Dave was in the extension part where most of the cooler students ended up. I personally didn't attend Indian Hills but a lot of my friends did.

DAN NAVARRO: Dave already had a reputation as "the hottest kid guitar player on the Westside." He was a teenager who could outplay his teachers. The Westside is a privileged, high rent district. One doesn't expect that a kid from there is going to really dive head first into rock 'n' roll, especially when it's likely his parents are going to pressure him to do well in school and go to college. . . .

MICHAEL ZIMMERMAN: Dave was just a cool guy. Girls always went apeshit over him. A classic stoner guitar player who always had the coolest fucking hair. Long, black hair cut a little heavy metal but then he let it grow out and it looked even cooler.

DAN NAVARRO: The other rock kid wannabes in high school would say, "Let me show you what I can do," and then Dave would show him what he could do and totally blow them away.

MICHAEL ZIMMERMAN: Dave Navarro was known as a teenage musical prodigy of sorts. But it was hard to get close or really talk to him. In high school, if you played music you were always in a secret competition trying to be the coolest, the fastest, the best. The first time I heard Dave play I was amazed, knocked out. He came over to a friend's house. We were all sucking up bongloads of pot and doing coke I had stolen from my dad's personal stash. Dave tooted some, too, before he played side one of Houses of the Holy, every note, lick, solo . . . all the songs in the same order as the record. When he finished he handed me the guitar and asked if I had anything I wanted to play him. I was stunned. Speechless. Demolished. I think I fumbled my way through *Dark Entries* [Bauhaus] and some old Bowie song. He was not impressed.

PUTTIN' OUT IN SHROOMSVILLE

MICHAEL ZIMMERMAN: I saw Dave play in a couple of bands. He'd been a major Deadhead. The first time I saw him live was at Madame Wongs West. It was some horrible hippie band, they sounded like the Dead meets Fleetwood Mac; bearded crusties in denim bib overalls and *Birkenstocks!* I also remember seeing Dave play in Dizastre, this heavy metal band. They played the Troubadour. It was a fun night.

MATT PALADINO: There was a brief disconnect of a few years between when I was seeing Dave at least once a week at some sort of family function or just in the neighborhood to . . . there's Dave sitting at a buddy of ours, Mike Ozair's house, smoking weed and jamming out on guitar. Mike Ozair went to Uni High with Dave. He took acid, pot, mushrooms, he was a major Deadhead.

MICHAEL ZIMMERMAN: Mike Ozair was always getting people together. He was the neighborhood party planner, an extremely charismatic leader type of guy. Mike would get these raves together and it's a legend around 80s Bel-Air and Beverly Glen . . . all-night acid parties [circa '85–'86] a good few years before acid house and the techno rave scene came up.

MATT PALADINO: There was this little remote brush clearing Mike found maybe half a mile away from any houses. Mike started having these stoner parties every other week during the summer, where everyone would come on mushrooms or acid or really stoned, bring beers and light a fire, like a camping party with a Moontribe kind of vibe. The Grateful Dead would be playing, natch. Somebody said, "Who's that guy playing guitar?" I was like, "That's Dave Navarro—I know him!" Dave was befriending kids a couple of years older than he was. Dave was really down with the inner core of the cool crowd, while the rest of us were like these really young wannabe kids lucky enough to get to tag along.

MICHAEL ZIMMERMAN: They called this enclave of druggies Shroomsville. It was a really cool walking trail behind these big houses around Beverly Glen and Mulholland by Angelo Drive. You had the laid-back stoner hippie-type people, and juiced-up leather rocker types on speed, you also had preppie types, students. I was the only goth-punk kid. It was a really cool diverse hang. I'd see Dave there all the time. The O'Connell brothers Tom, Jim, and Andy also had legendary parties. The O'Connells were north of Westwood Boulevard in those really cool houses. I'm sure at least one of Dave's bands must have played there, set up in the living room, or outside by the pool. . . .

MATT PALADINO: Mike Ozair was a really likeable guy, never mean, just like a big-hearted Israeli hippie guy who never turned anyone away. After school we'd go over to his house to get stoned. His little brother Danny was more my age so I was going over to see Danny at their house and Dave would always be there, guitar in his hands. He'd become Mr. Guitar Man for everybody. His whole life had become either playing guitar or taking a short break from it. Either jamming along or soloing over records, playing old rock songs, radio off, Dave playing, people singing: classic 60s tunes, Zeppelin tunes. With our generation it was 60s *and* 70s music. We liked the Dead, we liked Cream, Hendrix, the big 60s bands, but we also loved Deep Purple, Zeppelin, and the power rock bands of the early 70s. Pink Floyd was huge in this world. Dave would always throw in *The Wall*. It's not so easy to solo and lead on an acoustic guitar, but Dave knew all these Page licks *perfecto*. Dave totally rocked on the acoustic guitar. Everyone knew Mike O. He was the leader, the motivator that drove people to go see Navarro. If Mike said, "Hey, we're all going to this Dead show," everybody went. Same thing if Mike said, "Hey, we're going to see Navarro's new band play," everybody goes.

MICHAEL ZIMMERMAN: Mike Ozair sort of disappeared into deep Judaism then popped up again reinvented as a rabbi who doubled as a sort of New Age healer and "life coach" motivator type, who got busted and convicted of "oral copulation" with a fourteen-year-old girl.

ENTER: STEPHEN PERKINS

Date of Birth: August 13, 1967
Or: September 13, 1967

STEPHEN PERKINS (musician, member Jane's Addiction, Porno for Pyros): I was a Jewish kid from the Valley, just bar mitzvah'd, but attending Notre Dame, an all-boys' Catholic school, when I met David Navarro. Van Nuys High where I was supposed to go was just too rough.

DAVE NAVARRO: After St. Paul's I went to Notre Dame High School, where I met Stephen Perkins.

STEPHEN PERKINS: I immediately joined the marching band on snare drum. Dave was already in there playing bass drum. We made easy friends. He confided, "I'm not really wanting to be a

Stephen Perkins.
(Courtesy Rebecca Avery)

Mid-teen Stephen Perkins.
(Courtesy Rebecca Avery)

drummer, I'm actually a guitar player." "Let's get together," I said, "I've been dying to find someone." Music was a big part of it, but our friendship was sealed by the sense of humor we shared about the way we grew up together in Los Angeles. We became two teen guys making up our own music, our own soundtrack as we went along. . . .

DAVE NAVARRO: I'd pick [Perkins] up every day before school. We'd do coke, smoke pot, and split a six-pack, all before eight A.M.[25]

STEPHEN PERKINS: At first it was Gene Krupa. The guy with the big tribal tom-tom thing. Then I slowly turned myself into a rock drummer wannabe, hoping to land somewhere between Moon and Bonham . . . style-wise, I mean . . . not drinking myself into a short life!

REBECCA AVERY: I began dating Stephen when he and Dave were in this heavy metal band together. Dizastre had a bit of a following. People would come down to see them play at the Troubadour. They would really rock out and do a good show. They sounded close to Iron Maiden.

DAN NAVARRO: Dave had just turned sixteen, not long after his mother died, when Dizastre recorded in a little four-track demo studio in my basement that my cohort Eric [Lowen] and I ran. Eric engineered, I helped with basic production ideas. Gave them the name and the odd spelling. I was just going back to my old 60s' roots of . . . spell it weird and have some fun. It was pretty close to speed metal, moving along at a pretty brisk clip, but not as lumbering as heavy metal can be. God love him, Steve had difficulty keeping time steady through his fills. He was always so excited that when he would go into a fill, he would pick up. Not an uncommon event out of any drummer, but he was only maybe seventeen, sixteen.

Bonded over Iron Maiden worshippery. Members of Dizastre, a pre-Jane's teen metal band featuring Perkins and Navarro. (Jerry Jung)

Date listed on the Dizastre demo: 4/24/83.
Song titles: Lady Fate, Take My Life and Killers (Iron Maiden cover).
Personnel listed: Dave Navarro, Steve Perkins, Brad Jones, and Rico Quevedo.

REBECCA AVERY: When David was breaking my heart I called Stephen, crying on his shoulder. He was so nice and so sweet. I got to know Stephen really well after Connie died. Stephen was such good friends with Dave, we would just talk about him for long periods of time on the phone. We were concerned about him. We became close friends that way.

STEPHEN PERKINS: I knew his mom and I knew the guy that killed her. It was too shocking to even grasp, especially for a fifteen year old. As a best friend, I just tried to be there for him. We played music. We talked. Whatever it took to free ourselves from the pain.

REBECCA AVERY: Stephen and I would talk about Dave and how terrible it was and what could we do and then it sort of grew into a solid friendship. Stephen was very persistent in pursuing me. He just grew on me. He was such a ball of energy and love. We started dating and I fell in love with him. We were together almost five years from when I was like sixteen to twenty-one.

DAN NAVARRO: Dave was successful even with his first band. Dizastre's first show had like 400 people at the Troubadour. Dave and Steve were hot from moment one in terms of Dizastre having a huge outpouring at their first show. They didn't play many times.

REBECCA AVERY: I think there were sort of two bouts of them doing a lot of shows at the Troubadour.

WHO KNOWS A GOOD, RELIABLE DRUMMER?

DAVE NAVARRO: One night Stephen and I went to see Jane's Addiction and we just loved it. It was a really exciting show. It was in this dingy little upstairs room on Hollywood Boulevard. They had the energy and power that we loved about metal, with a total abandon that we didn't have any experience with. It was Eric and Perry and the drummer from Kommunity FK, Matt Chaikin, and I think it was Chris Brinkman, or it might have been this guy Ed, on guitar, who ended up in the Lovedogs.

STEPHEN PERKINS: Dave and Rebecca and I went to a couple of Jane's Addiction shows together and were completely knocked out. Dave and I knew right away that we could fit that spot better as musicians, but we didn't think that would ever happen, so we just kept on trying to make our own music.

ERIC AVERY: I remember them [Stephen and Dave] up front in the pit at the Black Radio show. They were a couple of metal kids, with long hair, and they were just rockin' out, fist-pumpin' the air while we were playing.

DAVE NAVARRO: I consider that show my introduction to the L.A. [post-punk] underground. I was hooked, and as soon as I got an opportunity to play with these guys I jumped at it.

PATRICK MATA: When I took off to England in '85, hoping for an indefinite stay, I left Matt behind, and he was really upset and hurt.

We'd all been doing lots of cocaine. Matt was friends with Eric Avery. So we were all hanging out and unbeknownst to me at the time, Perry apparently got Matt into heroin. When I went to England, he took Matt as soon as I was gone and started Jane's Addiction with him, my drummer of nine years. Matt didn't tell me anything about this. It's like he felt he was cheating on me or something.

JOSH RICHMAN: Perry badly wanted Matt Chaikin [Kommunity FK] to be the drummer. Perry was influenced by Killing Joke who were really percussive and tribal. . . . Matt as a drummer was also down with the Killing Joke groove, that's why Perry wanted him. . . .

PERRY FARRELL: I'd asked the Kommunity FK drummer to play for Jane's. Everybody in that [version of] Jane's Addiction had drug problems already, it seemed. Three rehearsals in a row, the guy won't show up, so you figure he ain't coming for the fourth. I started to ask around, "Who knows a reliable drummer?"

<hr />

REBECCA AVERY: I was telling Eric, "What about Dave and Stephen for this new band with Perry?" He's like, "Rebecca, they're just not our style of music. They're not what we're looking for." I was like, "But they're such great musicians."

Stephen Perkins, the "blue sky of Jane's Addiction."
(Courtesy Rebecca Avery)

Stephen and Rebecca at prom.
(Courtesy Rebecca Avery)

ERIC AVERY: We were on such different musical planets that I tended to think of Dave as my little sister's heavy metal friend. As it happened, I actually played with him and Stephen up at Dave's house a few years before Jane's, probably during my Flower Quartet days back in high school. They were really young. I remember playing in the living room at Dave's dad's house in Bel-Air. They wanted to play Iron Maiden covers and other stuff that just wasn't my thing.

STEPHEN PERKINS: Perry and Eric were into Joy Division, Bauhaus, Love & Rockets when I first met them. I was really big on hard rock. I was seventeen and Metallica had just come out. I liked the aggression, I wasn't too especially hip on the music, as much as feeling the explosive aggression of it all. As a drummer, I thought it was exciting.

REBECCA AVERY: In the end they went through so many people that Eric finally relented, "Why not? Let's have Stephen down and give it a shot."

PERRY FARRELL: Eric's sister was going out with this curly haired, mopheaded young kid with soft red boots and a bandanna to hold the curls together, and like this giant grin.

REBECCA AVERY: After Stephen saw Jane's at Black Radio, and I already knew he dug them, I told Stephen that Eric and Perry wanted to try him out. He was really excited about it. He really wanted that gig. He just played one song and Eric and Perry just looked at him and said, "Wanna join the band? You're in."

PERRY FARRELL: Stephen showed up with an eighteen-piece drumkit at the audition. He was ready to rock us with a double kick! We were from completely different worlds, but I felt this kid could just rock the shit out of us. He was from The [San Fernando] Valley. That's what the kids from The Valley looked like and that's what they sounded like. Stephen was the cream of the crop of those kids.

STEPHEN PERKINS: Some guys would just bring a little four-piece set to an audition. I brought like ten drums. The first song we played was "Pigs in Zen" and I started pocketing with them. I saw the smiles and their butts shaking, and I just went for it, and they offered me the job right away. . . .

ERIC AVERY: We gave Stephen a try first, and it worked out great. It was the first time we'd tried someone who was an incredible player. We only knew people who were sort of artistic, certainly not chops guys as players. Stephen not only had crazy chops, he was also totally open to us shaping him.

REBECCA AVERY: Stephen and I were like, "OK, now that's settled, now you've got to get our friend Dave in there, too! Just give him a shot is all we ask." And, of course, they loved him to pieces, too, first time they got together.

STEPHEN PERKINS: After I got in I promised Dave: I gotta get you in the band, I can't wait to get you in the band. Dave and I had a couple of extremely derivative heavy metal bands. By the time we caught up with Perry and Eric, we wanted to make music like what we were feeling. No more emulating other bands; we were dying to express ourselves creatively.

DAVE NAVARRO: They apparently had a problem with their guitar player, so Stephen recommended me.

STEPHEN PERKINS: They had this cat named Ed playing guitar; nice guy, but he wasn't Dave Navarro. I said, "Look, you gotta bring my buddy Dave down."

Dude, easy with the mascara. (Karyn Cantor)

Spiritual Perkins, the only non-addict.
(Karyn Cantor)

ERIC AVERY: It went so well with Stephen, we were like, "Let's give it a go with the other guy with mad chops." Same story.

DAVE NAVARRO: I got a demo tape of their songs and just learned them real fast and went down and jammed and was pretty much welcomed into the family that night.

PERRY FARRELL: Everybody knew how great Dave was, his reputation preceded him. What an incredible talent. Who wouldn't want him to play guitar in their band? What a stroke of good luck to find him!

STEPHEN PERKINS: The first song Perry, Eric, and I ever played with Dave altogether as a four-piece was "Whores," and at that moment, for me, the sound for Jane's Addiction was born. And it hasn't changed since. We were like these stoner teenagers with long hair, but we all got an instant sense of freedom from each other.

PERRY FARRELL: I thought, "Omigod, they're adorable." Stephen and David. I called them Jane's Teen Rock-a-Babes. They were like exuberant teenagers all the time. What great energy.

DAN NAVARRO: There was a lyricism—and fury—to both their playing that balanced Perry's outrageousness.

STEPHEN PERKINS: When you hear Dave's guitar, like John Frusciante, there's a sadness. But there's also gladness. Dave's an expressive person, an emotional person. And you can hear that when he plays.

PETE WEISS: Jane's Addiction could never have continued long without Perkins. You gotta have that one guy in the band that's just always there and can go with the flow. Because if so-and-so and so-and-so are arguing, Stephen is always there cool and calm. He'll always just show up with his drums and do the show with a big smile on his face.

DAN NAVARRO: There's an additional creative element beyond accomplished musicianship and youthful energy that can't be overlooked in the Jane's equation. Dave and Steve also helped make Perry palatable to those inclined to find him strident.

CARLA BOZULICH: David added a lot in terms of the writing, but he also added this metal edge which sealed the deal for the band and made them irresistible.

PETE WEISS: You can't undervalue Stephen's keeping that band together— of course there's no Jane's Addiction without Eric, either. . . .

THE ERIC AVERY DEEP BASS GROOVE LINE

STEPHEN PERKINS: Eric with his amazingly cool bass lines and his deep sense of the groove was the best. He was so solid I could go crazy on my drum parts. Eric enabled me to be "Keith Moon.". . .

ERIC AVERY: We had tribal drums and I was writing purposely simple four-note bass lines that I just repeated over and over. I would start playing that and everyone would jam on top of it. Perry or I would say, like, "That's cool. Can we maybe not have that thing there . . . maybe a little more of this and less of that?" Perry would write words, and it would all just sort of come together.

CARLA BOZULICH: The uniqueness of Eric's bass and Perry's voice together created the basic sound that is Jane's Addiction . . . without Eric there never could have been any success for Jane's Addiction. Eric had written the music on his bass, years before he met Perry.

CASEY NICCOLI: Eric could play superb . . . huge melodic grooves, but he couldn't make them into complete songs. Perry could cherry-pick the best grooves, and make songs out of them.

CARLA BOZULICH: Those bass lines are what turned into the music for ninety percent of the first two albums. These grooves were expanded and embellished upon by the others to make completed songs, something he

Huge melodic grooviness.
(Karyn Cantor)

could never have done himself—none of them could have done what they did without the other. At the time I don't think Eric could have come up with a melody line by himself that would have really worked, or a chord progression that would have fit.

FLEA: The music of Jane's Addiction revolves around Eric's bass playing . . . which is technically very simple. In all the songs, you really feel the bass at the center. He was no virtuoso at putting down fancy speed chops, but conceptually he was absolutely incredible, melodically and groove-wise. There'll never be anything like it again. It's one-of-a-kind bass playing.

ERIC AVERY: My first jam with Perry eventually turned into "Mountain Song." Later, Perry said he thought that I was either a genius—because I didn't do anything other than play the same notes over and over—or that I just didn't know how to play at all.

BOB FORREST: The bass [in Jane's] is just something that you're never going to forget. The bass is dark, spooky . . . the lead instrument. Like Joy Division. And David plays such solo-ey stuff that you need the bass to be there all the time. Most of their early songs are arranged jams centered around a bass.

ERIC AVERY: Peter Hook from Joy Division probably was the largest influence on my playing.

DAVE NAVARRO: Clearly Eric's bass lines were the signature sound. His playing provided a whole dynamic that transcends words. He had a grounded, repetitive, rolling sonic quality, but extremely melodic, that was unusual for metal-influenced players like Stephen and myself to connect with and add to.

FLEA: Eric is one of the greatest rock bass players ever. I'd put him in the top five or ten, for sure . . . up there with Jah Wobble, Entwistle, John Paul Jones, Jack Bruce, Mike Watt . . . for the bass lines of "Nothing's Shocking" and "Ritual." A lot of the songs start with just the bass. As soon as Eric would play two notes the crowd would just go nuts.

BASIC MUSIC LESSONS/CONCEPTS

PERRY FARRELL: I was a singer who didn't know how to play guitar. Casey taught me some basic song things, some basic chords on her acoustic guitar.

CASEY NICCOLI: I played self-taught guitar and I'd had a couple of lessons in music theory in high school. I couldn't sing, but I could play guitar. I knew a C, a G, and a D chord.

PERRY FARRELL: I discovered that writing on an acoustic guitar is a wonderful way to start. If you can get a song structured on an acoustic guitar to sound good, you can expand it out to electric surely. I wrote a lot on acoustic guitar. It's a beautiful experience to play acoustic at small parties. You're hanging out at somebody's house and you can always pick up an acoustic guitar and just kind of jam any old time.

BOB FORREST: Punk rock was getting an amp and playing as loud and fast as you can, but Jane's Addiction introduced acoustic guitars—or re-introduced them in a big way for the first time since . . . say . . . Zeppelin III? Acoustic guitars were slowly coming back in to hard rock because of the influence of Daniel Ash from Bauhaus and now . . . Dave Navarro of Jane's Addiction was doing it. . . .

DAVE NAVARRO: I'm much more impressed by Daniel Ash than by [the big chops guys] like Vai and Yngwie Malmsteen. I don't own any of those records and would never purchase one. But I'm amazed by their playing. Steve Vai does get incredible sounds. I'm not a sports fan, but when I see an incredible athlete I'm impressed.

DANIEL ASH: That's nice to hear. Dave Navarro is a much more technically proficient guitar player than I am. I always just treated the guitar as a piece of wood with six strings to make noise and write songs with rather than trying to copy Hendrix or whatever because I knew I would never be able to do that anyway. Hendrix had already achieved the maximum and I couldn't get close, so why go in that direction? I would go more in the direction of a band like, say, early Devo, which was sort of going the punk way of simplifying everything. The simplest things are the best musically, as are most things in life, but I think Dave plays a lot more like Page than he does me, that's for sure. I don't mean that as an insult, because the guy's great.

DAVE NAVARRO: Ash is no technical wizard, but he knows what's needed in each song, and that makes it so much more beautiful for the listener. Daniel Ash and Robert Smith of the Cure are my favorite guitarists. [The Butthole Surfers' Paul Leary is another influence], I love the guitar sound—how it's just kind of all over the place. I don't want to call it sloppy, but it's almost anti-guitar. I think the best formula for playing guitar is no formula at all.[26]

DANIEL ASH: I wasn't into Zeppelin at all. I appreciated Hendrix and I also loved Mick Ronson. Ronson could say so much more with three notes than anybody else could with three dozen. My favorite ever guitar solo is the end of "Moonage Daydream."

PERRY'S LYRICS

CASEY NICCOLI: Perry could take other people's words and rewrite them. Like if you said something funny, all of a sudden, it became a song. He kept tons of journals. He wrote all of the lyrics himself.

DAN NAVARRO: Perry captured that time period and the sense of things in his lyrics. No one else was doing that at that point. They were making a beautiful noise and it was rollicking and they were great to see live, but I wasn't getting the message [from any other band] the way I was from Jane's. What was being said was monumental: "Pigs in Zen," "One Percent," "Jane Says," "I Would for You."

STEPHEN PERKINS: When I hear Perry's lyrics, that's how I express my drum part.

ERIC AVERY: Just great fucking lyrics, that's where Perry's untouchable.

DAN NAVARRO: None of the A&R people could see or hear it at first. No one got it that Perry was telling stories about his childhood and his parents. Jane's was not only a thinking man's thing, mostly because of Perry's lyrics, it was also a "feeling" man's metal.

BOB FORREST: Emo-metal anyone?

THE STYLE SECTION

PERRY FARRELL: When you're in a rock band, your best stylist is your girl.

JANE BAINTER: Perry was really focused on one goal . . . to be a rock star dressed to stun. He was different then, but he wasn't as different as he was when he got his piercings, when he got his scarification and he began braiding his hair a year later. Perry was really into African tribalism and the ancient ritualistic arts of different cultures. He said the scarification was done by some anthropology professor at UCLA.

Perry Farrell was reportedly bummed that his African scarification cuts healed without permanent scarring, bushman style. (Chris Cuffaro)

DAVID J: Perry told me about his scarification, how he'd got 200 cuts on his body because he wanted to experience the ritual. Once you've gone through that kind of pain and you have this record of it on your body you can psychically tap into that experience to be stronger in the face of future adversity. He was very disappointed because the welts didn't come out like on black bodies. They didn't have that effect on his body.

If you look very close, he's got hundreds of these cuts on his body. It seemed like there was something very shamanic about it. He would really get into these other states of consciousness.

JOSH RICHMAN: He was [one of the] the first white guy[s] to have dreadlocks. [One of] the first to have piercings.

PERRY FARRELL: I got pierced because you're hanging around with a lot of art punks, and a lot of them were gay and into this mild to heavy bondage. They were so cool, I just wanted to adorn myself right along-side of them. Eventually I took all my piercings out. I was out there surfing with a tit ring, and the next thing you know I ripped my nipple off. And then every week one of my ears would turn into like a rose bud, it would get so swollen up. The clincher was, one night I came home from a gig blazing on acid, and I wanted to get my nose ring out but the membranes inside my nose had all swollen up. I tried for prob-ably four hours to get this damned aching nose ring out. I finally got it out the next day after I passed out and so I finally said, "Forget it, it's just not worth the energy."

JANE BAINTER: Xiola Blue, this girlfriend of Perry's before Casey, first wore her hair in braids, and she probably influenced him to put a ring in his nose and a bow in his hair. That immediately made him stand apart from everyone else in the scene. . . .

PERRY FARRELL: I would borrow corsets and things from Casey. You wore a blazer and a corset . . . with boots and a wacky hat and gloves, and you just went down Melrose to mix it up and meet some people.

INGER LORRE (lead vocalist, Nymphs): You'd see Perry peacocking on Melrose in Doc Martens with boxer shorts over long johns.

ERIC AVERY: Casey definitely had a huge impact on Perry and therefore a profound impact on us as a band. She has a great aesthetic sense so I'd check with her, "Is this fucking thing stupid?"

INGER LORRE: Perry and I both had that style thing going on at the same time. We never talked about it. He would say nice things. He'd say, "Nice hat!" and I'd say, "Nice gloves." We just nodded to each other: "You look good." It was never like, "Hey, Inger, can I borrow a hat pattern?" And I never said, "Hey, dude, stop dressing like me." When a man does it, it looks like his own thing.

DAVE NAVARRO: We were very much into thrift shopping. Garments became communal. On different photo shoots you'll see a hat that was Perry's in '89 become mine in 1990. Or some pair of pants that were once Stephen's on Eric. A lot of it looks goofy now, but it wasn't intentional. The visual de-unification didn't put us into a category which I think helped the longevity of the band.

CHARLEY BROWN: Perry's dress sense reminded me of an Indian, in a crazy top hat with his dreads and his pierced nose and this corset.

INGER LORRE: I was wearing long gloves past my elbows, because as a female, having tracks on those delicate sweet little arms is just not a pretty sight. Then Perry started wearing those same gloves and hats. He might have had one or two hats his own style, but the big, huge madhatter kind, he copped from me. There was no rave scene yet. I just always loved hats. I didn't have very much money so I sewed and made everything myself. Some things would come out half-assed and I would always make them in better materials so if they looked weird, at least they were made of velvet so it would give an air of richness. They came out looking madhatterish just because they would be leaning sideways and skewed because I had just started sewing. Then we had the thing where we would wear stripes with the hats and purple and green, the color schemes, magenta, and green and purple.

ERIC AVERY: The initial reaction from the business end was how are you going to package this? It's not Motley Crue. It's not Guns N' Roses. How do you market this? A guy in a corset with dreadlocks, another with pink hair who looks like a punk rocker . . . and then *two* heavy metal hippie guys from the Valley? We didn't make for a great, tidy package. People used to comment, "You guys are such a hodge-podge of styles, you look like four different bands."

DAVE NAVARRO: There wasn't a unified thread between us. Perry had a whole freakish look of his own, like some skinny, bugged-out goth surfer in whore makeup with flailing dreadlocks. Eric was more traditional punk rock, and Stephen had this crazy Afro hair thing. I was kind of a hippie kid, a little Deadhead gone heavy metal. But you

Perry and Casey. Contemplating the lilies. (Karyn Cantor)

throw us together and it was a patchwork quilt—it doesn't look like it makes sense, but it keeps you warm.

DAN NAVARRO: Perry scared the crap out of me at first. The girdle and the pantyhose . . . the dreads, the crazy doll makeup, and the nose ring, looking like he weighed 95 pounds; definitely not a conventional hard rock voice, not Sebastian Bach in looks. Perry was a freak from the point of view of the hair metal establishment. . . .

KARYN CANTOR: Perry and Casey definitely had an exotic hippie quality in their style. They were making jewelry and selling it at Grateful Dead concerts. I don't think they were particularly into the music, but Perkins and Navarro were! Dave was a total hippie.

THE JANE'S ADDICTION SOUND "ART BAND" OR "REAL ROCK BAND"?

PERRY FARRELL: Musically, there really wasn't a neat ilk for us either. There was metal, but we weren't extreme deathcore metal . . . and we sure weren't down with those shaggy poodle metal pop types either.

Art for art's sake. (Karyn Cantor)

There was punk rock, which wasn't getting major attention, but we weren't exactly punk anyway. And there was jangly R.E.M.-style collegiate pop-rock, but that wasn't us either.

TED GARDNER (tour manager Jane's Addiction, later became their manager): The hair band situation was starting to wane. Guns N' Roses were the biggest band in the world and Poison was still around. Nirvana hadn't come out. We were riding that pause between the death of one and the birth of another. Jane's Addiction was a very different style of band musically, visually. It didn't fit anything.[27]

INGER LORRE: Where Guns N' Roses were great seedy rock 'n' rollers, Jane's Addiction and The Nymphs were trying to do art. We used the punk ideology, but what we were doing was more planned out. Although some of it was obviously preconceived, most of it happened very naturally.

DAN NAVARRO: Jane's was the first possibility that a hard rock band had something of value to say instead of girls, girls, girls, party, party, party . . . Motley Crue-Ratt style. It may have been rockin' but it was just too clean, and I don't mean that as positive.

FLEA: Jane's did all this stuff that we just couldn't have done in the Chili Peppers at that time. Big, long, epic, classic rock guitar solos, slow beautiful ballads . . . pretty psychedelic stuff, acoustic guitars, hand drums, tambourines . . . they worked a much wider musical palette than any other band of the era. . . .

DAN NAVARRO: Writers were saying "thinking man's metal." Dave was going some places that none of the hair bands were going musically on the guitar. Alternative radio was very *boing, boing, boing,* synthy sounds and bouncy Depeche Mode sounds. The dreaded new wave. Hard rock was either anachronistic like Led Zeppelin was considered at that point, same goes for Deep Purple, The Who . . . or it was an endless stream of Triumph, Poison, Ratt, Warrant, Saga, Night Ranger. Hair bands.

ERIC AVERY: I remember the phrase "art metal" or that we were an "art band" but whenever they said that there was frequently an edge of derision to it, like that was the quickest way to discount something that wasn't proletarian enough, not populist enough for the rock 'n' roll masses. Some people didn't know how to differentiate us from the other bangy guitar hair bands topping the *Billboard* charts at the time. . . .

PERRY FARRELL: *Of course* we're an art band, and damned proud of it. Isn't music an art form, too? Art had gotten so far away from popular music.[28]

JOSH RICHMAN: Whatever it was, everyone was hyped up for this new jam rock style. . . . Perry was calling it "groove-metal." . . .

FLEA: As time went by this band Jane's Addiction definitely influenced us, particularly John [Frusciante] and I.

JOHN FRUSCIANTE (musician, songwriter, member Red Hot Chili Peppers): I was eighteen when I joined the Chili Peppers. I was caught totally off balance. I quit when I was twenty-two and I just thought everything's over. I needed time to do absolutely nothing and I needed time to have no responsibilities other than to experience life. Jane's Addiction guided me in ways that would be embarrassing to explain in detail, but their music was important to me during that period. I was figuring out what kind of feelings I wanted my music to represent.

With the song "I Could Have Lied" by the Chili Peppers, my intention was to write a guitar part that was the same vibe as the bass line on "Three Days."

DAVE NAVARRO: Jane's Addiction created its art through a self-destructive process, whereas the Chili Peppers create their art through the healing process.[29]

GOTH-METAL TRANSMISSION: The TVC15 Connection

Circa 1985–86

Motley Crue. Several veteran club scenesters earnestly believed at first that they were a parody dress-up joke band patterned on the Tubes, Kiss, and the NY Dolls. The archetypal obnoxious, beyond-punk big-hair "New Wave of American Pop Metal" counterpart to the NWOBHM phenom in the U.K., which spawned a million wannabes. Jane's Addiction eventually became a sort of feminine counterpart to this band and Guns N' Roses in the hard-rock sweepstakes. (Lynda Burdick)

DJ JOSEPH BROOKS: We were mixing the first Motley Crue record with Bauhaus and Sisters of Mercy [at the TVC15 club, another Joseph Brooks-Henry Peck weekly promotion that followed the closure of the original Fetish Club]. We thought this was going to be the next thing, glam metal. It was very much like the goth-death rock look. Christian Death was very close to what Motley Crue was looking like and doing. We started playing with that and then added Hanoi Rocks and New York Dolls and all this glammy metal sounding stuff . . . we put it together with Siouxsie. Siouxsie and the Crue are also connected . . . each band covered "Helter Skelter." The Crue had their first record come out on their own label, Leathur Records. We did a window display at Vinyl Fetish [record store originally on Melrose] for it and people were shocked. We took a lot of shit. How could you do a window display for this record? This isn't alternative; it's cheapshit Gazzarri's pay-to-play heavy metal! But we thought it fit perfectly with this punky gothic thing.

MIKE STEWART: As the DJ at Scream I probably was closer to the old Fetish format than TVC15, bearing in mind TVC15 came after the Fetish. TVC15 was trying to be more glam, metal, and rock. Joseph took out all the dancey stuff because he had already done that with Fetish and he was so over those two crates. He was trying to push the format toward what he liked, and he just really liked heavier guitar rock at that time. Scream was definitely not a "rock club" but it had some rock parts to it. The Scream became more popular [once it moved from Mondays to Fridays and basically killed off TVC15] because we had a more open format. We didn't specialize or push one way or the other. I'd play what I wanted that I thought people would dance to. I never played Motley Crue or Ratt at the Scream, that was way too rock for me. As rock as I ever got was playing The Cult's first record, which had all the big hits on it, but that was considered "alternative."

JOSEPH BROOKS: This was major crossover time. This new crowd would listen to the Banshees *and* Motley Crue. [Around '85, '86] I had the [Vinyl Fetish] record store and Henry owned Wednesdays at the Glam Slam [the pre-Roxbury Imperial Gardens sushi restaurant on Sunset]. People wore the appropriate kind of clothes that liked both kinds of bands. The kids that hung out at our store during the day went to all these metal . . . gothic . . . glam . . . clubs at night; people that ended up starting bands like Guns n' Roses, L.A. Guns, Faster Pussycat. . . .

The Glam Slam convened by pioneering rock club DJ Henry Peck at the Imperial Gardens, a sushi bar-restaurant on Sunset Strip, circa 1985. Eventually the same space morphed into the legendary Roxbury sleazepit immortalized in some daft forgotten movie. Peacocking, mooching, brawling, and slamming unlimited sake with beer chasers paid for by girls with day jobs became the weekly Wednesday ritual for a gaggle of gnarler dudes who eventually morphed from Hollywood Rose into L.A. Guns, Guns N' Roses, and Faster Pussycat. (Publicity photo)

8225 SUNSET BLVD.   EVERY WEDNESDAY   10PM-2AM   FULL BAR $5
DJ-HENRY FROM VINYL FETISH   TRASH GLAM PSYCHEDELIA PAST TO PRESENT

MIKE STEWART: TVC15 was at the Ebony Theater of the Arts on Washington, in a predominantly black area of Los Angeles. That's how we knew about it. It was just a seated theater and a little lobby. Two doors down there was this little gymnasium. We booked both rooms for the Scream and I DJ'd the main floor and had three bands play: Jane's Addiction, Cold September, and Damn Yankees. It was Scream's first night ever having bands, although the club had previously existed as a Monday night DJ-only promotion, first at the Seven Seas, owned by Eddie Nash. . . . Later, we moved it to the Probe for safety, a few weeks after the Cathouse took over Tuesday nights there. Jane's Addiction were brand new. They'd only played one or two gigs, if even that, but they said they'd help us out with some extra promotion. I didn't know what to expect. As soon as they climbed onto the stage you could feel the vibe in the room change instantly. Perry was standing motionless, striking a total Bowie stage pose, covered with this long coat. He drops the coat off his shoulders onto the floor vamp-style, just like a stripper, and he's completely naked except for a pair of nylons. You can see everything he has! So he grabs the mic and goes off at the crowd, like, "Hey, you . . . I'm Perry, man . . . and I came here to do two things: one, to rock the fuck out!" and he grabs himself; "Two, to show my cock off!" and he just went straight into the first song, probably was "Whores." The four guys on stage looked like they didn't belong with each other. Dave was so pretty he looked like a girl, Perry looked like the Domino's Pizza noid on drugs, jumping and vibrating and screaming and singing. The drummer Steve had this real kinky hair and looked like a stoner-surfer dude from the Valley. Eric was in the corner, the slow, but very sly Venice Beach guy.

DAVE NAVARRO: My first memory of the Scream was the Ebony Theater. Perry performed the whole show in a shopping cart, like literally we had a shopping cart on stage and I was wearing a floppy hat and a tie-dye and no shoes . . . some of that Grateful Dead influence still there!

MIKE STEWART: Perry brought this shopping cart on stage and while he's in the cart singing we were divvying up the money. We were already real nervous about the gig in general. Someone supposedly drove by earlier and said, "You guys don't belong in this neighborhood." I had a gun with me. We called it the Value-Pac. I hid it in a McDonald's bag. Bruce was out front when someone drove by in a Cadillac and threw a Molotov cocktail at the front door. Now the front door's on fire! Bruce came running in with the money. I said, "Shit, better get the dough!" and so I grabbed all the money in this briefcase and ran to my car and split from this hood as fast as I could.

"GONNA KICK TOMORROW" (1986)

FLEA: There was a very distinct, very L.A. music scene, and it was very quirky, and artistic, and bisexual, and punk at the same time; it was angry, and effeminate, and cool . . . that's what Jane's Addiction brought to the table. They also brought this macho heavy metal, this dirty rock 'n' roll thing together. Those two things had major links to two totally different parts of the L.A. music scene.

Into the Mystic. Prophet Peretz ponders the Stairway to Heaven. (Chris Cuffaro)

CASEY NICCOLI: When you're twenty-seven in rock 'n' roll with nothing really happening you think you're old. That's why Steve, Dave, and Eric were seven or eight years younger than Perry. He felt like he could mold them and they would forever do what he wanted. Eventually, they'd grow up, but by then he'd have gotten what he needed out of them.

PERRY FARRELL: I got into music kinda late. I didn't get into it to be a rock star. It seemed really cool to try to put together some creative interesting music—but not rock. I didn't even have a record player or a radio when I was growing up.[30]

DAN NAVARRO: I was aware Perry was quite a bit older than the rest of them. He was articulate, real interesting to talk to, and I was impressed by how polite he was. He was like twenty-seven or twenty-eight, and they were like eighteen–twenty.

PETE WEISS: People in our little L.A. scene of the 80s were following in the footsteps of the first punk rockers, we were the generation after them. We looked up to them, we liked their ideals. We took that shit to heart! A lot of us distilled the real message of it—and lived it out. We thought we were exactly like them because we rejected the status quo, we were inventing our own lives, creating our own lifestyles, not living by someone else's rules. We applied old punker ideas about leading the DIY life—just do it yourself 'cuz no other fucker will. Punk rockers spoke to us, they taught us you don't have to work within the mainstream to make your way. We also loved their music to pieces.

PERRY FARRELL: Punk was a catchphrase for so much more than punk rock. It didn't matter how old you were. It didn't matter how much training you had; you could enter at any level, do anything you wanted with it. . . .

THE BE LIVE SHOW

March 23, 1986

PERRY FARRELL: I would drive around looking for warehouses and find out who owned them.

CASEY NICCOLI: The Be Live show was another legend in early Jane's Addiction lore.

PERRY FARRELL: Bianca said she'd put up some money for a show and so we found a place. You set up once, do it once. If you can get out of there without cops arresting people and confiscating your money, you did a good job. You just started looking around for dilapidated warehouses that might need a little bit of spending money and you'd say to them, "How would you like to have a party here?"

Be Live flyer.

BOB FORREST: This was *years* before born-again psychedelia and electronic dance culture came out of the underground warehouse parties. . . .

PERRY FARRELL: I had no money of my own. Bianca put up for all these shows. Bianca always took the money with old black tape on her tits. That was to draw people in. Bianca always worked the door because she wanted to show her tits. We got Thelonious Monster and Jane's Addiction, we got a laser light show. Smoke machines. Spinning lights. PA. We set up in this warehouse on Beverly Boulevard near Silverlake. I found a place that does custom motorcycles, and I said, "Hey, man, how'd you like to display at a rock show?" This stunt pulled in like ten custom choppers, but I didn't tell them I was also having a transvestite dance review.

REBECCA AVERY: The Be Live show was just bizarre. So much prep work went into it, so much excitement. So much hope had been placed into this one night. It's going to be great. It's got everything! But in the end it was just awful, it was a big flop. Nobody came except us diehards, close friends of the band and a few others. . . .

CASEY NICCOLI: Hardly anybody showed up!

BOB FORREST: Luckily, our band had seven people in it . . . made it seem like there were more people there.

DAVE NAVARRO: It was a wild night, but an obvious financial disaster. Poor Bianca lost her shirt financially.

PERRY FARRELL: . . . literally, as well. She was strutting around with the cashbox topless, with duct tape on her nipples.

CASEY NICCOLI: We had fire-eaters on stage. We had a hot dog stand going, too.

ERIC AVERY: The guys in Thelonious Monster and Fishbone were there, and I think Anthony Kiedis was humping some girl in the pit.

CASEY NICCOLI: It smelled really bad. The hot dog cart was smoking. You couldn't breathe or see anything. We didn't realize there wasn't any ventilation!

BOB FORREST: We [Thelonious Monster] were playing at this weird storefront garage warehouse thing that Perry set up. It had the greatest PA and there was lights and a motorcycle exhibit with bondage girls all tied up. We played and Jane's Addiction watched us and then they were playing and we watched them.

DAN NAVARRO: Perry stripped down to sheer panty hose and nothing else. The opening act was a group of transsexual strippers.

PERRY FARRELL: It was quite the cast. Macho biker dudes mixed with punk rockers, artists, drunks from the Zero Zero Club, and Bianca's clients—bow-legged old guys in sweaters reeking of cologne, with white shoes and hairpieces. There were also some under-age, metal-rocker kids from the Valley, friends of Dave and Steve's. But the kids couldn't handle their liquor. One of them passed out, and when he woke up, his pants were down around his ankles, and somebody told him that one of the trannies had sucked him off.

DAVE NAVARRO: My friend drank himself into a blackout. I left him crashed on this couch, and when I came back later, his pants were down around his ankles and he was sound asleep with an erection, and there was a transsexual hovering over him. I kind of shooed him away.

PERRY FARRELL: The kid should have just gone with it, chalked it up to experience, but he lost his mind. . . . It was the old panic trauma, "Oh, no-o-o-o . . . my cock penetrated a man's skull . . . now I'm *gaaaaaay!!!!!*"

DAVE NAVARRO: It was our first exposure to this elaborately seedy, fabulously filthy Hollywood underground scene that we'd only ever heard or read about. I was, like, eighteen years old—in awe. I was over the moon. I'd finally made it at last.

PERRY FARRELL: That was the Be Live show. The name makes no sense, but Bianca, because it was her money, she had the say. She named it the Be Live. I still don't know what it means.

PAY TO PLAY

Circa May 1986

DAVE NAVARRO: Perry and I went to see whoever was booking the Troubadour who agreed to let us perform, but then asked us for money. We were stunned. We couldn't believe we were being asked for money . . . pre-sold tickets, deposits on microphones, or whatever they claimed it was for, but we were hungry and eager. We were in such shock that we paid it and went on our way to try and sell these tickets.

PERRY FARRELL: The whole pay-to-play plague was happening in Los Angeles where a band couldn't get a gig on Sunset Strip or the Troubadour without paying for rental of microphones and pre-buying the tickets. We were so against that we said, "Screw you all! Let's find a warehouse!"

Adorable Dave, dear to every woman. (Valerie)

JEAN-PIERRE BOCCARA (club owner-talent booker): From a club booker's perspective, most of the local bands were overexposed; always playing too much in the same geographical area, always diluting their draw. Some local bands played more than twice in the same week . . . and then kvetch there wasn't anywhere to play! Places like the Lingerie, the Anti-Club, the O.N. Klub, Al's Bar, the Brave Dog, Theoretical, Phenomenon, the Music Machine, plus my club, the Lhasa Club, although we were more diversified with spoken word, avant-garde cabaret, and live performance art. All these small bar-driven clubs were competing for the same bands, but I'll say it . . . it did create a thriving scene. None of these clubs had pay-to-play policies like the Troubadour in West Hollywood and Gazzarri's, the Whisky and the Roxy up on the Strip. Bands would argue, "How are we to develop a following if we don't play around?" The big daddies who ran the Strip turned it around; they put their foot down and made the bands pay *them* for the honor of playing their world-famous soundstages.

TEXACALA JONES: The very first places I ever played at were the Lingerie and the Cathay de Grande and they weren't charging anybody to play at those places, mister! The bands that I hung out with or played shows with just wouldn't do that, couldn't afford to, even if they wanted to. We played with the Sirens, Blood on the Saddle, Tupelo Chainsex, the Blasters, X, lots of other bands, even Jane's Addiction refused to pay to play. They played it our way.

DAVE NAVARRO: I made some flyers and underneath the Troubadour logo I wrote, "Where you pay to play." I handed out all these flyers at

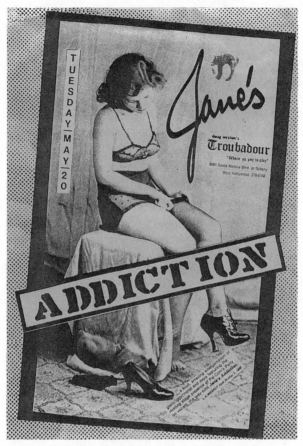

The Troubadour, "Where You Pay to Play."
(Courtesy Rebecca Avery)

Scream and the Cathouse. I also drove by the Troub and just threw a stack of them on the sidewalk. The following day they yanked us from the bill, so we got a whole bunch of people calling the club asking what time we go on and they were told that we'd pulled out. We looked at it as a small victory of some kind.

WALT KIBBY, JR.: We wouldn't pay to play. Hell, no. That's not the way to do it. The club scene was mostly done on just hard work. Just playing, promoting yourself, filling the clubs. If everybody knows it's the thing to go and see, if they know it's a good bill of bands, they'll go and see it.

TEXACALA JONES: Mostly all the hair bands did the pay-to-play scam. Maybe their parents helped them out and what not. Nobody I ever knew did that. We didn't really hang out with many metal people. We would play at dives like the Cathay and then Raji's and the Underwear Club [Club Lingerie] before it shut down. Music Machine, Al's Bar, Anti-Club, Club 88, those places didn't charge you money; only the Strip clubs got away with it 'cuz they had the cool address, they had the famous location. . . .

KURT FISHER (club owner): At Club Lingerie there was no pay to play. My booker [this book's author], Brendan Mullen, was always saying, "If you can't book a great show that people will come out for . . . then just forget it . . . go home . . . get out of the business. . . ."

POWERTOOLS, L.A.'S LAST MONOLITHIC MEGA CLUB

BOB FORREST: There were so many changes going on with the downtown scene. Jane's was the complete band of their time. They played in the lobby at Powertools. Sometimes acoustically in the siderooms. The residency at Scream came later that same year.

JOSH RICHMAN: I hung out weekends at Powertools. I was the guy with the no shoes, and the cane and the bowler or the cowboy hat. The promoters Matt [Dike] and Jon [Sidel] were my friends. One time they were doing a huge rock 'n' roll theme night. . . .

JON SIDEL: We were big on Area-style [legendary 80s N.Y. disco] shifting installations and themes. . . .

JOSH RICHMAN: I told Sidel, "Get this band Jane's Addiction to play the base of the stairs and everybody will be blown away."

JON SIDEL: Josh called me because we sometimes did live shows but rarely full-on rock bands with cranked guitars. We were a DJ-driven dance club with emphasis on r&b/funk, soul and hip-hop, sometimes with a little bit of rock thrown in, depending on [DJ] Matt Dike's mood. Josh said, "Check out this band that Matt Chaikin of Kommunity FK got goin' with Perry Farrell, the singer from Psi Com." We were producing a special rock 'n' roll theme night so I jumped for the idea.

JOSH RICHMAN: Sidel was like, "Matt from Kommunity FK is the drummer—dude, there'll be goth chicks!" Sidel and Dike were really into goth chicks but had been unable to get anywhere near them on their own. Now these two East Coast transplants had the hottest dance club of the decade on their hands. It didn't matter how the band sounded, they just prayed some goths would come down from Hollywood because the Psi Com guy and somebody from Kommunity FK had this new band.

BOB FORREST: I saw the first Jane's Addiction show on the steps of Powertools at the Park Plaza Hotel. The crowd was just ignoring them, walking past them on their way upstairs to dance [in the main ballroom]. That dance crowd just didn't care about any live band. They wanted to pose and listen to [70s and 80s] funk tracks with Matt Dike DJ'ing, hoping to get mentioned in *Details* or *La Di Dah*. Jane's set up on the steps, just a tiny combo busking away like they were on the street with only a few people watching. . . .

JOSH RICHMAN: Jane's set up on this beautiful marble floor, no stage at all, below these wonderful old chandeliers. There were 100 people sitting on the stairs gawking. . . .

BOB FORREST: Later, we played with them a few times in the side lounges downstairs at Powertools . . . big rooms with these amazing high ceilings, they had like these classic Masonic columns and carvings. . . .

REBECCA AVERY: They were like huge carpeted rooms with no stages. Just set up on the floor . . .

BOB FORREST: We had total freedom to decide our own set times and the length of them and we got to play anything we wanted.

DAVE NAVARRO: Sometimes I jammed with Thelonious Monster downstairs at Powertools. I'd sit in on a song or two. It was real loose and fun with those guys.

BOB FORREST: There was a medium amount of people there because we were like sideshow bands near the bar area; that's when the Jane's guys

Early Jane's line-up plays a sideroom at Powertools, a two-story,
multi-room pre-rave dance club with themed installations, which
convened weekly at the Park Plaza Hotel, MacArthur Park.
(Karyn Cantor)

got into more experimental acoustic things, something they were always real good at. People would come in to buy drinks and then maybe
hang for a few numbers then wander out again to peacock around the
lobby and the stairs under these old chandeliers. . . .

PERRY FARRELL: I remember these cool chandeliers, wrought iron . . .
beautifully crafted woodwork . . . the interior and the exterior [of the
Park Plaza Hotel] was a trip, an L.A. monument overlooking MacArthur
Park. Used to be some kind of Elks' Lodge back in its day. . . .

BOOTED FROM CLUB LINGERIE

October 1, 1986

WALT KIBBY, JR.: Melvis, this door chick from the Lingerie, was pissed
off at everybody and everybody was pissed off at her! When we

played Lingerie, we were all way under twenty-one, too young to get in anyway. She always tried to keep us in the back, and one time Angelo snuck out and ran upstairs just to see his father, and Melvis saw him and just threw him down the stairs and tossed him out! She was just a hard-assed chick. After a while all the bands started talking to each other about that club and what they were going to do when they were going there next. People looked forward to going in and messing up, like you had to go in there and prove something because they were such assholes, well maybe not all of 'em, but Melvis for sure. . . .

DAYLE GLORIA (DJ, Scream booker): I was DJ-ing at Lingerie the night Perry flew off the stage and jumped up on the bar, and knocked everything off. Every glass, all the ashtrays, the cherries, everything.

DEAN NALEWAY: Perry said, "Fuck it, I'm not doing this show." And I said, "Perry, you've got to. Important people are coming down, we can't get a rep as fucking flakes. You've gotta do this show." And he's like, "Dean, there's only one way I'll do it." And I'm like, "Anything, just name it, 'cause we gotta do the show," and he's like, "You let me run across the bar in the middle of the set." And I'm like, "Oh-oh." I said, "Perry, that's like a lawsuit waiting to happen." He's like, "That's the only way I'll do the show." I said, "Okay, but do it with only two songs left, at least get most of the set done."

DAVE NAVARRO: Perry jumped off the stage and ran down the bar and kicked everybody's drinks over and so we got blacklisted. . . .

CHARLEY BROWN: Perry got pissed off at something. It was like an antelope the way he leaped from the stage to that railing and made this spectacular jump to the bar. I remember being pretty pissed. The Lingerie was an important room at that time . . . and now he's got us booted from there. . . .

KURT FISHER: I don't think they were too worried about it. Many of the bands I 86'd from the Lingerie went on to bigger and brighter things, some became big-time legends: Gun Club, Top Jimmy & the Rhythm Pigs, Red Hot Chili Peppers—I remember tossing Fishbone and Jane's Addiction. El Duce and the Mentors. Thelonious Monster hit the curb a few times, too.

BOB FORREST: Top Jimmy and Carlos Guitarlos were booted all the time. . . . Jeffrey Lee Pierce also made Kurt's Hall of Fame Shitlist. . . .

PETE WEISS: Flea pissed all over the stage into the monitors at Lingerie, that got the Chili Peppers bounced for sure. . . .

DAVE NAVARRO: Stephen and I were like eighteen years old, so we weren't allowed in the Lingerie, except to play. It was strictly twenty-one and over. We'd be headlining there and be waiting in the car outside until it was time to go on. Since we had nothing to do, we got so drunk one time I blacked out and kicked the monitors off the stage and smashed my guitar and broke my equipment. Had I been allowed into the club in the first place I can assure you I would just *never* have gotten so wasted right before I had to play. . . .

DEAN NALEWAY: Later, the owner guy Kurt—still paid us some, but he took off for the shit that Perry and Dave broke. He said, "This band will never fucking play here again. But, I have to tell you, this was one of the best shows we've ever had."

WALT KIBBY, JR.: It was a good spot for a club, and there was always great shows booked there, and if you packed it, there was a good vibe, but some of the people running the door there were just horrible, man.

DENNIS MARTINO (bar manager, Club Lingerie): It became like a club, this weird all-male fraternity of bad boys. Getting bounced from the Lingerie by Kurt or Melvis [our over-heated platinum-quiffed star doorperson of the time] bonded these guys into a larger group which only increased their notoriety; it just made 'em get more popular! A few months later, Brendan would talk Kurt into lightening up and he'd promote a bunch of these bands together on special "amnesty" forgiveness theme nights . . . and there would be lines around the block to see them. . . . Worked like a charm every time . . . and Melvis would get even more pissy that her authority had been undermined!

WALT KIBBY, JR.: It was like, if you get banned from that club, that puts you up there. The Beat Farmers was another one that always used to get kicked out.

DAYLE GLORIA: Jane's was banned from the Lingerie so I said, "Come and play for me, I don't care if you break anything."

THE SCREAM (1985–89)

Circa November 1986 through 1987

Jane's Addiction plays regularly at the Scream and explodes locally (basement of the Embassy Hotel, 851 S. Grand, downtown Los Angeles).

CHARLEY BROWN: We got kicked out of virtually every club we played, which is why we played parties so much, and why Scream became our main L.A. play.

JOSH RICHMAN: The scene that [was gathering] around Jane's was ancillary to this thing that was going on with Guns N' Roses and Faster Pussycat, L.A. Guns and Jetboy. Those bands were playing the Troubadour and the Strip, but Jane's was selling out the Lingerie, the Palace in Hollywood, the Country Club in Reseda; they also got the Lhasa Club and the Powertools downtown art crowd. Then, they started to play regularly at the Scream.

BRYAN RABIN (club promoter, party planner, PR guru): As just another scrappy little teenager finding myself in L.A. [mid-to-late 80s], Jane's Addiction were really exciting. At the time they broke, the predominant thing was heavy metal, which was gross and disgusting. Poison, Warrant, Motley Crue, and others come to mind. Punk rock, the more intelligent wing of aggressive hard rock had been marginalized years ago.

JOHNNY NAVARRO: It was pretty girls lined up around the block and guys lined up to see the girls and then everybody goes in to see the band. Smarter, more creative pretty girls really loved Jane's; chicks with sharper intellect who generally found Motley and Ratt dumb and repugnant. . . .

FLEA: To us, all the new hairspray bands were just ridiculous. The whole glam metal pop thing didn't make sense to us. We didn't even pay attention. It was a totally different world.

BRYAN RABIN: Sunset Strip was a horrifying mess, this gross metal thing had taken over when "alternative" still really meant something. It wasn't just another banner at first, another mall chain marketing niche, it wasn't just another dopey radio or MTV format. The Scream became such a phenom in L.A. . . . it was such a great alternative that everyone kind of glommed onto it as if it was their own.

PAUL V.: Nothing had really crossed over yet, but in those days it was like, "Who cares about alternative?" It was just sort of "Oh, that's that weird music that's on college radio."

BRYAN RABIN: People were living outside the line and experiencing different things, creating their own art and music. Jane's Addiction spearheaded the scene in a way that needed to happen, no matter how small that window was.

MIKE STEWART: Suddenly in the late 80s everyone liked everything. It was bizarre how everything opened up all of a sudden. There were all these small factions: punk rockers, mods, rockabillys, the goths, all the different factions, but the timing of Scream was just right: We were able to draw a little bit of everybody. They all liked looking at each other and hanging out together again and it all came together at one time.

CHARLEY BROWN: The Scream booked mostly the same headlining bands that were already doing the circuit, except they'd go after-hours, it was weekends only; that was its main appeal. . . .

MIKE STEWART: Scream lasted from December '85 till '89 at various locations. I thought of the name because I loved this photocopy I saw of the famous Munch painting and my best friend Steve Elkins created the logo. I thought it was a really disturbing image and a great name for a club. My first flyers used that exact painting. We were first at the Seven Seas, then the Probe on Mondays before we took Fridays at the Berwin. After we moved to the Embassy we hired Dayle Gloria to help with band booking and stage management. We booked all the bands by committee at first. There was definitely a crossover between bands that would regularly headline Lingerie and Scream because the Lingerie was a lot more alternative than any other club at the time. Then the Music Machine in West L.A. jumped in on the action, and they were raiding many of the same acts. . . .

JON SIDEL: Two blocks away from the Scream at the Embassy, the Variety Arts Center would be having these awesome national touring

FRIDAYS at the BERWIN
6525 Sunset Blvd.
18 and over

SCREAM

The Scream, with second location address. Promoters Mike Stewart and Bruce Purdue moved from a hostile neighborhood, which firebombed their club while Jane's Addiction was inside playing one of their first shows (the occasion also apparently marks the first time that Perry whipped out his member onstage). The Scream began to blow up after moving to the Berwin Entertainment Complex on Sunset Boulevard, following a sold-out show with Siouxsie and the Banshees at the Hollywood Palladium, literally a few blocks away, when the two savvy promoters promoted Scream as the after-party hotspot.

bands like the Butthole Surfers, The Replacements, Husker Du, Red
Hot Chili Peppers. Bands like that who were regarded as "alternative"
could sell out two nights there easily. It was just an incredible time.
One night the Beasties and Run-DMC did this spontaneous jam [at one
of the dance clubs held at the VAC]. They got up on stage unannounced with the DJ [Afrika Islam] and there was only one mic to go
around, so they were just passing it around. Afterwards, we'd literally
walk up the street to Scream to catch Jane's Addiction . . . they'd play
all night while some people danced to records in another room . . .
sometimes the whole area would be heaving with like three or four
thousand people between both places. . . .

MIKE STEWART: We could see each other from the two buildings, it was
like having not one, but *two* Danceteria-style clubs, like two club mini-
malls within two blocks . . . this was downtown L.A. of the 80s. . . .

KARYN CANTOR: After Scream moved into the basement at the Embassy
Hotel in downtown L.A. it became an integral part of Jane's career.
Playing there constantly, people seeing them a lot helped to consoli-
date and expand the fanbase they'd already accumulated fom all the
different little music scenes they'd touched on. . . .

MIKE STEWART: Perry told me he loved that space because it was sweaty.
People were like a bunch of bugs rubbing their wings together and creating this energy together. It was a nasty room for me. It was always
hot and you felt like the dirt was dripping on you.

PERRY FARRELL: Fire marshals would come in and break things up. It
was really cool; it was one of the first clubs to have a separate video
room. They built rooms where you could see . . . *strange things.* Anything went. Then they moved it to a hotel right downtown so it had
this air of danger. Outside, kids would get mugged. Everything was
busting out wild. Because I didn't have to play every night. I could go
all out when I did. I would break ribs and ankles, get black eyes, shit
like that. I can't do that now. You've got to pace yourself. But you can
really impress people breaking limbs. . . .[31]

MIKE STEWART: There was a certain core amount of people who'd go to
Scream no matter who played, probably about 500. We averaged probably around 1,000 to 1,200. If the band was bigger we'd go up to 1,500. In
the beginning Jane's Addiction benefited from Scream's basic draw. I'm

sure in the end we benefited due to Jane's Addiction's draw. On our last night we drew 3,000. A really good night would be 1,500–2,000 people. That main room could hold 1,000 so you're talking 1,000 sweaty people. People would do their drugs on the patio or have sex in the bathroom or in the dark video room, others just wanted to dance to the records and have a good time. There are a million stories about Scream and what went on there. We kept going until 4:00 or 5:00 in the morning.

KARYN CANTOR: Perry and Casey would go to the Scream and get treated like the royal couple of the scene. . . .

PERRY FARRELL: You knew you were going to see the same people every Friday at Scream. Afterwards, you went back to somebody's house until the sun came up.

DAYLE GLORIA: Jane's played monthly at Scream [from mid-'86, well into '87]. The club grew with them. We grew together. I kept booking them because if somebody would cancel, it was like, "Let's call Jane's Addiction." They became like the house band.

PERRY FARRELL: The club clicked and we clicked.[32]

Scream becomes home to Jane's
Addiction. (Karyn Cantor)

ON-STAGE BRAWLIN'
JANE'S ADDICTION IN NEW YORK
SCREAM NIGHT AT THE LIMELIGHT

Circa early January 1987

CHARLEY BROWN: Every time we left town they broke up.

ERIC AVERY: It was the first time Jane's went on a trip. We were taken by Mike Stewart and Dayle Gloria. They were trying to open up a club, Scream East, in New York. The Limelight space.

MIKE STEWART: The New York gig created a lot of drama.

Scream East flyer.
Mike Stewart: "There
was a lot of drama in
New York."

CHARLEY BROWN: The best show they ever broke up on was at the Limelight. The band got in a huge fight onstage. Ian Astbury and Billy Duffy from the Cult were in town trying out their Led Zeppelin stuff for the Electric album. The Cult were huge then and we were nobody.

DEAN NALEWAY: So the Cult guys jump up [at the finale of Jane's set] and Dave hands his guitar over and the Cult guy was playing it for a while until Dave suddenly snapped. He went up and unplugged the guy in the middle of a solo . . . just ripped the guitar back from the guy . . . and started wailing on the solo like a madman . . . this was beyond Spinal Tap!

CHARLEY BROWN: Billy and Ian came out with Eric and Steve and started doing Led covers. Backstage, Dave was incredibly drunk. He staggered out and unplugged Billy, and Duffy was left just kind of strumming on air, like, "What the fuck just happened?" Then Perry came out all jealous and they had a fucking major rip. He was ready to kill the whole band. He and Dave got in a fistfight.

ERIC AVERY: There was a huge tussle and I remember drums getting knocked over.

CHARLEY BROWN: They just went wild. Perry threw Dave into the drums and the whole set just fell apart.

TOM ATENCIO: Every night was theatre with Jane's Addiction.

PERRY FARRELL: I never thought pro wrestling was high entertainment. Led Zeppelin is high entertainment.[33]

GETTING SIGNED TO RECORD LABELS
WARNER BROS. ERA
COMPARISONS TO ZEPPELIN

Circa January 1987

AGENT AVA: I told Perry everybody's calling KXLU, asking when they could get music in the stores. He said I can't talk about that right now because there's some stuff in the works. I just knew at that point it wouldn't take long before they would go straight to the top.

DAVE NAVARRO: KXLU was the first local station to play our music. The first time I heard us on KXLU—I think it was the "Mountain Song" demo—you would have thought I was signed up to be on the first civilian flight to the moon. It was just the biggest deal. I was so excited.

ERIC AVERY: I was prouder of hearing a song that I made on KXLU than on regular radio. . . .

STEVEN BAKER (Warner Bros. Records executive): I was driving to work [at Warner Bros.] listening to KXLU and they played . . . "Jane Says." The first thing that struck me is, God, it sounds like Led Zeppelin. . . .

DAVE NAVARRO: Of course there is a [Zeppelin] influence there, you can't help an influence that you've grown up listening to. It's second nature when you pick up an instrument to play like a particular person but I'm not going to say I'm duplicating it. I think I have my own style. Then again our bass player really does hate Led Zeppelin.

ERIC AVERY: I was totally perplexed when people referred to us as like Led Zeppelin. In retrospect I can see some aspects of it.

PERRY FARRELL: We probably do sound something like Zeppelin. But I don't sing or look like Robert Plant. They compare me more to Iggy Pop but I don't move like Iggy Pop. I don't deny the feel. I really do love funk, more than rock.

ERIC AVERY: I also shared a love of funk [with Perry], which makes sense on the surface with the Peppers and Fishbone in a way that doesn't immediately with Jane's. Perry and I both really liked rhythm-based music like funk and rap.

PERRY FARRELL: These guys [Stephen, Dave] like metal, so that's where that blend comes from, funk and metal, and that's also what Zeppelin was doing. One thing we never play is blues, and that's something that Zeppelin did. Our music has a very hard vein, it's very raw rockin'. So how do you get an intelligent audience out of that? I'm really into the poetry, and the slower stuff, and I don't want that end of it to drop off.

DAVE NAVARRO: A lot of people compare the band to Zeppelin and the Doors. But if you listen to what Eric's doing in Jane's Addiction, it's very English, kind of . . . Bauhaus, Joy Division. That kind of stark, intellectual stuff.

STEVEN BAKER: I called Anna Statman [A&R rep at Slash Records] and asked her about this band Jane's Addiction. Our messenger came back from her office with a four-song demo. I thought it was great and played it for Roberta Petersen, one of our A&R people, since I wasn't from the A&R department, but I knew she liked hard music.

❦

DEAN NALEWAY: It was a team. The three of us, Charley [Brown], Pete, and myself. We started Triple X together in late '85 as a record company that branched out into management. We were out in the clubs all the time looking for new bands to build a roster. We'd already staked out a few bands when we saw Perry handing out flyers, and we were like, "Pretty interesting-looking guy. Who is he?"

CHARLEY BROWN: I was out every night in clubs and saw Perry first and then dragged those guys out to see them. I was director of sales at Greenworld [a record distributor] and Dean [Naleway] and Peter [Heur] were the buyers, but the company was going down and we knew it. I showed those guys how to get fired so we could get unemployment, like a six-month window of cash to start Triple X. We had $100, our credit cards, and we hocked everything to get that [Jane's Addiction live at the Roxy] recording happening.

DEAN NALEWAY: We wanted to do a three-record deal with Jane's at first. They were unknown, we had a little bit of clout. But Perry had his eye on the big picture. He knew that three records for us was too much.

CHARLEY BROWN: We had them signed for five records for 5,000 bucks and then Perry brought up managing the band. I felt that was an incredible conflict of interest and that I could get them a better deal. I suggested we do one record and split it 50–50 and I'd go on and manage them. That's how the Triple X Management wing of the company came into being. . . .

PERRY FARRELL: At the same time Warner Bros. Records was hot for us.

STEVEN BAKER: We wanted the band bad.

PERRY FARRELL: [Warner Bros.] weren't sure about us [at first]. Some people didn't get it, others said they were crazy not to sign us. Typical big-table rock-business talk. They assigned Ted Templeman's sister to be our A&R rep [Roberta Petersen], but first we met with Lenny [Waronker], Mo [Ostin], and [Steve] Baker. I liked them. It felt safe because of who had previously been on the label, people like Hendrix and the Talking Heads. And I thought, "There're some artists for you." If I'm not sure about the men, I'm always sure about the artists. Lenny had the posture of a guy who's perpetually concerned and he had this endearing worried look, especially when he was listening to the music and thinking about things.

CHARLEY BROWN: At first, the L.A. music industry didn't understand Jane's Addiction in the slightest, which is why we stuck our record out there. The industry basically hated them for the first year we were working with them.

DAN NAVARRO: A famous A&R guy told me, "I could listen to your cousin play all night and day, but I'm not going to sign a band where the audience is going to be turned off because the lead singer wears a dress or a girdle or some crazy effeminate thing like that. They're going to turn off the very audience that's made for them." I thought, OK, fair enough. I don't agree with you, but fair enough. So it was really heartening to see Triple X and Warners really believing in them enough to let them be who they were.

BRUCE DUFF (musician, journalist, PR honcho): One A&R bigwig said he felt that Perry's image simply would not appeal to the kids most likely to go for [Jane's] their music. Another manager called Perry "the Birdman" with a derogatory tone of voice. Everyone who didn't like the band said they just "couldn't get into the singer."

PERRY FARRELL [to Bruce Duff in May 1987]: So what does that mean? Does that mean I should calm myself down? Does that mean, like I better behave myself? Oh, fuck it, I've thought 200,000 light years ahead past whatever that fuckin' guy was. I've thought and thought and thought, it's all I do; that's why I fuckin' am going crazy. All I do is think. I know what's up. Half the people are gonna hate my guts and half are gonna like it. You want everyone to like you? If you don't have controversy you're not living, because everyone's trying to homogenize. So you step out of line, you're making a problem. It doesn't bother me. That's what rock 'n' roll is all about. You better be ahead of everybody else—really far ahead—even to the point of being absurd, slightly.[34]

BRUCE DUFF (writing in *Music Connection*): The important thing isn't so much that [Jane's] nabbed a major record deal, but that—for a left-of-center band—signing with WB is the ideal deal. This is the label that let Husker Du self-produce a two-record set, that let Prince develop slowly over four albums, that had the guts to sign the Replacements. This could be the start of something big.[35]

PERRY FARRELL: There were all these A&R people at the Roxy in January, but we were already recording for ourselves. It was a little of a slap in the face.[36]

STEVEN BAKER: The Triple X indie album came out after we made the deal with Jane's Addiction.

CHARLEY BROWN: Soon everybody copied us with the fake indie release while they're already signed to a major label. Exhibit B: the Soundgarden record on SST. Soundgarden was already signed to A&M when they released it. Geffen did the same thing with Guns N' Roses, put out a fake indie record on their own bogus label Uzi Records, or whatever . . . it was like a blatant major corporate ploy to basically buy out the "alternative" scene, to purchase instant indie street cred. . . .

PERRY FARRELL: We told Warners we definitely wanted to sign, but we wanted to come out on our own label or an indie first and then grow organically from there. It just made more sense. We said, "We appreciate all the money you're offering, but we need to come out on Triple X with a live record first."

BIDDING WAR BEGINS

January–May 1987

PERRY FARRELL: Things were hot. Record companies were all buzzing around.

CHARLEY BROWN: We couldn't get anything happening until we all came together at the Music Machine show [January '87]. The band broke up but was still obligated to do one last show and it turned out that's when all the A&R people showed up and that's when everything got hot. Don Muller was great, Marc Geiger's assistant. Muller would come to all the early shows, but he wouldn't have any authority.

ERIC AVERY: All of a sudden, we had MCA, Capitol, and Geffen feting us with dinners, but we knew we were never going to sign with them because Warner Brothers was just the right place. It was like visiting a college dorm. You could walk down the hallways and hear music blaring out of everyone's office. What a great vibe. We just knew it was the right place for us.

DAVE NAVARRO: I don't remember much about the bidding war. All I remember was they took you to Hamburger Hamlet on Sunset for record-label dinners back in the 80s. Always the same place. I don't know why.

HEIDI RICHMAN: Guns N' Roses and Poison were signed quite a bit before Jane's. However uncool that may be to some—it definitely affected how things went down in the business side of the new rock 'n' roll faces of the 80s. . . .

CHARLEY BROWN: Irving Azoff, who got called "The Poison Dwarf" behind his back, was one of the big guns coming after us. Goldie Goldsmith was his point person at the time he was running MCA, which had this terrible rep as "The Music Cemetery of America," and so one of the things they were trying to beef up was their rock roster. They were just throwing silly money at us. I had a meeting with Irv and Goldie to hear out their pitch of why they were the right place, but I knew I wasn't going to go there. No way. It was all just a charade. We knew we were going with Warners, but the only way a new band has any power in a record deal is if the label wants the band more than the band wants to put out a record . . . in other words, the band has the ability to walk. I had to create competition. Play these fuckin' sharks against each other.

DAVE NAVARRO: We went with Warners because they offered us more creative control. Other labels offered more money, but [with Warners] we could basically do what we wanted, production-wise, and with artwork and videos.[37]

CHARLEY BROWN: Azoff was the classic little guy with a gigantic desk to compensate. He also had a miniature basketball court in his office. While he's running down all the great things that MCA was going to do for Jane's and all the money they were going to give us, this weird little fellah, like out of a circus sideshow with a big head and stubby little legs, is shooting baskets and Goldie had to rebound. It was hilarious to watch this big-time A&R dude having to scramble under tables and fetch like a dog. Irv says to me, "You may have heard that Goldie is going to be changing companies but you know he won't really be changing any time soon—he knows I'd have his arms and legs broken." He's . . . like, little big guy East Coast gangster talk, very funny, straight outta *Goodfellas.*

DEAN NALEWAY: Their hearts and minds were already set on Warners. We could get anybody on the phone, from the top man down, which impressed the hell out of Perry. And the Warners deal gave them 100 percent creative freedom. But we played around anyway and milked it for some good meals.

PERRY FARRELL: I never ate so well in my life. . . .

CHARLEY BROWN: Tom Zutaut, Geffen's point guy, didn't come out of his house for three weeks after he didn't get the band . . . and he would never sign a band that I worked with after that. Where is he now?

INGER LORRE: Hah-haha. . .

PERRY FARRELL: I knew I wasn't inevitably going to end up with David Geffen, although that was the informed bets. We would have gone with Geff's company if we could have worked with David direct. I was just so tickled to meet him. I remember the amusement in his eyes. I'm the kind of person who is probably up his alley. I'm not afraid to be myself and sometimes I'm kinda flamboyant.

   We almost could have worked together. Too bad. It would have been fun. Unfortunately, I sensed we wouldn't be seeing very much of this man as soon as the blood dried on the scroll.

JIM BARBER (record exec-manager): I'll never forget sitting in on this meeting when Charley and Perry came to talk with Fred Bestall at Big Time [Records, a fairly prominent indie at the time]. It was the hugest charade of a meeting I've ever attended. They were so high on the big bucks they knew they were getting elsewhere that a Gigantor $40K Big Time commitment wasn't even going to cover their catering bill for the album.

CHARLEY BROWN: I negotiated the biggest advance that had been done at that point. We tied Guns N' Roses because Warners wouldn't go beyond what Geffen gave them. They gave us the exact same deal. It was about $250,000 or $300,000.

INGER LORRE: The Nymphs got a crazy amount of money for our first record [she claims $800,000]. We never would have gotten signed or got anywhere near what we got without the momentum created by Jane's Addiction.

ENTER MARC GEIGER

MARC GEIGER (agent, co-founder Lollapalooza): We [Triad Artists/ William Morris] were interested in Perry. It started with Psi Com. I had gotten a tape. Thought it was quite good—very goth. Went and saw them play at Club Lingerie. And then they just broke up and Perry formed Jane's Addiction. Don Muller, a co-worker at Triad, had gotten an early tape and thought it was fantastic.

CHARLEY BROWN: Geiger hated us at first, but when the bidding war started, he miraculously fell in love with us overnight.

DAVE NAVARRO: We went to see Marc Geiger at his office, this huge booking guy. I didn't really know what that was, but Perry thought he was going to do everything for us.

MARC GEIGER: Dave and Perry came by our offices to drop off this tape and package. And then Don went and saw one of their first gigs and said you gotta go see 'em. . . .

DAVE NAVARRO: We all got decked out and created this long impressive band bio with pics, reviews, and artwork and stuffed it all into this manila envelope with our five-song demo cassette. Finally we get the call "Mr. Geiger will see you." So we walk in and hand him the envelope, and he takes the cassette out, throws it on a pile of others on his desk, and takes the envelope with the rest of the shit inside and just drops it in the trash can. We were so fuckin' *mortified*. We painstakingly put care and time into creating stuff specially for this guy and we felt like we just got pissed on. He was the hotshot behind the desk who was like "I'm all about the music, I don't need your little package. . . ."

MARC GEIGER: We signed them pre-Warners before they even recorded the live record for Triple X. We were their booking agents for all live shows and touring, from the beginning all the way to the end of the first breakup.

STEVEN BAKER: Don and Marc from Triad Artists, being the consistent agents for Jane's Addiction, were a huge part of the fact that we [Warner Bros.] could eventually be successful with that band.

JANE'S RECORDS LIVE AT THE ROXY

January 26, 1987

DEAN NALEWAY: We invited everybody down for a show at the Roxy. We put up everything we had to make that live record [1987's *Jane's Addiction*]. We even sold our cars.

MATT PALADINO: The Roxy was fucking packed. I never really got into Perry, but I went to see Navarro, as did all my friends. I probably knew half of the people there from the Shroomsville parties. Mike Ozair was like, "We're all going to see Dave and then, hey, it's party afterwards at Shroomsville!" The big draw of kids in the pit—not the record industry people who were crawling everywhere—was primarily for Dave and probably secondary from Perkins. Perkins was a popular guy at Notre Dame. I had some friends who were a couple of grades under him . . . and they were all there rooting for him, too.

CHARLEY BROWN: Perry was outside the Roxy hanging out at the Rainbow parking lot when this big old limo pulls up, and out steps Jack

Live at the Roxy. (Karyn Cantor)

Nicholson, so Perry runs up to him going, "Jack, Jack! We're playing here, we're playing here! Can you come in and introduce us? It would be so-o-o great!" Jack just took two steps back and was like, "Whoa, back off, buddy, back off." Who wouldn't be scared shitless of some freak in a corset and a silver jacket with dreadlocks flying, running up to you. . . . Perry was just too much! The bodyguard got all puffed up and Nicholson scuttled away as fast as his pins could carry him. . . .

BOB FORREST: When they played the Roxy everyone I knew that played music in L.A. was there. Fishbone . . . the Denney brothers from the Weirdos . . . all kind of feeling the same thing. Like this is rad. Anthony [Kiedis] and I were watching and it was just so mesmerizing and powerful. It was everything that everybody who had bands hoped to accomplish. It gives me chills still—how great they were. We walked out to the car and Anthony was all quiet and I was all quiet and then he said, "What are you thinking?" And I said, "I'm thinking why I even [bother to] play music." And he said, "Yeah, me too." And he just started the car and drove away. They were that far ahead of everybody else.

CHARLEY BROWN: We made the live record for $4,000 and we went $1,500 over budget which almost killed us. Everybody was calling us. There were several hundred people on the guest list.

DEAN NALEWAY: There was just major label ridiculousness—fighting over seats, and "Why aren't I sitting over where so-and-so's sitting?"

CHARLEY BROWN: I was intentionally cruel to industry slime, the more I abused them the more they kissed my ass, and it was a total bluff. They had no idea it had been set up to record live. Jane's did two sets. They opened the night all-acoustic, followed by a couple of bands, then they came back on and totally rocked out full-on electric.

PERRY FARRELL: I behaved like a prick and cussed out the entire record industry in the audience. I was telling everybody they needed to lose weight. I was like, "Fuck you all, you can all kiss our ass." It was typical overwrought histrionics from a pissed-off band that's got the world in the palm of its hand. But we made sure to put on a great show because it was being recorded.

CHARLEY BROWN: I was trying to shop the deal so I was horrified. I was thrilled and horrified at the same time! Notoriety was much better than being ignored, but was there a limit to the abuse these industry cretins would take?

DEAN NALEWAY: Most everything was live, but there were a few mistakes, and a few things we had to fix up like somebody screaming in the background that we had to get rid of, and that was about it. Light on overdubs. Almost 100 percent live. Mixed by Ethan James at Radio Tokyo Studios. I think the audience applause dub is from a Los Lobos show, or maybe it was Ricki Lee Jones show 'cos of some miking error in the room.

DAVE NAVARRO: On our first album there's a cover of "Sympathy for the Devil." And personally—people get surprised and shocked when they hear this, sometimes angry—I hate the Rolling Stones. Always have, always will. I like what they've contributed to the industry, but I would never put on a Rolling Stones record. We ended up singing "Sympathy for the Devil" as a joke, and we played it live and it ended up on the record. I can't believe that one of my least favorite bands is on my first record.[38]

ALBUM COVER

PERRY FARRELL: The album covers are just dreams. In some cases they are beautiful memories.

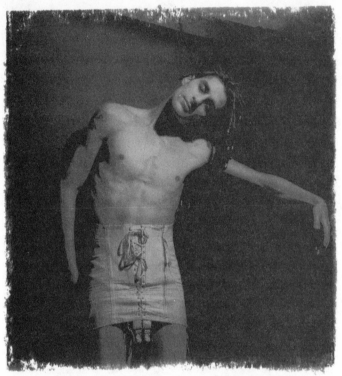

Outtake from the cover photo shoot for Jane's *Live at the Roxy* record. Perry Farrell: "The first cover was the corset and the nose-piercing. A painting." (Karyn Cantor)

KARYN CANTOR: I shot the cover for the first album, which is a picture of Perry's chest that he had painted after the black and white photograph. I took many of the live shots on the outside of the album, and then I shot the pictures of Jane on the inside, and I think there's just a picture of the corset he was wearing on the inside of the album as well. . . .

DEAN NALEWAY: For weeks he was painting this thing until he finally ran out of paint, and didn't have money to get any more, so he touched it up with Wite-Out because we were pushing and pushing him to finish this cover. We did one pressing that was clear vinyl. This was before UPC codes. That first cover with no UPC code and clear vinyl is the big collector trophy.

JANE'S ADDICTION AT U.S.C.
JANE'S ADDICTION FLIPSIDE INTERVIEW
FLIPSIDE FANZINE #52, SPRING 1987 [39]

Jane's Addiction were interviewed at USC in January 1987 by Al and Lawrence Livermore shortly after a rowdy on-campus gig with Bulimia Banquet.

PERRY: I like when things kind of go to hell. . . .

STEPHEN: When the light went out I thought people were taking my drum set into the audience.

ERIC: It didn't go enough for my liking.

PERRY: I myself like to see violence sometimes, and then other times I just want things to turn into a great show. I think every man wants to see some violence.

STEPHEN: But not when people start trashing. . . .

PERRY: But at the same time I want to see people into it. I want a reaction of appreciation and letting us do our music. When it gets like that [trashing], the music goes to hell, and that's my first concern. I can't speak for everyone, he likes riots [Stephen]. I like the tribal, ritualistic thing where people don't hurt each other, but they are moving up and down with each other. I'd rather see that than people turning on each other. A spiritual thing, where people are out of themselves, not inhibited physically—but aren't violating each other . . . 'cause that's not productive, the world's already fucked. . . .

STEPHEN: I like to see people let go this much, especially at the University of Spoiled Children. [Ha ha]. When people go ape shit that's the biggest compliment we could get. . . .

PERRY: I have [been attacked on stage], at Fenders some girls were pulling my pants off!

ERIC: You must have hated that!!

PERRY: We could play those [hardcore punk] shows if we did all of our fast stuff, but that's not all that we do. We'd be cutting ourselves short.

STEPHEN: Punk rock isn't fast or slow, it's. . .

DAVID: Just bad!

STEPHEN: No, it's an attitude, it's not a speed.

PERRY: Well it wasn't, but I think it is now. "Hardcore" . . .

STEPHEN: But "hardcore" isn't anything like punk rock, hardcore is . . . what's the word . . .

PERRY: Predictable . . . regimented . . .

STEPHEN: There's a certain code that you have to dress by, and listen to, and that is the opposite of what punk rock is—a state of mind where you can do your own thing, and it doesn't matter what society or any authority figure thinks about it.

PERRY: I myself am ready for something else. Not different than what I'm doing, but I'm ready for a change in the attitude of the youth. I would like to attempt to start a new attitude slightly. More of getting together, and easing up on each other. It's all got to be torn down again and started over. Everybody is looking at each other with such scrutiny—it's gotten so regimented. I think there is something happening now.

STEPHEN: The 60s were a real good learning period for us. We all thought life was beautiful, we had JFK, and things were looking up—we looked at the future optimistically. We are at a time now where we can see that didn't work—it wasn't reality that we all love each other. . . . Now it's a good time for something new to come out because there is a good balance between optimism and what's happening now. . . .

PERRY: I'm looking for more of a forceful optimism in the decade to come. Like the reaction I want from a crowd is as a community, it's aggressive, but not upon each other. Now they hit each other, what are you going to accomplish when you go to a show and people are hitting you? The reaction I wanted was not to have people turning on each other—but it seems to be a hard habit to break. Especially if they go to a show and hear fast music, they immediately think "I know what to do here."

ERIC: Plus, when they're slamming they're not paying attention anyway....

PERRY: Yeah, and neither are anybody else because people are concentrating more on the crowd than the music. The first thing I want to maintain is artistic integrity with the music—but sometimes it falls short in situations like that. We never played standard punk-rock beats or standard speed metal beats, we try to go past it.

STEPHEN: The bands you play with have a lot to do with the crowd.

PERRY: I've seen so many bands that just aren't that good, but people are just smashing all over the place. If you've ever seen Fela or gone to a reggae festival, the feeling that they leave with is so much better than that reaction, because people are in such a good mood and they just want to groove. Women are there, guys are there, the feeling is much higher. I couldn't classify it. I have thought out my life—and I have thought about the stars and the moon. . . .

ERIC: I wouldn't say I like metal, I'd say rock. Four years ago I was in a metal band.

PERRY: I'm more into black music and African music, so the contrast and variety is there. That's what I think keeps this band from falling into the category of bands that can only do one thing good. It's easy to make people slam, but it's harder to make them literally enjoy slow, beautiful music. That is a higher art. And to be able to do both is very rare. It's kind of like life—you don't always walk around wanting to fight. You fall in love. What are you going to do, deny your feelings? So if a band can touch every single feeling that you have, then they are for me. I'm in love, you know? Then I feel like I want to kill somebody. Sometimes I want to be serious, sometimes an idiot. All the great bands have touched on all of these and done them well.

I was in Psi Com for a long time (that basically fell apart because of religious beliefs), and I was underground, I put my own record out. But this band is way more popular, and I don't want people to think we are not street credible because something might happen in a big way with money. I've basically been a street kid all my life. But wait till you see what we do with our money, it's gonna be really creative as far as helping people. The rock star shit is fucked. I hate that shit. People come up and think "rock star" because we're getting popular, fuck that shit.

This is on the record. If you EVER see me do anything different, you can come and fuck me up the ass, man! My artistic integrity and the whole band's artistic integrity comes first. And as far as popularity it can become contrary because . . . I get nervous sometimes because of the popularity, but I'm not going to slow down. I've never gone to be a commercial guy, and never have gone out to try to get the record companies to fall in love with us.

"JANE SAYS"

PERRY FARRELL: "Jane Says," we never put that out as a single or a video. That's the one, of course, that gets played still today, but just to screw with them we wouldn't put a video out on it and we wouldn't play it live. We figured that's the one thing we don't want these guys to have. You can't have the same mentality these days. You wouldn't get anywhere. I'm amazed we got anywhere at all.

JANE BAINTER: The Sergio [in the lyrics to "Jane Says"] was a drug dealer who lived near the Wilton House. He was an El Salvadorean who was like seventeen or eighteen who came to Los Angeles with his younger brother who's only thirteen. They were alone in the big city. Most of the local Salvadorans were refugees who sold drugs to send money home to their families during the war.

BOB MOSS: Sergio was just a drug boyfriend. He wasn't any real damn boyfriend. The TV was stolen and they blamed Jane and Sergio for

ANGELO MOORE: I have no recall of jamming in the living room, but I remember this crazy party after some gig . . . at Perry's house on Wilton. That's the first time I took mushrooms. I saw a blue electric mask over my face and just started trippin' outside my body. Me, Chris, Norwood were there, some of the other guys from Fishbone. Jump with Joey was there, and . . . Gaz Mayall. (Karyn Cantor)

taking it to hock for drugs. That was the assumption of the anti–Jane contingent. They didn't like Sergio at all. He wasn't welcome at the front door so he'd sneak around the back and holler up to her bedroom window.

PETE WEISS: I copped on St. Andrews many times, and that's what the neighborhood kinda felt like. It's like the guy with the bell on his cart or whatever, but you know east off of Beverly and stuff, that's what that neighborhood sounds like. But yeah, that song really uh . . . nails it. . . .

JANE BAINTER: I was strung out by now, and Sergio was using that to manipulate me. One of the strongest incentives for me to finally get off of drugs was that other people can have control over you so easily, and it's just so stupid. When I think of Sergio, it was manipulative but it was really survivalist. We were all very poor and we were all in survival mode. So if you're hiding the TV, that's money and that's power. Not like anybody cared. I don't even remember watching TV over there. It's the idea, that this was something that somebody owned.

BOB MOSS: You know the lyric "Have you seen my wig around?" That was another thing for real, man. Jane had her wig phase. Underneath she had super-short bleached blond hair, but she used to wear this long, dark wig a lot. She just had this weird personality quirk where she needed to change costume and be a different person. It was just something she did without really explaining it. She wasn't an actress so she wasn't a natural performer. It was more personal. Jane was naturally very sweet. It all seemed pretty benign, though I never asked her upfront what was up with the wig.

CASEY NICCOLI: Jane was bizarre. . . .

ERIC AVERY: Sometimes we'd do acoustic jams on the porch at the Wilton House.

DANUSHA KIBBY: Flea and Angelo would come over a lot and jam with Perry. We had a huge wraparound porch and they would play outside on it. I met a lot of cool local people through the parties and barbecues. . . .

JANE BAINTER: It was very communal in a hippie-ish way. We were into cooking and the guys would sit out on the front porch and play acoustic guitars and bongos. . . .

ERIC AVERY: We played barbecues in the backyard and that was the beginning of people starting to dig us. I'll never forget when Jane asked us if we'd play a sad song for her, and I had to shake my head and say, "Jane, we just got through playing 'Jane Says,' one of the saddest songs in the world."

JANE BAINTER: When I was in college, my parents had gotten divorced and my mother and her new husband moved away. They sold up in the U.S. and bought this house in the south of Spain. I had the opportunity to go but couldn't because I was so strung out and everything was so bad over here. It was this idea, this big reward of mine that if I could just kick I could go to Spain. Spain became like a metaphor for sobriety and a better life. . . .

PERRY FARRELL: "Jane Says" wasn't even released as a single, but it became its own anthem. . . .

DAVE JERDEN: When I first heard "Jane Says," I just thought it was another good song they'd written. I didn't know it would become like a sort of modern rock "Stairway to Heaven."[40]

DAVE NAVARRO: It's not long enough to be the new "Stairway."

GUNS N' ROSES

SLASH (musician, member Guns N' Roses): When I first became aware of Jane's Addiction, Guns N' Roses, at least for me, was pretty much in its own bubble. We just did our thing and fuck everybody else. I liked Jane's, though. I respected them because they had their own trip and they were sort of wild with that footloose thing going on. I think Perry is fucking great. I love Perry and David and Stephen. They're all fucking awesome. I don't know their bass player that well, but they're just great musicians. . . .[41]

PERRY FARRELL: Maybe there was a bit of posturing between the two bands in the early days. I admire their accomplishments and I'd love to see them back together. I think it's really a shame that they don't play together anymore. Look, I've got a guy who won't play in my band, either.

SLASH: We rehearsed in the same little hole in the wall off of Santa Monica and Vine. One day those guys were coming out as we were going in and it was sort of like one of those high school things where two football teams quietly face off. We never exchanged words.[42]

ERIC AVERY: Perry, Casey, and I went to see Guns N' Roses together at the Troubadour. I remember walking out and sitting on the curb smoking a cigarette, waiting for them to come out because I was just so uninterested in Guns N' Roses. And they followed soon after with the same feeling.

CHARLEY BROWN: We hated Guns N' Roses. Guns were our mortal enemies as far as scenesters and stuff. The first Guns record came out right before ours, and, oh, man, Perry was just nearly losing it. Guns were suddenly getting all that attention. We kept telling him, "Perry, calm down, dude . . . you're gonna happen, you're gonna happen . . . it's just gonna happen in a different way."

JOHNNY NAVARRO: Dave and I listened to Guns N' Roses and NWA a lot. Those were the cassettes in our tape player all the time when we went to score drugs. They became our official cop records. I still can't listen to those records without remembering that time.

HEIDI RICHMAN: Guns N' Roses had a crazy rivalry with Poison, but not particularly with Jane's, as I remember it. Guns and Poison both came up through the same club scene, more or less, but were so incredibly different. Guns N' Roses were somehow a reaction to something.

PETE WEISS: G N' R and Faster Pussycat were a whole scene apart from the generic pay-to-play hairspray bands; if anything, G N' R even seemed to be a reaction *against* them. I remember Axl Rose trashing all the posey hair bands . . . he didn't want to have anything to do with that scene, either . . . his crowd at the Cathouse was beginning to blur into the Poison-Ratt crowd and Axl wasn't diggin' it. . . .

JOSH RICHMAN: There was no wimpy prefab geekiness about G N' R in the beginning. They were absolutely the real thing. . . .

HEIDI RICHMAN: Their extreme surliness, the brattishness, was coming much more from a punk sensibility, whereas the guys from Poison moved out here from Pennsylvania to become rich rock stars who got all the chicks. They were all about being glamorous and having fabulous blond exotic dancer girlfriends and hangin' out in the jacuzzi with champagne every night at the Playboy Mansion. Guns N' Roses certainly didn't form with those illusions.

SLASH: Guns attracted punk rockers, pickup drivin' heavy metal dudes, fuckin' preppies, skate kids, and the Allman Brothers stoner crowd. I mean we got fucking tattoo guys, college students, bikers, office workers, glam rockers . . . dude, we had cops, strippers, surfers, marines coming . . . and on and on, you name it, man . . . just this bizarre fucking mix of people.[43]

PETE WEISS: The metal kids, the glam kids, the art punks, the goths, the gays, the longhairs . . . the whatevers, all rallied around Jane's because they appealed to all these different things. They were who they were, and it just attracted all these diverse groups.

SLASH: With Jane's you got bizarre people coming, too. The only thing Jane's and Guns had in common was that both bands were never part of any one scene. There was no scene as far as we were concerned. Jane's got their own crowd, but it wasn't like the whole fucking Sunset Strip thing. Or like the L.A. punk thing. Even the Peppers were more L.A. than that. Guns hated everybody, we weren't part of any scene, either.[44]

JOHNNY NAVARRO: Jane's and Guns N' Roses both kind of ruled the town but then Guns went up to this other level, like stadium rock, which Jane's never really wanted to do at that time. It was like, "We're with the art alternative crowd. We have street cred."

JOSH RICHMAN: Jane's would end up at the Cathouse. You'd see Perry in his girdle and long droogie gloves with pancake and dreads looking like no one else in the building. Everybody else is all gypsied out in bandannas and leather.

JOSEPH BROOKS: Later, I was resident DJ at Bordello [offshoot of Cathouse], promoted by Riki Rachtman Thursdays at Peanuts [iconic dyke bar in West Hollywood]. I played some stuff that I wouldn't necessarily play at Cathouse. I started mixing Jane's with the regular rock set and people really went for it. I was playing "Trip Away" and "Mountain Song" and "Pigs in Zen," "Whores," lots of stuff . . . people were certainly dancing to it and the dance floor was packed. There was a crossover happening for sure. The same people who wanted Guns N' Roses were now starting to listen to Jane's too.

⟡

March 5, 1987

Jane's wins in two categories, "Best Underground Band" and tied with Redd Kross for "Best Heavy Metal/Hard Rock Band," at the first ever *L.A. Weekly* Music Awards show at the Variety Arts Center.

ERIC AVERY: The *L.A. Weekly* gave us like the best heavy metal award. I was like, "We're *heavy metal?* Dude, I just thought of it as expressionistic music . . . unlike anything else that was going on!' What was thought of as metal at the time was all kind of feline . . . Ratt and Poison? Warrant? Candy Ass? No, thanks. . .

THE SCREAM GOES FULL SHRIEK

Circa April–October 1987

Not since the early punk days in the late 70s at the Masque in Hollywood has L.A. had a music scene like this, with its own bands and culture. And Scream has been at the center of it.

FROM THE PRESS RELEASE FOR *SCREAM: THE COMPILATION,*
A TEN-BAND ANTHOLOGY OF SCREAM REGULARS, INCLUDING
JANE'S ADDICTION, RELEASED BY GEFFEN RECORDS, OCTOBER 1987

PERRY FARRELL (to Steve Hochman and Jeff Spurrier in the *L.A. Times*): It's late at night . . . it's good crowds . . . it's young people . . . it's sweaty . . . and it's dark. It's not the cleanest place, but it gives you a chance to rub up against people. People are like insects who need to rub up against each other to communicate. . . . [45]

DAYLE GLORIA: [Scream was] nine or ten miles away from the Strip in downtown L.A. where only the more adventurous rocker types would go. The Cathouse, where Taime Downe and Guns hung out, was more of a sleazoid tattoos, strippers, and rock 'n' roll kind of thing. All the Cathouse guys looked like Bret Michaels from Poison and the chicks were slutty Tawny Kitaen types. At Scream, all the guys looked like Ian McCulloch [of Echo and the Bunnymen] and the girls were all Siouxsie clones.

HEIDI RICHMAN: You didn't get many of the poodle-haired Valley people at Scream that you did at Cathouse, but then on the other side of the coin, you got goths, punkers, you got people coming from a different side of it.

Live at Scream, location number three. The basement at the Embassy Hotel, downtown Los Angeles. (David Hermon)

DAYLE GLORIA: Guns were playing to the whole Whisky-Gazarri's-Strip thing. We represented the anti-Strip at the Scream because of the darkness of a lot of the things we were doing.

MIKE STEWART: My DJ sets included Bauhaus, the Banshees, Virgin Prunes, Cocteau Twins, Lords of the New Church, the Cure, and other early goth stuff; we also threw in old Zeppelin and some classic punk like the Buzzcocks. The Cult's "She Sells Sanctuary" was a big song, at least one of the Sisters of Mercy songs was always big. The Monday club was the dance part of Scream. Whatever was new was on top of my format. The Cult was always at the top.

ERICA PAIGE: The Cathouse played up the rock side of it. It wasn't a punk-rock club. The Cathouse was a really nice merge of different scenes. The Scream was more a conglomeration of different kinds of people.

PERRY FARRELL: Both scenes were great and wild in their own ways. . . .

JOSEPH BROOKS: Scream had that sensibility of wanting to be more indie. No selling out—they had that punk-rock do-it-yourself indie thing going. Scream had its roots in goth and death rock. If I think of Scream, I think of Sisters of Mercy. That's the soundtrack. Cathouse came out of a more rock thing, a New York Dolls–Hanoi Rocks kind of thing.

MIKE STEWART: They were two different scenes completely, but it did meld together once in awhile. We did book some of the same glam bands. Some of them crossed over into our crowd. Faster Pussycat played at Scream. A lot of the Strip bands played, but they would warm up for a Red Lorry Yellow Lorry, or the Lords of the New Church, they'd open up for Jane's Addiction.

ERICA PAIGE: Everybody went to the same clubs. It didn't matter if it was your scene or not, you went anyways, usually because Cathouse was the only thing going on Tuesdays . . . and Scream was it for Fridays . . . if you loved rock 'n' roll, or even if you didn't particularly, but just wanted to step out for the night. . . .

PERRY FARRELL: The Cathouse was much more of a hetero male hag club for the exotic dancers who love them, with a glam slant on it, and . . .

BRYAN RABIN: . . . *lots* of silicone booty.

ERICA PAIGE: The Cathouse was mostly about metal guys and stripper girls. Lots of stretch pants, big belts, T-shirts.

HEIDI RICHMAN: Guys were dressing like Hanoi Rocks with the gypsy hats and the scarves.

JOSH RICHMAN: Cathouse bands like Guns N' Roses, Faster Pussycat, Jet Boy . . . Nikki Sixx was calling 'em the "gypsy junkie" bands. . . .

JOSEPH BROOKS: People who dressed to go out at Scream would certainly fit in at Cathouse. They were wearing somewhat similar clothing. Maybe the colors weren't as black at Cathouse. At Scream black was it. At Cathouse you'd find girls in white cowboy boots. You'd *never* find that at Scream. At Scream they were wearing pointy black shoes, witchy. Girls [at both places] had big hair, but it wasn't necessarily dyed black. At Cathouse you'd find girls that were bleach blond. You wouldn't find too many bleach blondes at Scream.

DAYLE GLORIA: The headliners went on really late. We didn't have a curfew. As long as the bar was shut for alcohol by two. Nobody cared. Sometimes we closed out well after five A.M. One night Perry played with a bag of shit in front of the stage. He just put out a big plastic bag filled with poop—we didn't know what kind of poop, human, dog, or other animal. We just thought that was so weird. I still don't know what the deal was. Jane's would do "Whole Lotta Love." I used to beg them at the end to do it one more time until finally Perry refused.

BRUCE PURDUE (DJ, club owner, Scream co-founder): We were sort of like three clubs rolled in one . . . a dance club, a video club, and a live music venue. . . .

ERICA PAIGE: I met David one night at the Scream. I didn't know who he was but he just kept coming up and saying hi. He seemed really nice, a really sweet guy. I didn't think anything more of it. I went to leave and he made up some cute lie that he couldn't find his keys and needed a ride home so I gave him a ride on the back of my motorcycle. But I didn't go out with him right away.

INGER LORRE: Dave and I had a very tempestuous, short-lived relationship. We fought all the time. We were both on drugs and hung out a lot. Somehow we ended up sleeping together. It was, a one-night thing and then we felt really uncomfortable and our friendship kind of ended after that. What really made me mad is that he borrowed my card to get drunk. I would just give it to him because at the time I had some money because I was modeling. He just took it and cleared out the whole fucking account! Never give a junkie your card.

ERICA PAIGE: Dave and I were in very different worlds. I was going one way and he was definitely going another way, but he was pretty persistent, he called and called and called. Problem was I was just getting clean and he was going in the complete opposite direction. He was the exact opposite of what I was looking for, but he was really sweet. He would often come visit me at the Scream and sometimes sit at the door and work with me. He was also very funny.

"HELLO, I'M A DRUG ADDICT." THE—UH—PRURIENT DRUG SECTION

PERRY FARRELL: I picked up a [drug] habit hanging out with the underground. . . .

JANE BAINTER: Dave was just like, cookie cutter, "Hello, I'm a drug addict." We all were really, you know, suckers for drugs. Just like made for drugs—we were all made to fight that battle.

JOHNNY NAVARRO: Dave told me a lot of people at the Wilton House were doing dope. The first night that Dave did heroin himself, Jane's played a show at Scream and they all went back to the house afterwards. He was with a girl, this foxy black chick. Next day, he was sick as a dog and he told me the chick had skin-popped it in his ass for him. I hated that he was going down that road. What the hell could I do about it? First of all, I'm a diehard alcoholic that did coke all the time. Who the fuck was I to talk? Somehow in my weird backward Calexico–San Diego brain, I thought that if I could go in there and relate to him, I could grab him from the depths of this darkness with a big, burly, brotherly arm and pull him out.

PERRY FARRELL: Once I started hanging out with the kids in L.A., it was a whole new world. I was landlocked but still carried my surfboard with me everywhere. I became a fully addicted drug fiend. Surfing just kind of went out of my field of vision. When you're a junkie, you're cold constantly. Now the idea of going in water repelled me, whereas it used to be the first thing on my mind.

WILLIE McNEIL: All of a sudden, probably like '86–'87, coke just became very socially out of vogue. It really fell out because people either got strung out or grossed out. After '87, if someone pulled out some coke at a party, everybody would kind of snub you . . . you were on your own. It was like, "What are you, an out-of-control coke pig, or what? Disgusting! Cocaine? Are you serious? Yee-uk, *man!*"

JOEY ALTRUDA: All the cokeheads were gradually becoming alcoholics and heroin addicts, or all three. . . .

PLEASANT GEHMAN: Heroin was really taking its hold during the early to middle 80s and continued into the 90s. This was all pre-Guns N' Roses, pre-Hanoi Rocks. After the Joneses [from Long Beach and Orange County] all the guitar players were trying to act out like Johnny Thunders.[46]

JOEY ALTRUDA: Remember The Joneses? The Joneses were the first of it. The Joneses, Mike Martt, Tex & the Horseheads, and The Little Kings (the Charlie Sexton–Nick Ferrari connection from Austin, Texas) . . . this whole group that were all like notorious heroin bands.

PERRY FARRELL: There are certain sacrifices you make when you're a heroin addict. Like having any kind of life.

INGER LORRE: Heroin was *everywhere.*

CASEY NICCOLI: Eric was probably a junkie before any of them.

ERIC AVERY: I was so naïve about drugs. The first time I was dope-sick I didn't even know I was dope-sick. I didn't really get strung out until we got signed and things got rolling.

JOHNNY NAVARRO: Dave would shoot all day and then kind of be sick all night and then kind of get well in the morning. That was the way it went for like months and months on end.

PERRY FARRELL: Being a junkie can be a drag. Some people piss me off and they're just potheads, they're just lazy. I'll take everything that's happened to me and everything that didn't work out . . . every trauma the band's been through . . . and put it right on my shoulders because I know that it must have been a drag to sit there and watch a guy nodding off, not available.

DAVE NAVARRO: Heroin ruined my dreams. It turned the thing I had worked my whole life for into the thing I wanted to get away from the most.[47]

BOB FORREST: Pete Weiss had the best heroin connections in L.A., these really good China White and Persian connections, so everybody went through Pete, which obviously made him into a very popular guy with the L.A. music community, but Pete wasn't dealing. He was just the guy who knew where to get it. They'd all go over to Pete's house and then he'd call someone. . . .

PETE WEISS: I never scored for those guys in my life! I just happened to share whatever I had because they were my friends. If someone's sick you help 'em out; you didn't charge them for it.

FLEA: As a drug abuser at that time myself, I remember it being a total trend. [Jane's] definitely nailed that aspect of the scene, during a time and era that I was into drugs. Isn't that always a sort of pathetic concept in the drug addict world? Everyone's always saying, "Oh well, I've been really good lately, and it's just this one time," and I remember always thinking, "Just shut up and get fucking high." We're all doing drugs and we all know it's bad for us, but we want to do it because we like it and we're going to do it because we're going to have fun tonight. And we're going to get high and we're going to take off our clothes and we're going to do whatever the fuck we're going to do.

DAVE NAVARRO: I admit I personally totally blew it with drugs back in those days. My intake was certainly a factor in the eventual demise of the band the first time around. What do you want me to say? There was always five pounds of heroin, all the booze and coke you wanted, all the strippers you wanted—all looking for nothing but guys in bands. And I wasn't even old enough to legally drink yet?

JOHNNY NAVARRO: I was just as bad as he was. He came out of rehab and he had that look and next think I knew we were both loaded again.

CASEY NICCOLI: At first it was fun to get high and do art. When we first started dating, we did dope together a few times, long before it became a problem. It was just us getting high, to open up our creativity, sitting around doing art and making Christmas cards for our friends.

DAVE NAVARRO: In Jane's I felt very unsure, very uncomfortable. By the time we were successful I was so down in the depths of despair that I didn't experience any of it. Perhaps the level of success we did reach enabled me to get through the destructive side of my [heroin] use quicker, because I was able to spend more money and go down faster. Whereas, who knows how many years it would have gone on had my habit been $50 a day?[48]

MARC GEIGER: Three of the four members—not Stephen—were very into heroin, as well as many other things, and it was clearly a big influence on the band and their behavior. Perry definitely believed that drugs fueled creativity.

STEVEN BAKER: Perry was always trying to experiment. He was advocating a lot of interesting stuff. Drugs were amongst them.

CASEY NICCOLI: Perry was more of a crack addict, or coke addict, than he was a heroin addict. I became a heroin addict when he started touring because I didn't like being alone. I didn't plan on it.

It just happened. It took me a long time to get past it. Perry would come back from touring while I was strung out. Then he would get high with me for a couple of weeks.

JOHN FRUSCIANTE: Before I'd had any serious drug experiences I would hear stories and it just seemed like Perry was living on the edge. I was really proud of him for that. We were so used to Anthony having all his anti-drug raps in interviews and stuff. We were at a rehearsal and there was an issue of *BAM* and there was an interview with Perry in it and they asked him, "What are your experiences with heroin?" and he said, "It was great!"

PERRY FARRELL: I didn't get into this to make sermons or set up structures for others to live by. My intent has nothing to do with teaching. It's to amuse myself on this completely boring planet. Listen, I'm very happy. Every day is different for me. At least I'm not in some box eight hours a day.[49]

FLEA: [It was all about] sexual freedom, the freedom to say, "So what if I'm on drugs, this is great." And then someone could say, "Well that's really bad to say that because then it makes people who love you, kids, think they should do drugs and that could ruin their lives." People have to make their own decisions with what to do, and I think if someone comes out and says, "I do heroin and I love it and I'm having the time of my life and 'waa-hoo'," they're at least telling the truth. I'd way rather have that than some full-of-shit dickhead like Rush Limbaugh hiding it while preaching that everybody else should be locked up. . . .

PETE WEISS: I think Perry coming out and saying heroin is [great for creativity] . . . for him it probably was, but how could he know whether it was the events and influences around him, or if it was the heroin? It was all happening simultaneously so maybe he just thought the great stuff was the dope, and thought, "Maybe that's what's making me so creative." Maybe the lesson is that he can now say, "This is what drugs did to me and my band, I thought it was a good idea at the time, but now I know it wasn't. I realize I made a mistake and said the wrong thing. I can't take it back, but I wouldn't suggest it to anyone now, especially young kids and teens."

PERRY FARRELL: People who do drugs want me to hail it. And the people who don't want me to hang myself. They want to argue, "Yeah, but what about kids out there?" My opinion is [that] drugs can be beneficial and are necessary, [but] if they're used improperly; just like a ski, you're gonna break your leg or even worse. So if you don't wanna ski, don't ski. I wouldn't advocate being a drug addict to anybody; it's a waste of time. Life is short. Get carried away. Be smart so you live to see another day.[50]

CASEY NICCOLI: With heroin, I just couldn't stop.

PERRY FARRELL: The whole point about drugs is to wake up and tell the story. It's just like surfing—the whole point is to get out of the tube. Nature put 'em here and, as many claim, God is in control of Nature. If he wants them here, who am I to argue?[51]

BOB FORREST: [The scene] was very pro-heroin. I personally thought everybody should be on it. I wound up losing my teeth and pooing in my pants for the trouble! But Perry never got to that level. He's very controlled, very kind of moral . . . extremely disciplined.

CARLA BOZULICH: I was so impressed that Perry seemed able to control his drug use.

CASEY NICCOLI: He could go on a little dope binge and then go out and run ten miles. Perry was able to walk away. Just bounce right back and start touring again. He didn't stay strung out when he toured, whereas Dave was always strung out on the road. Perry did a lot of coke on the road, because promoters supply a lot of coke, but as far as being a junkie, he really wasn't a junkie like most junkies are. He was like a part-timer. But with coke, he had a harder time [quitting].

JOHN FRUSCIANTE: Even though Perry talked about drugs and gave the impression he was some kind of drug addict, and he obviously smoked a lot of weed, I don't think he was ever a heroin addict. He would just go on drug binges and then not do them for a while.

PERRY FARRELL: I am narcissistic, extremely, and I love feeling gorgeous, and when drugs get to the point where I feel I've lost the edge and I'm a piece of shit, my better senses tell me I'll never get laid again; no one else will ever adore or love me, so take a break.[52]

JANE BAINTER: I don't know if he was shooting hard narcotics like meth or coke or smack during his time at the Wilton House, but when he did it was all done in a very exploratory way. He was pro-drugs . . . pro-exploration, pro-experience, pro-experimentation . . . pro *any* drug. . . .

PERRY FARRELL: I will not try to impress you as a functioning drug addict—many people are, they think it's really cool. And it *is* kinda cool if you can take those kinda drugs and put them to good use.

JOHN FRUSCIANTE: Perry once offered to do a debate with Henry Rollins. He said, "Hey Henry, how about we do a debate on television where I'm pro-drugs and you're anti-drugs?" And Henry freaked out. He's like: "I'll kill you! If we did that I would *murder* you!" We were all surprised about what an unfriendly reaction Henry was having. I think Perry thought it would be like a friendly heated debate . . . because they have differences of opinion, but Henry did not have a friendly response.

JOHNNY NAVARRO: Dave and I got even closer when we were loaded. In modern psych terminology it was called enablement, back then it was called a running mate. He always had a girlfriend as his primary running mate but I was his secondary running mate, if you will, and sometimes I slipped into the primary position because a girl isn't always what you want when you need to fix. Dave and I would always help each other out. We would score downtown Los Angeles, not St. Andrews. That comes from when Perry was living in the Wilton House and all that.

CHARLEY BROWN: After they got the advance that's when it really started. Biggest all-time rock cliché. First thing they do with the money is stop writing and buy the heroin indenti-kits; they'd already become rock stars before they'd earned out a penny.

JOHNNY NAVARRO: We used to score our shit on the street. You would think that the guitar player in Jane's Addiction would have a dealer set, a reliable steady connect, right? We didn't have a dealer. We would score our shit on the street every day.

JOHN FRUSCIANTE: Forgive me for saying something that is maybe not true, but I think heroin might have been their main muse . . . it seems to me that heroin must have coaxed the writing of some of these Jane's Addiction songs, especially with Dave.

JOHNNY NAVARRO: Dave OD'd on the road a couple of times, he OD'd during the recording of *Ritual* a couple of times. Our street connects pretty much dried up when the sun went down because the cops get busy in the dark. If you can't score you have to make sure you have enough to last you through the night.

PERRY FARRELL: I'm simply writing the way Bob Dylan did when he said he married Isis, man. I'm just dreaming it all up. I mean, did Dylan *really* go riding in on a horse on the fifth day of May in the drizzle and the rain? I don't think it's anybody's business if I choose to sit there and bang myself on the head with a board . . . if you don't get anything extra for being healthy, why should you be penalized for being a little sick?[53]

FROM AN INTERVIEW BY BRUCE DUFF IN *MUSIC CONNECTION* MAGAZINE

Circa May 1987

MUSIC CONNECTION: Are you really signing with Warner Bros.?

PERRY: We *think* we are. If we don't sign with them, you're gonna see three dead bodies. . . .

STEPHEN: . . . with X's on them.

PERRY: The papers are all like there and everything

STEPHEN: It's an 80-page contract.

DAVE: We've seen the contract.

STEPHEN: It's like a book.

PERRY: And we know everything about that contract, too, by the way. Oh, yeah, you think anything's gonna get by us? Man, I'll watch your spit fly!

DAVE: We discussed producers and stuff like that.

PERRY: Actually, we prefer a pushover.

MUSIC CONNECTION: Someone you can boss around?

PERRY: Oh, fuck yea!

STEPHEN: We have the best ideas.

PERRY: Actually, I shouldn't say that, 'cuz hopefully we'll get somebody who's a great person to work *with* us. It's just that if a producer thinks they're gonna go in there and tell us at all what's the final say they got the wrong band. They'll find that out.[54]

MARC GEIGER: Ultimately, Perry always got everything he wanted.

CASEY NICCOLI: When he put his mind to something, Perry always got things done. He was a leader. He stuck his nose into everybody's business and sometimes he pissed people off, but he always got what he wanted.

NEW MUSIC SEMINAR (NMS)

July 1987

CHARLEY BROWN: We were in New York for the New Music Seminar where there are massive showcases and hundreds of bands in all the clubs every night for a week. It was their first year before the record came out, and it was a big deal, big showcase, and we had gotten a real cool slot. It was like a one o'clock showing at the Ritz, and we were really stoked.

KEITH MORRIS (former vocalist, Black Flag, Circle Jerks, West Coast punk rock icon): Jane's was playing a showcase at the Ritz with Flesh for Lulu, New Model Army, and That Petrol Emotion. The guys from Flesh for Lulu were assholes who made it a point to push the entire show back, causing Jane's Addiction to go on way after two A.M.

CHARLEY BROWN: Flesh for Lulu apparently had an early ten o'clock slot, and pulled the petulant rock star thing because nobody was there to see them, and so they did a no show, but then their agent begged me to let them play before us. Just for fifteen minutes he promised. For "the cause." Like a fool, I let them do it due to those stipulations, but then Flesh for Lulu took total advantage. . . .

ERIC AVERY: Stephen even lent them cymbals, or something, in good faith. . . .

JON SIDEL: Jane's got bumped to the end and everyone left and we were in this big empty hall. There were like twenty people there, fifteen of them friends of the band, but they still went out and played their asses off anyway. There were punch-ups backstage. Tension was everywhere. It just set the music even more on fire.

KEITH MORRIS: Flesh for Lulu wouldn't quit and they played a full-length show. There's like six people left to see Jane's. Rick Rubin was one of them, Jon Sidel was another. And they played probably one of the greatest shows I've ever seen them play. It was just unbelievable.

CHARLEY BROWN: Flesh for Lulu played for nearly an hour by the time I got the sound guy to shut them off and drop the curtain in the middle of the song.

ERIC AVERY: We were sitting at the side of the stage just steaming.

CHARLEY BROWN: Perry is by nature a very excitable guy—especially when someone is stealing his thunder. As soon as the curtain went down, he just tore across the stage and slugged the singer hard on the nose and, he had like this huge honker, and the shit just hit the fan, just everything broke loose.

ERIC AVERY: When they were finally done, Perry just went after their lead singer. BOOM!

CHARLEY BROWN: Nasal blood gushing everywhere. Bloody cymbals flyin' around. Rock 'n' roll carny, a guaranteed freakshow, presented by your compere for the evening, ladies and gentlemen . . . Perry Farrell, that demented dizzy droog in diva drag [starring in] Jane's Addiction versus Flesh for Lulu! Lulu's road manager was the classic obese Limey gorilla stereotype in a Hawaiian shirt with jeans fallin' down his ass complete with hairy butt crack showin' . . . and he's got Dean by the throat pushed up against the wall with his feet dangling. It was fuckin' g-r-reat! A knock-'em-down, all-out hillbilly brawl; bare-knuckles, teeth, spit 'n' blood! We called them *Flush* for Lulu for the rest of the tour. It was total rock 'n' roll to the bone. Bands just don't do crazy shit like that anymore.

ERIC OD'S AT THE CHELSEA

CHARLEY BROWN: After the Flesh for Lulu dust-up we went back to the Chelsea Hotel. We were staying there because we had this thing about Sid [Vicious]. We just left the guys to do their thing, and sometime before dawn, Peter [Heur] and I went out for a bite, and that's when we saw this ambulance pulling away from the Chelsea. I said to Peter, "What asshole chump was possessed by the spirit of Sid?" Soon Dave called me kinda teary that Eric had OD'd. We all charged down to see Eric in this medical center. He came "this close" to dying. Perry was super-pissed. It cost a lot of money to get him out of there.

ERIC AVERY: Dave saw me off [from the Chelsea] in an ambulance and then hopped in a cab and got there [to the hospital] before the ambulance! The cab driver drove like a maniac and beat the ambulance there. Dave got irate at the emergency room insisting I was there and they kept saying, sorry, no one here of that name. It was embarrassing, so passé of me, especially being a bass player like Sid was!

CHARLEY BROWN: After we sprung Eric from the hospital everybody was buzzing about this unannounced show Perry had set up at the Lismar Lounge in Alphabet City, which was sort of a Hell's Angels' dive bar. Perry's brother Farrell [Bernstein], like his father, was a jeweler. Farrell had strong ties to the Angels; he fulfilled their need for jewelry emphasizing skulls and Germanic iron crosses, but I don't think he was ever actually initiated. Perry worshipped him. That's why he took his name. We were in a club where absolutely *nobody* gave a shit about Jane's Addiction. Afterward there was an altercation . . . with this Angel guy.

ERIC AVERY: The day I got out of the hospital, that night we played in a bar. Perry said something snide about how I was in the hospital this morning and here he is playing a show. He gave me a public "atta boy" kind of thing.

CHARLEY BROWN: Farrell Bernstein had the Hell's Angel hook-up to look out for us, a little bit of security, which was another reason why we picked it down there, the Lismar Lounge . . . where G. G. Allin, the crazy, trainwreck guy would play when he'd get to New York. . . .

MIKE STEWART: I was in New York for the New Music Seminar, a couple of months later [after the debut of Scream East], hanging out at the Lismar Lounge, right around the corner from the local Hell's Angels HQ. I knew a couple of people from there from doing Scream, so we're hangin' out at this grungy old grebo biker bar with these fucked-up hard-core glam bands playing, like the Lunachicks would be there. Lismar was the size of the Viper Room. It was disgusting, like CBGB-style gross disgusting. Dark, dank, dusty, dirty with fucked-up bathrooms. They had tattooed girl bartenders, or maybe they were drag queens— who knows—that looked like they'd beat the crap out of you. One of them was in the Cycle Sluts from Hell. Hell's Angels and rastas hanging around everywhere. It was really intimidating if you didn't know somebody who hung out there.

CHARLEY BROWN: Playing in the corner of some filthy Hell's Angel toilet in some rat-infested New York cellar had a sleazy, dangerous edge, which Perry loved.

MIKE STEWART: Jane's Addiction was hanging out with us and Rick Rubin is also there. So Rick tells me behind their backs, "I only like Jane's Addiction because of that Dave Navarro guy. If you could get me Dave Navarro, I'd be forever in your debt, Mike." I said, "Dude, what are you asking me to do? You want me to tell Dave Navarro you want to sign him out of Jane's Addiction?" He just thought David was a rock god. He said, "Oh my god, I need that guy. I could make him a star." I just remember telling Rick these guys were my friends. They're such an amazing band I wouldn't want to see them break up, but I'll tell David because it's his right to know, but I hope he doesn't do it. I mentioned it to Dave. It wasn't a good thing, thank goodness. I was personally so relieved that he didn't.

ERIC AVERY: Rick Rubin had never been a fan of Jane's Addiction. He just didn't get it. He tried to get Stephen and Dave to leave. He wanted them to do something else because they're such great players. Rubin's like the big heavy metal guy of the day, and so, of course, he just wasn't diggin' on the likes of me, and especially Perry . . . and Perry really hated him for that. When Perry found out about Rick's agenda to raid both Perkins *and* Navarro, he was super-pissed. . . .

MIKE STEWART: Rick probably wanted Dave for Danzig . . . or maybe it was the Four Horsemen, remember them? What was the other guy? Chris Goss? What was his band? [Masters of Reality] Maybe Rick thought Dave looked hotter to young girls, and would go good with Chris, who knows what the fuck he was thinking. . . .

CHARLEY BROWN: . . . if it wasn't Danzig, it was some other male cretin act from back East I can't remember. So, like . . . everything's going pretty cool that night [at the Lismar]. Dave and Steve met a couple of girls. Suddenly this well-dressed black dude comes in the bar. The Big Hush falls over the joint. Guy's a little drunk, tries to order a drink, but the bartender won't serve him, right? So this major rip breaks out, and they booted his ass out, and everything gets back to normal for a minute or two, but now he comes runnin' back in wavin' a fuckin' *Glock!* Oh, shit! I pushed Dave and Steve and the girls underneath the table.

ERIC AVERY: I was still out of it. . . . I don't remember anybody menacing us, but there were a lot of mean-looking biker dudes hanging out, but they just seemed cool for the most part. . . .

CHARLEY BROWN: The Angels had these hidden mechanical knives up the inside of their wrists, always ready to go; they could snap out blades from under their sleeves in any major standoff and literally hack their adversaries to pieces! If the other guy had a gun, as in this instance, he might be able to smoke one or two of the Angels before the rest of 'em got to him and opened up his throat, right? The dude obviously knew it . . . and so the guy slowly backs out of the bar, cussing . . . and he hops in a cab. Everybody runs out and jumps on their bikes and speeds after the taxi. They're gone for like an hour or whatever, and when they get back I try to talk to one of the Angels. I says, "You know that crazy black dude with the gun about an hour ago, what happened?" He was like, "Listen, smart guy, nothing happened, OK!??" Then he starts shouting real loud, "Nobody was here! He doesn't exist! He never existed! Get the hell away from me!" I was like, "OK. OK. OK."

MR. MOJO RISIN':
Dark Vibe in the Tradition of The Doors and the Velvets

JIM MORRISON: Wanna see my rig? Is that any way to behave at a rock 'n' roll concert?

PERRY FARRELL: Summertime, and a young man's cock gets hard. Blow jobs on stage? Those are good. Not every night, though.

DAVE NAVARRO: We can't help but capture some of what L.A. is.

PERRY FARRELL: How many of you like [being] pressed up against other men? Does it turn you on?

PERRY FARRELL: Have you ever once thought about sucking a man's cock? A kid says, "Yeah." "He has? Now we're getting somewhere! We've all been lifted."

PERRY FARRELL (between songs at the Universal Amphitheater, Studio City, Los Angeles): *The next orgasm I have, I'm going to lift everyone to a higher place, I'm going to a place that's free. Who wants to come with me? I want to know true freedom.*

JIM MORRISON: When sex involves all the senses intensely, it becomes a mystical experience.

FLEA: For Los Angeles, the list of bands who capture and help define the times in their music goes something like this: Love, The Doors, the Germs, X, Jane's. You can even draw some comparisons between Jim Morrison and Perry.

PETE WEISS: Sometimes they'd encore with this awesome medley of "L.A. Woman" (Doors) going into "Nausea" (by X) and "Lexicon Devil" (Germs).

DAVE NAVARRO: We're from here, I was born in L.A. Eric and Stephen were born here. We make music based on our environments.

MARC GEIGER: It was a different age. People were a little more easily spooked [then] . . . the vibe surrounding Jane's seemed to come from a really dark, drug-intense place. It was really just Perry's way of expressing art.

FLEA: Those Jane's guys have a major darkness to them. They're very polite, they're nice, cool, caring people, but they definitely have a part of them that's dark, a part of them that's mysterious and afraid; a part that is angry and all of those things that make up what we call dark. It's also an aesthetic that they really embraced because they were good at it. And they actually played that way. It was beautiful.

DAVE NAVARRO: When I listen to music that's really dark, I get this overwhelming sensation that I'm not alone, that I'm not crazy. It's a little comforting.[55]

ERIC AVERY: We were certainly concerned with things dark, all of us. With the exception of Stephen, we were all dark people. The drugs and the lifestyle and . . . the twisted gallows humor.

CASEY NICCOLI: I don't think Perry meant to study the darker end of the occult. I think you find that out when you study it.

JOSH RICHMAN: When they [Perry and Casey] would get dark they would get real dark together, too.

PERRY FARRELL: Just playing with darkness, that's like half an idea. I need to know more. I want to know about lightness.[56]

DAVE NAVARRO: Sure, I enjoy dark music, but I don't think of the band as "dark," it's too multidimensional. "Then She Did" is a very dark song about death, but then that same album has "Been Caught Stealing," which is very poppy and upbeat and tongue-in-cheek about an experience Perry had as a kid and now he's laughing about it; but nobody wants to say we're a goofy, carefree band, they gravitate toward the darkness. There's also happiness and joy. Listen to "Summertime Rolls," it's an amazing, beautiful song . . . and "Jane Says" is a true story. . . .

ERIC AVERY: We were concerned with passion, expression, and experience. There are certainly sweet aspects to what we did. "Summertime Rolls" comes to mind.

PERRY FARRELL: I enjoy going to the end of the pier and looking to see what's over the railings. We had a lot of adventure, dark adventure you might say, but it doesn't mean that we're not good people, and it doesn't mean that we don't know where to stand. You've got to experiment with this life.

MARC GEIGER: Stephen was the odd man out. He was the good kid from the Valley who was an unbelievable drummer and a happy, peacekeeping influence.

STEPHEN PERKINS: I'm a very positive person, I'm not at all dark. I'm the blue sky in Jane's Addiction. I'm happy to be that role. That's how my drum parts sound. Percolating, bubbly, bouncy, 'cause that's who and what I am. That's my expression. Some people might think that I play a lot. I'm just being myself. I talk a lot. I feel a lot. That's me.

PERRY FARRELL: Stephen wasn't a drug addict. He's a great, great spirit and it comes across in his playing. Stephen is one of the sweetest people you'll ever meet, and, remember, this poor guy had three horrible junkies in his band forever and the guy always put up with it. He'd hear bad news about us, the kid would just fall apart. The look in his eyes was like telling a kid he couldn't go to sleepaway camp.

STEPHEN PERKINS: The dark and the light. I think the movement of Jane's Addiction is generally positive; it's a movement of children, future, sunshine, fresh air.

∘⨳⨳⨳∘

STEVEN BAKER: Perry was constantly advocating sex.

PERRY FARRELL: Ask around. I'm not a prude.[57]

STEVEN BAKER: His dick was frequently hanging out of his pants after one song.

DAVE NAVARRO: It happened quite often where something naughty popped out from his clothing. . . .

PERRY FARRELL: I used to whip my cock out all the time. I did it because it was just something to do. And then it became a thing. As long as I could whip out my dick, I knew I was alive.

CHARLEY BROWN: I made him promise he wouldn't do it anymore. I mean I loved it, the outrage of it, the showmanship of it, it's just I didn't want it to get in the way of what was happening musically. I thought the music was really magical . . . and, remember, the same thing helped kill off Jim Morrison's stage career twenty years earlier. Now we're slap in the middle of this puritanical revival.

It's PRMC time and the Tipper Gore Show [mid- to late 80s]. This flashing shtick of Perry's was flirting with danger. . . .

DAVE JERDEN: The Doors were never able to come back after Morrison's arrest for onstage flashing. . . .[58]

MAKING THE MARK ON SEATTLE

October 24, 1987

Jane's Addiction, Green River at Scream.

JEFF AMENT (musician, songwriter, Green River, Mother Love Bone, Pearl Jam): Green River was Stone Gossard and I with Mark Arm and Steve Turner who went on to form Mudhoney and our very last gig was at the Scream at the Embassy Hotel in Los Angeles, sometime during fall of '87. We opened up, Junkyard from Austin played second and Jane's headlined. Stone and I were on the side of the stage when Jane's was playing, totally mesmerized by the interaction between the band

and the crowd. There was just something about the way Perry connected with them. The audience was singing along to everything. They knew every word to every song. It was the first time I had seen an alternative music show where it was like the most reverential hard-rock crowd. That night Jane's Addiction showed us that you could do something totally different and make it work, which basically caused Green River to break up since the other guys didn't dig it as much as Stone and I did. Our drummer hated them. When we got back to Seattle we just knew we wanted to do something else, something with less limitations, something that had endless possibilities and that's what Jane's seemed like to us. It really inspired us. It seemed like they could go in any direction. They could have been The Cure or they could have been Led Zeppelin, or anything else they wanted to be; that was exactly the sort of open-ended band we wanted to be in, and so Stone and I formed a new band, Mother Love Bone.

BOB FORREST: It was obvious that Mother Love Bone liked Jane's Addiction. Somehow those two bands seemed to have the same kind of concept: mixing the metal we grew up with and punk rock . . . they also both hooked up with the indie DIY punk attitude at about the same time.

JEFF AMENT: We soon hooked up with Andy Wood [from this band Malfunction] to be Mother Love Bone's lead singer. I first saw Malfunction probably around '83 in Seattle. It's amazing how similar what Andy was doing then to what Perry was doing in terms of the campiness. Andy strutted in pancake makeup and was throwing out a T. Rex, Freddie Mercury vibe. Like Perry, Andy was also super funny, yet at the same time sexually ambiguous. Half the crowd didn't know if Andy was for real or if it was a joke. Jane's had a lot to do with what Mother Love Bone became; they helped define what Stone and I wanted to do musically, to be a heavy groove hard-rock band with some arty leanings.

PERRY FARRELL: The first time we went up to Seattle, we were hanging out and partying with the Mother Love Bone guys that eventually became Pearl Jam. That was the pre-Nirvana era. There was one brewing, but it wasn't like a fully blown band scene yet. We had a great time up there, we really revved up the kids in Seattle.

ERIC AVERY: I always really liked Seattle as a place on tour because it had a different energy.

Postcard to Dayle Gloria from Mother Love Bone, the
proto-Pearl Jam band Jeff Ament and Stone Gossard
were inspired to form immediately after seeing Jane's
Addiction live. (Courtesy Dayle Gloria)

PERRY FARRELL: There was a really great community that was responsive
to what we were doing. The crowd felt like it was lit up and electrified.
You could feel its warmth. They were aware of the feeling that was happening in the country, with the music, with us—they were so onto it.

BOB FORREST: Jane's Addiction and the bands out of the Seattle scene
and . . . even Guns N' Roses . . . were among this new breed of rock
bands who said, "We're going to mix it all together and it's going to be
this new hybrid gumbo of metal, hard rock and punk. . . ."

JEFF AMENT: There were many other different things going on, but if there was any direct influence [on our scene] by Jane's Addiction it was that; whether you were a punk rocker not afraid to play a big heavy riff or if you were a heavy guy not afraid to pick up an acoustic guitar.

ERIC AVERY: It just seemed like everybody was in a band, a carryover from the early punk rock days which I never experienced first hand, but the idea of it had carried on in Seattle just like it had in L.A.

PERRY FARRELL: One of the great shows we did during that era was in Seattle. We have footage of it in our short film—go to *Soul Kiss* and you see where I'm wearing a big green hat and a pair of white glasses. Those glasses were stolen from the kid in Mother Love Bone, who eventually overdosed [Andrew Wood]. May he rest in peace.

ERIC AVERY: Seattle always had cool clubs, there was always live music going on there all the way back to the 50s and 60s. Now there was an explosion of rock clubs and people playing in each other's bands. Such an incredibly interconnected web of creativity and out of it pops all these new bands like Soundgarden. I just loved their grooves, they were super heavy and cool.

CHRIS CORNELL (lead vocalist, songwriter-lyricist, Soundgarden): Seattle was a very autonomous scene. [Jane's Addiction] were liked, but the bands that were really heroes of the Seattle scene tended to be really aggressive, post-punk indie bands like the Butthole Surfers. So for any L.A. band to make any kind of impact at that time was huge because if you were a band from L.A. and weren't Black Flag, nobody wanted to know. When the [*Jane's Addiction*] Triple X record came out everybody knew about it, everyone knew what was going on, everybody had the record.

STEVEN BAKER: Seattle's so-called grunge scene might not necessarily have been influenced musically by Jane's but I think the band was definitely a big part of that scene's inspiration.

CHARLEY BROWN: If Jane's hadn't happened, Seattle wouldn't have happened in the same way that it did. The scene was bubbling up and Soundgarden and Mudhoney were the first ones out there, but they were too paranoid of the L.A. music-business people, and they hesitated, and missed the window.

CHRIS CORNELL: I had a very difficult time making the decision that maybe it would be OK to sign a major label record deal because it never seemed to work out. Our audience went to "mom and pop" indie record stores. They didn't go to Tower or the other big chains, they didn't buy records that were on major labels.

JEFF AMENT: Soundgarden was a little closer with punk rock . . . they didn't want to turn their backs on the early punk-rock scene in Seattle, but Stone and I always felt a little bit of a separation in terms of what was going on with that crowd and what we wanted to do. We were unapologetic about saying, "We want to sign to a major label. If we're going to be in the business of selling records, we want the opportunity to sell lots of records. Sorry, but we just don't want to beat our heads against the wall for the rest of our lives to sell a few hundred records." Of course, once we did sign with a major, it became like, "Why the hell did we do that?"

CHRIS CORNELL: Jane's had a pretty big cultural impact on the Seattle scene by doing exactly what they wanted as artists; plus being irreverent about the industry as a whole . . . that personally influenced me because it helped solidify in my mind that I could do the same thing on an indie level.

JEFF AMENT: We always associated Los Angeles with heavy metal and hair bands and I think in some ways L.A. was a big turnoff at that point in the mid-80s. Punk rock had largely died out down there so L.A. was the last place we wanted to be. After the Jane's show at the Scream, Stone and I were kind of like, "Maybe L.A. wouldn't be such a bad place to be, after all." Jane's set the example. You didn't have to do it completely DIY. You could take that same ethos and push it on to the major labels. . . .

CHRIS CORNELL: Musically Jane's also had an impact on Soundgarden. . . .

JEFF AMENT: I bet if you talked to Kim Thayil [from Soundgarden] he would say no, but I think there are elements of Soundgarden that are very similar to Jane's.

CHRIS CORNELL: Jane's helped open doors slowly but surely, as much as the Chili Peppers, the Butthole Surfers, Husker Du, The Replacements, and many other bands that weren't out of Seattle.

JEFF AMENT: In Seattle we always looked at Minneapolis and Austin as the two music scenes. There was Husker Du and The Replacements and everything that was going on in Minneapolis, and then there was the Butthole Surfers, Scratch Acid, and Really Red in Texas. X and Jane's Addiction were the two L.A. bands we looked up to the most. To me the bands that stand out as breaking it open nationally were Husker, The Replacements, and Jane's. . . .

ERIC AVERY: A more universal analogy would be like if you pass a lighted match through gas it will go up in flames. I think the Seattle scene had all the ingredients and everything was already there in place to create that kind of scene. But some things that moved through had the kind of cumulative rub off effect that helped spark it . . . bands like us, L7, Butthole Surfers, the Pixies, Ministry, Nine Inch Nails, Fugazi all had an impact . . . and before us it was Black Flag and the SST bands . . . Meat Puppets, Husker Du, Sonic Youth, maybe Dinosaur Jr. . . .

CHRIS CORNELL: Jane's also helped open doors for commercial airplay. Our first A&M record got some rock radio. Now there were stations playing Jane's and Soundgarden; that was absolutely the first time they'd ever played anything that wasn't really commercial or straight heavy metal.

CHARLEY BROWN: The sheep in the music industry hated us at first, until they realized that this was happening, so once they didn't get Jane's, they started milking the Seattle area for the bands that opened for us, like Soundgarden. . . .

STEVEN BAKER: Someone called me after the first Alice in Chains record asking can you get these guys on the road with Jane's Addiction? They wanted to market AIC not as a regular, down-the-middle rock band but something with a different point of view. . . .

TED GARDNER: If Nirvana was the bomb Jane's destiny was to touch the blue paper.[59]

CHARLEY BROWN: Nirvana ended up getting the credit, even though they never claimed to actually be from Seattle . . . and that's not a diss on their music or Cobain's talent. . . .

CHRIS CORNELL: A lot of people think that rock 'n' roll changed in the early 90s when Nirvana showed up and everyone had a big hit. But it didn't really work that way.

CHARLEY BROWN: Jane's got mired down because we were the first ones cutting through.

DAVE NAVARRO: I became a major fan of Nirvana. I didn't have any resentment about them becoming much bigger than us. I thought that they were fantastic. But I think that in some ways we contributed to their success in terms of opening doors. Some of those Seattle guys today will probably agree.

PERRY FARRELL: I never had a bad feeling about Nirvana because their music was compelling and strong. But I had a bad feeling about myself. In six months, the world had just spun itself a whole new yarn!

TED GARDNER: There were lots of bands around prior to Nirvana; the Melvins for sure, and a lot of other bands like the Pixies that were strong in their particular town. Jane's Addiction was a very strong L.A.-based band, as were Soundgarden and Mother Love Bone in Seattle, and Smashing Pumpkins in Chicago, Nine Inch Nails in Ohio, Fugazi in D.C., and so on. . . . .[60]

ERIC AVERY: Someone told me that you have to see this band, they're like the new Jane's, and it was Smashing Pumpkins.

STEVEN BAKER: Perkins told me the first time he went to Chicago Jimmy Chamberlin from Smashing Pumpkins said that when the Pumpkins opened for Jane's [during '88] it was his first gig with the band, and that immediately afterwards, like literally overnight, Corgan revamped the Pumpkins' whole onstage style, their entire approach to music changed.

ERIC AVERY: I remember Don Muller sitting in the back of a car saying, "I don't know if I want to do this anymore. I have all these bands that nobody cares about and I really like them and they're great. But who wants to hear from them?" The bands he was naming were the bands that he eventually went to the top with, like Soundgarden, Alice in Chains, the list is crazy. It was the next wave. . . .

HENRY ROLLINS (singer, bandleader, author, actor, publisher): Jane's was the only band I saw in those times who had that I-will-follow-them-anywhere type of crowds. The band had struck a nerve with people and the response was intense. There were a lot of great bands around at that time, but Jane's had this powerful tribal thing happening with their fans.

FLEA: Without a doubt, to me, Jane's Addiction are the most important rock band of the 80s . . . up until Nirvana came around.

TOURING WITH LOVE & ROCKETS

Circa October–December 1987

STEVEN BAKER: They weren't just sitting around waiting for the world to come to them. Before the album even came out they were on the road with Love & Rockets. . . .

CHARLEY BROWN: It was costing $10,000 a week to put them on the road with just me and a roadie and a motor home. Warners paid for this before we'd even signed. Love & Rockets audiences hated us throughout the country.

STEPHEN PERKINS: The English Goth movement was on top of us at the time.

CHARLEY BROWN: We played San Francisco before we drove to New York to join Love & Rockets. San Francisco always hated L.A. and L.A. bands. We were opening for Until December, which was like this horrible New Wavey Human League kind of thing, arty farty, really cheesey 80s New Wave. Perry and Dave were being brats, like dissing them and making fun of them the whole time they were getting ready. Perry was mouthing off on this tirade against Until December saying how lame they were and how fuckin' lame the club was and then all of a sudden the PA just goes off. I went fucking ballistic on the sound guy. Next thing I know three bouncers grab me and heave me out of the club. So I'm getting up and dusting myself off like an Old West saloon kind of thing, right . . . and then it was like BAM! SPLAT! The rest of the band

Love & Rockets. Bauhaus minus Peter Murphy.
Tour-mates with early Jane's whose audience
was largely indifferent to the openers, although
a good time seemed to be had by all in the end.
(Fin Costello)

comes flyin' out the doors one at a time, thrown out. And then all our equipment comes flying out after them!

ERIC AVERY: I remember our manager, Charley Brown, going to collect for us one night in Arizona and coming back to us and us going, "How much did you get?" He just replied, "Uh, I got choked." We were like, "What!?" "He fuckin' *choked* me!" We could see these really red marks on his neck.

CHARLEY BROWN: We were at this crummy toilet of a club in Phoenix— not the Mason Jar—but it was the same slimeball of an owner, trying to expand his empire by opening another filthy little public sewer with a stage and a bar. Nobody knew who we were. There were like ten or twenty people, and during those kind of shows Perry always mouthed off. So, now this guy wants to stiff us on our guarantee, the lowest form of bottom feeder life in club or concert promotion. That happened quite often at the beginning, and so tonight I've had it, tonight I'm gonna try out alternative collection techniques. I decide to raise my voice. I'm like hollerin', shouting real loud at this tiny little thing, this creepy little troll, like under five feet, who now starts blowin' this fuckin' whistle, and now these two Neanderthals grab me and hold me, and he starts strangling me and then he calls the cops. And the cops are gonna arrest me for assault and I'm like, "See these hand marks around my neck?" They literally ran us out of town, and because he was in with the cops he didn't have to pay us. Our all-powerful Triad agency was going to get us our money, but they never did.

PERRY FARRELL: One tour we're playing some dive club in Phoenix, trying to get paid while this guy is choking our manager and pulling a gun on him. Next, we're selling out Madison Square Garden.

CHARLEY BROWN: Going across the desert to New York, we were camping the whole way and throughout the band was fighting. Perry and Dave would exchange hate poems. Perry would leave writings on the table so that Dave would discover them. I can't remember what they said. Perry's into humiliation, always has been. He's into S&M, not too much the physical pain, but he likes to psych people out with his superiority. Dave would go off somewhere and be crying and Perry would go sleep in the snow. We had a motor home and rather than sleep in the motor home with Dave, he'd go crash outside under a blanket or something.

ERIC AVERY: Perry was often under the impression, and evidently he's still this way, that there were conspiratorial designs against him from everybody. That we really put thought into how we could undermine him. Like me and Dave were moping around thinking, "How can we fuck up Perry's day?"

CHARLEY BROWN: Dave and Perry were both constantly showing off what great artists they were, insulting each other with poetry, showing how clever they could be with their insults.

ERIC AVERY: Dave wrote in a journal or a diary something about he thought that he'd look cooler under a light show rather than jumping around looking like an idiot. That was innocently left out and Perry read it and interpreted it as talking about Perry . . . like, "I would rather look like Dave Navarro, cool under a light show, than look like Perry, an idiot jumping around." What he was really referring to was our band versus Love & Rockets. We would see Love & Rockets looking really cool and reserved and we'd get up there and jump around like idiots, by comparison. Perry may have truly believed that Dave left that out on purpose so that he would see it and get the dig.

DANIEL ASH: Jane's Addiction was very different from Love & Rockets. . . .

CHARLEY BROWN: Everybody was there to see Love & Rockets. The first show at Long Island University people were just screaming to get off the stage and throwing all sorts of crap at us. That was pretty much the whole tour. Jane's was just a local L.A. phenomenon up to now. Suddenly we're playing 5,000–10,000 seaters. The biggest crowd they'd played in front of was at the Scream. We lived like dogs with one beat-up motor home, one crew guy, and myself. Everybody's been fighting the whole way across the country. We get there, expectations are high, and the audience *hates* us. Gaaah.

ERIC AVERY: I just remember making a lot of extra change every night. We would get pelted by irate fans who wanted Love & Rockets to come on. They hated us, especially on the East Coast. . . .

CHARLEY BROWN: We opened for them at the Beacon, one of the finest venues in New York, and everyone was standing out in the lobby and I had to go out and pretend I'm a fan and say, "That's a great band in there, they're fucking awesome. Get in there!"

KEVIN HASKINS: I think it was the *Earth, Sun, Moon* album when we toured with Jane's.

DANIEL ASH: I remember hearing a cassette of their stuff and David saying more than any of us, this is the band, this is great.

DAVID J: I told Daniel this tape just turned up from [our booking agent] Marc. He wants us to think about having this band on tour as support. So we put it in and loved it instantly. We thought, "This is the real thing." We played it over and over again. The more we played it, the more we liked it.

MARC GEIGER: There were dates with Gene Loves Jezebel, Love & Rockets, Peter Murphy, The Cult and so on. I'd say the goth thing was the musical bent of Eric and Perry. At the very beginning the goth scene was where they felt the most kinship, not only musically, but vibe-wise. I don't think it was a strategy. The band had such strong character they made you look at who was taking to them. We just went with that. Our instincts were that this band could not be looked at as a regular hard-rock band—even though they played hard rock, so to speak—we kept them darker. We kept the bands they played with dark.

DAVID J: We loved Perry's voice. We thought it was lyrically interesting, very androgynous. We loved the space in the music and how you'd have the juxtaposition of these soft, psychedelic, pretty parts and it would just explode into hard, almost metal music with a punk edge to it. Lyrically it was interesting, too. The drums were amazing. The bass playing was incredible. It just held together. It was very, very colorful.

DANIEL ASH: As soon as we saw them live, we were wondering why we were headlining. We thought they were fantastic. They really reminded me of the chemistry of Bauhaus. Not musically, just the personalities in the band and the way they interconnected.

DAVID J: We became fast friends and bonded with them like no other band we had been on the road with. We used to hang out in each other's dressing rooms jamming a lot. They used to do two different sets, regular electric and acoustic. They were doing the acoustic set in the dressing rooms. We just thought that was great. They really warmed our audience up. It was very complimentary. We had great times on the road, traveling, after the shows we would hang out with each other. . . .

DANIEL ASH: My lips are sealed. . . .

DAVID J: There were many obvious parallels between Perry and Peter [Bauhaus lead vocalist-co-songwriter Peter Murphy]. Peter was probably less conscious than Perry of the American Indian and the early Californian shamanism traditions, but Peter would naturally go there. Like Peter, Perry was very provocative. Inevitably, some violence would erupt. It was always impressive the way he would deal with it. He would never throw a punch or become physical. It would be something from the crowd and he'd snuff it out very quickly by saying a few words or give a particularly glaring look. I remember being aware of this friction, which was somehow very necessary to both groups.

DANIEL ASH: I could see a little bit of that same electric friction in Jane's Addiction that existed in Bauhaus.

December 1987

DEAN NALEWAY: At Cal State–Irvine, Perry didn't want to open for Love & Rockets anymore, so we had to talk him into doing the show, and he said, "Okay, but I'm gonna whip my dick out." And we're like, "Ohhhh, we never heard that."

DAVID J: Perry flashed his knob in California at a big gig. He got his bonker out for the crowd.

CHARLEY BROWN: It was the biggest show of the whole tour, our first, and homecoming for everybody. We were still nobodies at this point. Love & Rockets were rock stars with semis and massive crews and everything, and we had a minnow, our little motor home, and this one metal-head roadie guy Sarj, who hated Jane's music, and myself.

REBECCA AVERY: Perry was getting temperamental and for whatever reason didn't want to go on that night. It's a little late! Here we are, everybody's here in their seats. They weren't getting the same response they were used to at the Scream when people were flipping and going nuts over them. Love & Rockets audience were just kind of uninterested, they thought Perry was just too weird. There was also a little booing. Just a few people would yell, "Fuck you, get off the stage, you crazy freak" or something really nasty, but I don't remember it being that big a deal, it didn't seem like something he couldn't have easily handled. It wasn't like a thousand people yelling, "You suck!"

CHARLEY BROWN: Perry didn't want to go on because in his mind the band was broken up. It had nothing to do with not wanting to open up for Love & Rockets. It was the last show. He'd just had enough of it and said fuck it. He was ready not to play.

REBECCA AVERY: Of course, the show had to go on in the end, so he was like, pouting, "Fine, but I'm doing it with my dick out."

CHARLEY BROWN: We were spare-changing their crew the whole way, literally panhandling for help, so the last thing I wanted to do was fuck up their big moment. But it was a big moment for us, too; French TV was there filming, and so Perry came out in these wafer thin stretch pants, kind of bicycle pants, made out of balloon material.

DEAN NALEWAY: He had his usual corset on over these rubber pants that he'd cut a hole out of so his penis could hang through. . . .

CHARLEY BROWN: . . . at a very strategic moment the pants burst, and being the showman that Perry is he continued for at least two more songs to a packed house.

DEAN NALEWAY: By the end he'd thrown the corset into the crowd and he was dancing around with his dick bouncing up and down. Campus and city cops streamed up in droves to arrest him for indecent exposure. Perry ran upstairs to the dressing room, and we had to hide him in a closet until they gave up.

CHARLEY BROWN: It was like one of those classic Lenny Bruce–Jim Morrison moments where the pigs are freakin' in all corners, ready to shit-can the show and arrest him for obscenity. I panicked, ran up to Casey, and demanded her panties, which she quickly gave to me, and I ran to the stage and slingshotted them to Perry . . . which he slipped into and played the rest of the show in. As soon as they finished their last note, cops were all over our shit. French TV was trying to film it all. Cameras were coming at us and cops were violently pushing them away. They drug us outside and Perry was cowering like a little kid holding up these sweaty fragments of rubber, saying, "It just broke, I didn't know what to do." I got the job of calming the cops down and making it all go away. Thank God he didn't get arrested. After they let him go, I was still dealing with the cops. I was dealing with Love & Rockets and I was dealing with their tour manager. I was dealing with our agent because it flipped everybody out.

DEAN NALEWAY: We were like, "No, no, it wasn't on purpose. His pants split." The cops were like, "Okay, well, we need to see the pants to make sure that they ripped." And we're like, "The pants are on him, and he's gone! He's already left the building." Finally they let it go and didn't press any charges, because they couldn't prove it wasn't accidental.

PERRY FARRELL: I would always just tell them my pants split. So they have to kind of think about it. I used to always wear rubber, so I always had the excuse. When rubber splits, it really splits.

NOTHING'S SHOCKING ALBUM

Circa January–April 1988

Nothing's Shocking sessions at El Dorado Studios, Los Angeles

ERIC AVERY: Warners put together a group of producers that we just kind of picked through. The guy who did Guns N' Roses' *Appetite* album was on it, but we were like, "Not right for us."

PERRY FARRELL: I liked Dave Jerden's work on [the Brian Eno/David Byrne album] *My Life in the Bush of Ghosts*, so I was excited to work with him.

DAVE NAVARRO: Dave Jerden is fantastic. He was a great producer. We had a great experience with him. We steered the ship a lot [ourselves] and Dave's job was to capture it. And I think he did that very well.

ERIC AVERY: Jerden was such a fucking godsend for me personally. I'm so glad we chose him. He really helped me in every way. I remember him saying, "You're gonna be around for this. What's going to happen to you for the next couple of years . . . get ready for a hell of a ride. Strap yourself in, man, and keep your eyes open."

DAVE JERDEN: I totally jumped at the chance to make a record with them. What other band since X . . . and then, even further back, The Doors and The Velvet Underground, could have segued from songs about killers and despair to singing beautiful tender love songs about summertime? Perry gave me a tape of all these bits and pieces of music. It had this feeling like our entire culture was in there, distilled into one idea and that idea became *Nothing's Shocking*.[61]

STEPHEN PERKINS: *Nothing's Shocking* was a combination of everything in the world today. Even back then there was reality TV when [serial killer] Ted Bundy was representing himself in court.

DAVE JERDEN: Perry has always been interested in the dark side, and with Ted Bundy, I don't think you can get any darker than that. He said he wanted to use some Ted dialogue in the song and we worked it in.[62]

DAVE NAVARRO: We had this song, "Idiots Rule," that Flea and Angelo Moore and Chris Dowd from Fishbone came down to play on. They had this horn section part worked out that took a Jane's Addiction song and, somehow, within one pass of tape, turned it into a Fishbone song. So Perry trimmed away some of the fat and it became what it is now. That was my first memory of Flea.

DAVE JERDEN: During the making of *Nothing's Shocking* Bob Ezrin came by. He said, "Don't try to make a record that people will like. Try to make a record that people will hate because then you're not in the middle. If you make a middle-of-the-road record you're nowhere. But if you make a record that, let's say, fifty percent of the people vehemently hate, there's going to be fifty percent of people who absolutely love it." I thought, just make it aggressive, and mean, and weird, and nasty as you wanna be. You never know what's going to please people, but it's easy to go up and slap somebody in the face and piss them off, always works, and that's what I think we did with that record.[63]

ERIC AVERY: I don't even know if I would hold Perry responsible as much as I would hold the machine responsible. It was an unstated thing that it operated like a partnership . . . that is until it started to take off. We had a meeting to figure out the publishing. I wanted it to be split equally between everyone—I tend to believe in the U2 model where no one person is changing his lifestyle dramatically over anybody else—but suddenly Perry wanted fifty percent for writing the lyrics straight off the bat, plus another portion of the remaining fifty percent for the music. I was sort of going to bat more for Stephen and David because I'm sure I could have gotten a much larger piece of the pie. We were stunned. Dave, Stephen, and I wound up getting 12.5 percent apiece.

PERRY FARRELL: The songs Eric wrote were good songs; they were very simple. They were basic grooves.[64]

CASEY NICCOLI: Perry could argue, "Well, without me, it would have just been a great bass groove in his garage forever."

REBECCA AVERY: It was a band of four members and everybody contributed. Eric wrote a lot of music, "Mountain Song," "Had a Dad," "Jane Says" and came up with some ideas for lyrics, not specific lyrics, but lyrical *ideas* for songs. For example, "Had a Dad" had to do with Eric finding out that he had this different biological father. He came up with the guitar for "Jane Says." And "Summertime Rolls" . . . two of their very best signature songs.

ERIC AVERY: I remember showing him a poem by Sylvia Plath called "The Companionable Ills" and there's a line in it about how stirrups inspired the spirit out of the mud. Something like that. I forget exactly. We were talking about it and that became "Ain't No Right." Perry wrote something like, "I am skin and bones, I am pointy nose, and that's what makes me try," which was born from that poem.

REBECCA AVERY: Eric would say, "I have this idea" and then Perry would take that and pen the actual lyric. He'd tell Perry, "This is what I'm thinking musically. This is the feeling of it."

ERIC AVERY: I came up with the guitar for "Jane Says" and "Summertime Rolls." The guitar part for "Jane Says" was probably by some guy I jammed with many years before. Then I put the chorus on it so it was sort of born from a jam. But the lyrics were totally Perry on "Jane Says." That was such a flash of brilliance of his, that's where his genius lies.

DAVE NAVARRO: We did everything totally different from song to song. Some came from Eric's bass lines, some from guitar, some came from Perry, some came from drum riffs, and some of them just came from free-form jams. There was really no formula.

ERIC AVERY: It was all jams initially, but there was also a crafting aspect of each other's ideas. David and Stephen brought the "metal" element. . . .

REBECCA AVERY: Eric was never like, "I want my due, I want my credit for this and that." He just wasn't like that.

ERIC AVERY: I thought of my role as assistant creative director, because I wasn't the most musically proficient and I didn't write songs in the traditional sense.

PERRY FARRELL: Musically, I help with arrangements, but I could never play as great as them. They're experts at their instruments.[65]

DAVE JERDEN: I drove to work at the studio one day a little late and Perry was already in his car in the parking lot with Stephen and Dave, and they were pulling out. Perry says, "The band just broke up. There won't be any record. See ya!" And I was like, "*Wha-a-t!?*"[66]

ERIC AVERY: Warner Bros. called an emergency meeting because Perry said it was going to be his way or no way.

REBECCA AVERY: Wanting to take more than half entirely for yourself and to give the others 12.5 percent each, that's shitty. I just remember feeling like no one's standing up to him. Nobody's saying, "That's not OK." They didn't want it to end there. They were all so fucked up. Eric was still using, so was Dave. In the end Perry got what he wanted.

ERIC AVERY: We actually broke up for a day. Perry said, "It's got to be this way or I'm walking," and we said, "Let's walk." But we compromised and obviously kept going. David made a T-shirt for our next show that had 12.5 percent spray-painted on it.

REBECCA AVERY: It's like Perry completely destroyed the team spirit forever that day, and I'm convinced they never really came back from that. . . .

ERIC AVERY: It had a profound effect that's for sure. It really upset Stephen. There was a fracture internally. From what I understand, David and Stephen have since been fine with that kind of behavior from Perry.

ANDREA BRAUER (copyright attorney, no legal or personal relationship to anyone connected with Jane's Addiction): If Perry wrote all the lyrics to a song and further contributed to one or more of the melody lines, according him the lion's share of songwriting would not be out of synch with industry custom. If, however, at the time the song was created, the prevailing attitude regarding songwriter splits was "all for one and one for all," then any attempt by Perry after the fact to adjust those splits would not be justifiable. One thing is certain: When a band parts company on less-than-friendly terms, everyone has their own version of events. It's extremely difficult to know for sure what's fair.

MARC GEIGER: As much as people are naive, potentially, about money, there's clearly a factor of money that always enters into these things.

STEVEN BAKER: It was a very emotional trauma, but they carried on.

CHARLEY BROWN: We got about halfway through *Nothing's Shocking* and then Perry got all possessed by money and I got kind of nauseated with the pseudo-rich thing and called him a money-grubbing egomaniac, not the best move. They wanted limousines to take them to a photo shoot. That's one of the things I got in a fight with Perry about. I was like, "Fuck, man, we're not a limo band! That's against everything I thought we were supposed to be standing for!" I come from the straight world of old-fashioned Midwestern values that you don't spend the money before you get it. First you have to tour like dogs and actually sell these fuckin' records, and lots of them, before you see any real money. That's what all of those fucking lame-assed bandanna Strip bands that we hated were all about. Perry was kind of faking it during that period . . . he really was that far south of what was happening. . . .

ERIC AND PERRY FALL OUT

MARC GEIGER: Perry and Eric just fell out.

ERIC AVERY: Things got really bad between me and Perry.

PERRY FARRELL: We had divisions. When Eric decided to become clean, I didn't decide to become clean . . . probably had a lot to do with it.

REBECCA AVERY: It was weird and getting weirder. Ever since the big showdown over the publishing, things were getting more uncomfortable with everybody in the band all the time. Somewhere around there Eric got sober.

PERRY FARRELL: One minute one guy was healthy and clean and suddenly that meant that nobody else could be unhealthy and unclean. But that's not the way life works.

ERIC AVERY: During the process of getting clean I started to say I'm not comfortable doing this thing or that thing and that created even more hard feelings.

PETE WEISS: People do drugs and someone in their circle doesn't do drugs. Even if the person who is not doing drugs will tolerate the people doing drugs, the people doing drugs only want people who are doing drugs around them. They shut out sober people.

JOHNNY NAVARRO: Junkies put up a wall around everyone else who isn't a junkie. If you don't run with them, you're excluded.

DAVE JERDEN: They were going through a really tough time personally. Dave was still having a rough time with the death of his mother.[67]

REBECCA AVERY: There was friction between everybody except Stephen. Stephen was the only one that was going, "What the hell is going on, guys? What happened? This is all going to hell in a handbasket, nobody's talking to anybody." Individually he was OK with Dave and Perry and Eric. They were all not talking to each other.

PERRY FARRELL: It's not like I can't say hello to Dave or Eric, but on a personal level, we're not friends. By that I mean I don't hang around with them on my days off. Maybe because I'm the oldest, I take on certain responsibilities. But I enjoy it; it's my forte. I *am* a control freak, but that's because I care.[68]

FLEA: They were having troubles with Eric, and Perry was talking to me about playing bass. This was before *Nothing's Shocking* came out. They definitely already had some sort of dissent in their camp at that point. I don't know what they were squabbling about.

ERIC AVERY: Our relationship deteriorated into an unspoken standoff; kind of like the Cold War, where both sides knew that all-out war would be devastating. It created this weird détente, this non-verbalized agreement not to escalate. So we never did. It's surprising with all the out-of-controlness that he and I never got physical with each other. We didn't even yell. In more roundabout, passive ways we'd say things to hurt each other's feelings.

CHARLEY BROWN: The guys always fought, they always broke up whenever we left town. They were at each other's throats. Perry and Stephen always got along, but Perry and Eric, and Perry and Dave were always at odds, sometimes at the same time, sometimes intermittently, sometimes each one would change sides with Perry and go against the other.

DAVE NAVARRO: We happened to have a very emotional lyricist and we're a very emotional group of guys creating music, so obviously it's going to come off that we don't all feel exactly the same way from day to day about each other and what we're doing. They were ugly times— some of them. I'm not going to deny that.

ERIC AVERY: Throw hard drugs and alcohol into a mix of enlarged egos and what do you get?

CASEY NICCOLI: Early on in the band, Eric got drunk one night and tried to pick up on me. We were both really wasted. When I told Perry what happened, he basically stopped liking him. Perry just never got past that. He hated Eric forever because of this stupid incident. I'd kissed him back, but I was just drunk. It was nothing. Just stupid puppy-love stuff.

PERRY FARRELL: But did she tell you he also went on to confess his undying love for her? That was uncalled for. I'm the kind of guy that doesn't try to steal girlfriends. C'mon, man, you *never* try to pick up on your dear bandmates' girlfriends—even in rock 'n' roll, man. I mean, *please.*

ERIC AVERY: It was just so silly and petty of me. That thing with Casey was just another indicator of me wanting to have a little part of his world or something. And his reaction was just so indicative of that same dynamic between us.

BOB FORREST: The two of them just don't have the right personalities to get along.

CHARLEY BROWN: It was all about jealousy, creative and personal jealousy. Dave was a pretty boy and was getting all the attention from the girls and from the guitar playing. Dave was not nearly as smart as Perry or Eric. Dave and Steve came out of this dumbed-down metal genre, which by definition we all hated, especially Perry. I mean, Perry was getting a lot of girls, too. They were all getting girls. It was more about attention. For Perry it's all ego. From hindsight, it's very clear that if it hadn't been that way, the band just wouldn't have worked.

ERIC AVERY: I admit I had a jealous feeling about how creative and interesting and everything Perry was. And I think that Perry had some similar feelings for me. There was kind of a mutual admiration, but also a jealousy of each other's powers and strengths. Rebellion is often brought about by a feeling of intimidation where you're going to have to assert yourself whether it be a cop, or an institution, or a personal relationship. There was an element of that with me and Perry.

STEVEN BAKER: Perry was an authority figure within the group and maybe that caused some issues amongst the other guys by virtue of his seniority. . . .

ERIC AVERY: I resented that he was getting all of the attention and all the power and so it would make me act like a prick. And me acting like a prick would then upset him and then he would retaliate. It was like a textbook deterioration of a relationship.

PERRY FARRELL: Maybe Eric felt he wasn't able to make enough decisions for the band.

ERIC AVERY: Perry was meeting with the label people and they were asking him for things, rather than me, or anybody else in the band. Geiger was also just dealing with Perry on business matters. I don't think any of us was interested in dealing with the business side because it was really Perry's gig at that point.

CASEY NICCOLI: Perry would openly, even on stage, put Eric down. He did it to be mean. He did it cause he thought he could. It was funnier than shit, because Perry is really funny. Maybe a lot of it, Eric didn't hear, because things were so loud onstage.

ERIC AVERY: I didn't take any personal affront to snide things Perry may have said [about me] from the stage. I thought it was part of that show, like the way you make fun of your cronies—your friends—and you fuck with them or whatever.

REBECCA AVERY: We were all like, "Perry, shut up and just play. We came to see this great band and hear the music, not hear you pontificate and be the prophet to all of us." One of those times Eric left the stage and he said, "You don't need me, I'm going over there, call me when you want some music."

ERIC AVERY: There was a lot of obvious eye-rolling onstage, little exchanges between me and Dave about what Perry was saying and there was just this kind of plainly exhibited rift going on.

PAUL V.: The chaos and interfighting, the tension and all the other dramas that were always going on in this band only added to the subversive allure for me because it was volatile and dangerous, while the music manifested this weird energy that always surrounded them. I think audiences during that era definitely picked up on that, it added edgy mystique. . . .

DAVE NAVARRO: Somehow the inner tension of the band translated to the audience and the listeners.[69]

ERIC AVERY: Some of our weirder fans really dug that about Jane's Addiction.

BRYAN RABIN: The guys in the band looked to Perry as a father figure because a band is a gang or family. It was really apparent to me they were onstage pleasing him. But it didn't feel like a one-man show either. None of it could have existed without all the parts of it together. They were playing with so many different types of imagery, so many different sounds, and really blurring lines in what they were presenting. Jane's also felt like performance art. Perry was the visionary, the driving force, creatively and . . . he physically towered over the rest of the band. He was this incredible modern-day shaman, that's for sure.

PF RUNS DOWN THE DIRTY VOODOO

PERRY FARRELL: We wanted groupies. It was a time when you could still get out there, screw your brains out, meet a girl a night, literally. It was great. And through that period of the AIDS epidemic, it started to become more and more of an issue and eventually not smart, not a good idea. But in my life, that was the time for it, and I don't know if there's any more time for it—I would say no, there's no more time for it.

REBECCA AVERY: Sometimes Perry's weird shit-faced raps were amusing, many times it was just plain embarrassing, like drunken barroom talk that didn't make any sense at all. Perry was getting worse and worse with his onstage rantings and ravings. He'd just be really fucked up on bottle after bottle of wine and he'd be talking and talking. We saw him gradually developing this messianic complex.

CHARLEY BROWN: One of the most unnerving times for me managing Jane's was in-between songs when Perry would talk. Sometimes he'd sound just like a fucking idiot. Sometimes it was hilarious. Perry can be very, very funny.

Li'l ole wine drinker, he . . . (Chris Cuffaro)

REBECCA AVERY: Perry was talking shit to the audience all the time. Telling whoever to fuck off. He would get drunk and start going on these crazy riffs. You'd just start going. "Oh, no. What's he gonna say this time?" "Pigs in Zen" was just a classic where he would just riff. You'd see Eric and Dave looking at each other and they'd try to start the song back up again.

CHARLEY BROWN: Once during this long, twisted, psychotic version of "Pigs in Zen," there was this overweight chick kitted out in some kind of Madonna hooker setup . . . way over made up, way underdressed, and Perry just started singing "Pigs in Zen" to her, and he was like "Come on, just show me some titties," and he goes into this taunting thing and just gets her in this whole S&M kind of insinuation thing.

PERRY FARRELL [to a club audience in '89]: She said to me, "Perry, come on. Can you make it hard?"

I get haaard . . . when I see my woman's titties. I got no problem gettin' hard with that woman's titty. She said, "Perry, watch this." I said, "No problem watching that." Not with that woman's titty. She said, "Perry, do I look alright?" Man, you look alright, with them titties, anything looks alright. I can't help myself when I see those titties. I JUST . . . WANNA . . . FU-U-CK!!

—THE STONE, San Francisco, 4.11.89

Oh, baby . . . I just wanna fuck! I know about pain and suffering and being cold, but I just wanna fu-u-ck!

—THE SCREAM, LOS ANGELES, 1.26.87

I know about PAIN! I still wanna fuck! I still wanna fuck! I still wanna fuck!

—THE COTTON CLUB, ATLANTA, GA, 2.8.89

You're all just so fucking horny. That's why . . . you wanna jump up and fuck . . . me! This is the part of the show where somebody comes up and sucks my cock. It ain't a tough one to tackle, but I'll tell ya, when the shit starts shootin', ya better look out, cause uh . . . uh, well, I dunno, I'll fuckin' piss somethin' or other . . . Fuck me or fight me. I'll wake up next morning with a big ol' dick and I'll say I WANNA FUUCK! Man, I like to make it long . . . last long . . . make my balls

hurt real bad. I WANNA FUCK! The pig is led to slaughter . . . the pig, the pig, the pig . . . the pig with your daughter. . . .
—PARAMOUNT THEATRE, SEATTLE, WA, 3.29.89

How many girls have clitorises that have been stimulated to orgasm?
—THE STONE, SAN FRANCISCO, 4.11.89

Fuck all the assholes! Fuck 'em up the ass. The ass is behind the penis. If you're female it's behind your vagina. There's a use for an asshole . . . it gets rid of all your shit. But the penis, it's a dick . . . it's big and it's thick. It's for cumming up a twat . . . but it doesn't hurt to occasionally fuck an asshole. You need an asshole, huh? I mean how would you take a shit without one.
—LA ULTIMA CARCAJADA DE LA CAMBANCHA,
MEXICO, DF, 6.90

What's up, sluts? I like your drinkin' and your attitude. . . .
—TEATRO TENDASTRISCE, ROME, ITALY, 4.1.91

I'll fuck three women and put 'em all up there! You don't believe me? Try me!
—MT. BALDY, CA, 7.7.90

Let's all hold groins on this song. . . .
—MT. BALDY, CA, 7.7.90

After a while you become numb . . . [to hard sex] . . . and so now we bring you a little bit of death.
—WAR MEMORIAL, ROCHESTER, NY, 5.91

God is in your scrotum!
—MADISON SQUARE GARDEN, NY, 5.1991

ARTWORK CONTROVERSIES

DAVE JERDEN: We finished the record and then the real trouble began. When we turned it in, someone at Warner Bros. was saying, "We're concerned about this record. It doesn't sound like anything else." It

Cover of *Nothing's Shocking.*

was the time of Guns N' Roses and the metal-lite thing. And this was before they'd even seen the cover![70]

PERRY FARRELL: I get a lot of things from my dreams, because in that state, you're either having a nice conversation with yourself and nobody can get in the way, or you're having a nice conversation with maybe a spirit guide. And a dream came to me—the Siamese twins with their hair on fire rocking on a swing.

DAVE JERDEN: Perry used the record company assets and then learned from them how to do it himself. For instance, he hired somebody to do the sculpture for the photograph on the cover of *Nothing's Shocking*. He just watched closely how the person worked and then fired the guy and did the sculpture himself.[71]

Perry casts Casey's head in plaster for
the *Nothing's Shocking* cover.
(Karyn Cantor)

PERRY FARRELL: I found a person who did body castings, 'cause I wanted a perfect replica. He put Casey into a full body and face cast. We spent the whole day, and she sat there, but she was completely stoned, so maybe it was a little easier for her, 'cause you know what happens when you nod off. It's a rocking chair, but if you look closely, it rocks side to side instead of back and forth. We had that made. We took the picture ourself, we did all the artwork ourself.

STEVEN BAKER: In 1988, nine of the eleven leading record chains refused to carry *Nothing's Shocking* because of its cover [which featured the Farrell–Niccoli painting of two naked, conjoined nymphettes].

PERRY FARRELL: Well, obviously nudity doesn't fly well at Wal-Mart.

STEPHEN PERKINS: We had to issue the record covered with brown paper.

PERRY FARRELL: Record companies wouldn't even mess with people like us anymore. You don't really see bands that go that far too often. I wouldn't mess with people like that, if I was trying to make a living. If I wanted to have a group of people that I wanted to work with, I sure wouldn't have chosen us.

PAUL V.: Perry didn't give a fuck if his record wasn't sold in Wal-Mart. Who wants to sell a record in Wal-Mart? The record company does. Yeah, great, everyone will make back their investment and maybe the band will make more money, but at the end of the day who gives a shit if a Jane's Addiction record can be sold next to the gun rack?

SOUL KISS

Circa August 1988

MODI FRANK (filmmaker, videographer): By then Casey and Perry lived in a storefront off of Santa Monica Boulevard by Vermont. Chickens were squawking inside the house while Casey was gluing paper flowers together. She was so high that I gave her a bowl full of crepe paper and scissors and said, "Here, cut these up into flowers. . . ." Five minutes later, I'd turn around and she was in the same scissor and hand position. The scissors had gotten no closer to the paper.

PETE WEISS: The big lesson for the music industry of Jane's Addiction was that it all happened off the radar. It happened despite the worst intentions of the industry. The *Soul Kiss* video completely circumvented MTV.

STEVEN BAKER: The genesis of *Soul Kiss* was we financed a video of "Mountain Song." It had Casey's bare breasts displayed in it and MTV wouldn't play it. Probably for a couple different reasons: One, they didn't give a shit about the band to begin with. Second, the video had some censor issues.

TOM ATENCIO (rock manager, one in a series of Jane's Addiction managers): The band and Perry always hated MTV. He would always stick something in there so that it couldn't be aired.

STEVEN BAKER: Perry said, "I want to release it as a single on video." He was like, "OK, so MTV won't play my video? Fuck it, we'll sell it to break even. Let the kids who like us see what we're doing." Then he added twenty-plus minutes of band footage. It's commonplace on DVDs now . . . live performance plus backstage footage. What Metallica was doing at that time. Just price it super cheap. But it was a first at Warner Bros.

CASEY NICCOLI: *Soul Kiss* was my first film project. I made the first Jane's Addiction video, which had some nudity on "Mountain Song." It had Perry and I laying on a bed together. And Perry didn't want to take the nudity out, it was only like five seconds of it, so in order to release that video, we did like a twenty-eight-minute short documentary and we featured "Mountain Song" in it.

MODI FRANK: The so-called naked breasts in "Mountain Song" are from the dummy! The label guys freaked out. They were like, we can't have naked girls' breasts. I'm like, but it's not a girl, it's a fucking *statue*. "Mountain Song" was considered ground breaking because the videos on MTV at the time were Scorpions, Iron Maiden, and Def Leppard . . . big-time heavy metal . . . huge productions, in front of massive crowds. . . .

DAYLE GLORIA: They shot "Mountain Song" at The Probe with a chorus line of dancers on stage wearing diapers . . . throwing peanut butter and jelly sandwiches at the crowd. It was crazy slapstick fun. . . .

MODI FRANK: The label people thought Perry was totally insane, so they hired a director behind his back to do another version of "Mountain Song" while me and Perry were doing our version. The label hired KK Barrett, who never even met with Perry . . . [who] had no idea that KK was doing this.

KK BARRETT (musician, art director, production designer, videographer): I was asked to work on a version of a video for "Mountain Song," which Andrew Ducette was directing for Warners. I only found out later it was without the blessing of the band. Andrew told me the band wasn't happy about their non-involvement and proceeded to stage their own version. I think Modi got me to shoot additional camera because I had been shooting a lot of Super 8 and had a few cameras. I got to work on both versions. . . .

Perry shreds the Probe club with the satanic Diaper Guy. (John Eder)

MODI FRANK: Perry wanted to do this poetry reading at the Probe [a former all-male club in Hollywood] with Casey lying dead on the table and he was going to read all this poetry to his dead girlfriend. Perry wanted girls and guys in diapers! He wanted waitresses to come out with trays of Tampaxes. On the Tampax in blood it would be written "God Is Dead." The girls would throw the Tampaxes into the audience.

DANUSHA KIBBY: Perry or Casey had this idea that we would make peanut butter and jelly sandwiches and that me and Karyn would dress up in 50s waitress outfits and toss them into the audience to provoke something. They spent the whole day writing "God Is Dead," or some other weird saying in red ink on little pieces of paper, then rolled 'em up and put strings on them so they looked like tampons and we put them in the middle of these peanut butter and jelly sandwiches. They were going, imagine how great it's going to be, imagine their reactions, but the audience didn't get the idea, the stunt backfired. It was totally anticlimactic. It just got so late and people were really tired. We started tossing the sandwiches and all the kids were just eating them! Yummy! They were supposed to throw them back, it was supposed to become this confrontational big shock-value thing, like a crazy foodfight, but nobody threw a sandwich back. It was more like, Oh wow, I got one, and everybody's just like starving because it's like two in the morning.

MODI FRANK: Perry also wanted two topless chicks in the balcony painted in Fellini makeup, all white with black nipples. Perry told me it was all about performance art. Angelo was going to do some poetry, and then Perry was going to do some poetry. The band was only going to play a couple of songs and then the waitresses and the diaper men were to come out. Casey said, "We want to shoot Perry making out with the band." Everybody was willing to make out with Perry, no problem. Stephen and Dave were, but if you look closely you can see Eric cringing.

PERRY FARRELL: We figured it [Soul Kiss] would definitely trip people out. Just to mess with people. And because the shots were quick, it would cause your eye and your interest to go in—was that [really] them kissing each other?

ERICA PAIGE: Everybody was making out with everybody on the set. I thought it was extremely funny. It was totally intended to cross the line. Casey has a real dark sense of humor. She's hysterical.

REBECCA AVERY: That was very, very weird where they're all kissing. It's me and Stephen kissing and Dave and his girlfriend kissing and then they all start kissing each other. My brother and my boyfriend kissing each other on camera, how weird was that?

BRYAN RABIN: Take the sexuality out of it, gay or straight. I think that it was about expressing themselves and blurring out those lines. I don't think he did those specific acts just for shock. Yes, it was provocative and yes, they knew that they would freak some people out. Yes, he knew they were theatrical acts, but I don't think that he thinks in such black-and-white terms. I think Perry lives in a completely different place and I think he really does believe what he speaks.

REBECCA AVERY: But it's rock 'n' roll, whatever, I guess. Eric giving his book report from the toilet. There again he's fucked up. Just watching that and seeing him scratching himself was too weird. Dave and his eel. It was a fake eel. He had put it in the tank specifically for twisted comic effect.

MODI FRANK: There were no dressing rooms at the Probe, nothing with a mirror in it. I had to stick this fancy makeup guy in a broom closet with these two dopehead chicks selected by Perry and Casey. I'm downstairs prepping and he [makeup guy] comes running out of the broom closet shaking and crying and screaming at me in front of everybody that he's never going to work for me again. I said what's wrong? He said, "Those two chicks have track marks on their arms and it touched my sponge." Then Perry goes, "I want me and Casey in a bed of roses naked like we're dead." OK. We finally get the flower bed ready and Casey and him get naked. Perry kept saying, "What do you think? Do I have a big dick? Can you see it at that angle? Do I have a big cock?" I'm shooting in Super 8 with no sound and I go, "Yes, you have a big dick, quiet, you're supposed to be dead!"

BOB MOSS: There were a lot of regular rocker/stoner people there, no Hollywood art punks or Melrose fashion freaks in sight. They were stoner kids really into the fact that Jane's kinda vaguely sounded like Zeppelin, dude. They assumed it was going to be a full-on Jane's Addiction concert because that's how Perry billed it on the flyer. Maybe chaos was the point because chaos was what he got. It was a crazy night.

The "Mountain Song" video shoot at the Probe, host club to the promoters of Scream and Cathouse at different times. (John Eder)

MODI FRANK: Perry didn't bill it as a poetry night. He billed it as Jane's Addiction. People expected the band. I almost punched a guy out in the front row because he was yelling right into Angelo's face to get off. Perry comes out and says, look this is Angelo Moore, he's one of the greatest L.A. band guys ever, give him a little respect.

BOB MOSS: Glen Meadmore was one of the performers besides myself. Angelo Moore, a few other people were hired. The "Diaper Guy" was my given character! One of the girls from the scene was the "Diaper Chick"—we were both the "Diaper People." It was sillyassed fun until this crowd of front pit gnarlers turned awful bellig'. "Who the fuck is this fag in the diaper? Where's Jane's Addiction?" Shit, man . . . there was nowhere to go. There's no dressing rooms at the Probe, nothin'! I couldn't go to the men's room. People in that audience would have dealt with me and my "faggot ass" real fast. I had to use the women's room to clean my makeup off!

MODI FRANK: So now Perry goes onstage to do his stint. The shout-out is coming from the audience: "Shut up and sing!" Perry gets pissed off and was heckling them right back, "You don't know what art is. This is art. We worked really hard to put this together. You don't appreciate anything."

BOB MOSS: Perry got pressured to bring the band out. Finally they cut the show short. They ran out and I had to run out with them and dance with my partner and they scrapped the rest of the show. They didn't even do a full set, but I guess they got a good take of "Mountain Song," right? Otherwise, the whole night was an abortion.

MODI FRANK: Finally he threw his hands up and said: "Fuck it, let's play." And so Jane's ended up playing a whole set that was just stunning. The dancers came out and threw the tampons. The night finally exploded into a full-blown Jane's Addiction set. The audience went nuts. They finally got what they wanted.

❦

Circa September 1988

PERRY FARRELL: We went to Dayle Gloria's place for a barbecue and there's Iggy Pop on the floor listening to our record—"Pigs in Zen."

There's one of my idols, listening to our music. I got too nervous, so I just left. Didn't know what to say, didn't know what to do. Dayle followed me with Iggy and said, "Where are you going? I want you to meet Iggy." He said, "Man, I think you guys are hot stuff, I want you to come on tour with me."

REBECCA AVERY: That was such a big deal at the time, "Oh, Iggy Pop thinks Jane's is cool." They were all so excited about that.

JANE BAINTER: Perry talked about Iggy a lot . . . until he got a tour with Iggy and it overshadowed the whole previous thing because the experience was different than the inspiration.

DAYLE GLORIA: I flew to New York and met them there when they opened up for Iggy. It was great. And then I went back on a train with David and immediately bought dope and did heroin for the first time on a rooftop in Greenwich Village with Eric and David. I threw up all the way through the Village.

Circa Spring 1989

STEVEN BAKER: The head of the promotions department at Warners saw Jane's Addiction for the first time at the last show at the Anson Ford Theater [in April, 1989]!

PAUL V.: I'm like doing cartwheels off the halls of Warner Bros., like, "Please pay attention to this band! They're the next *Led Zeppelin*." I was so desperate I was reduced to speaking in their terms of lame hype lingo because there were a lot of old-timers who thought like ZZ Top was alternative. Nobody ever got fired from Warner Bros. in those days. You'd have to run over the CEO's kid before they'd even consider it. Part of the problem was that there were too many lifers there. Lots of clueless dead weight coasting along pulling down these huge salaries.

STEVEN BAKER: I remember playing the first album for our radio guys. I purposely only picked the harder rocking stuff like "Mountain Song" . . . things that I thought would have appealed to the rock promotion department.

PAUL V.: These guys came from Top 40, where if you want a record on the radio you're going to grease some palms. That doesn't necessarily mean cash is exchanged, but flyaway trips, free dinners, all this stuff you have to do. I don't so much have a problem with the process. Fine, that's how it works, but it was just the arrogance and there's no allegiance to the band. Here we are with *Nothing's Shocking* and one of the all-time greatest songs ever written and recorded, "Jane Says." I'm sitting there going, "My god, this should be a massive, massive hit. How can you not feel and hear this song?" The company eventually did the single but it never saw the light of day outside of KROQ. There was no video for it.

STEVEN BAKER: Roberta Petersen and I were in Ted Templeman's office, because Teddy had these huge speakers. It was also the right setting symbolically for these guys because Van Halen, the Doobie Brothers, the artists that were important to these people and our company were overseen from there by him. We played about four, five tracks. The last note was dying away and Roberta and I are like, "Isn't this just great?" but all these guys could say was, "Oh, thanks, we have to go to a Van Halen rehearsal" and they just walked out. Not like, "That's great, that could be a single, we're going to get behind this." Not even a single word of encouragement.

PAUL V.: Even if a radio station loved the band and played them and then the band came to town one or the other stations who started to play them also wanted tickets. The bigger station would shut out the smaller station and then the smaller station would stop playing the band because the record company didn't step in and slap the hand of the big station. Who loses? The artist and the fans. This was driving me crazy, and I really didn't want to do it. I loved the music but hated the process of getting it played. Basically, you have to kiss ass. You have to talk to a lot of these radio guys. They want everything, and they'll give nothing. This was still when the format was in its infancy. It's a thousand times worse now.

STEVEN BAKER: We just sat there going, "We're fucked." It was incredibly disappointing, and it also showed you kind of where it was at. We thought, "We're not playing you guys this quirky new wave thing that new stations could never play, we're playing you a hard rock record with a unique point of view." The part of the company that could have been supportive was just not there for them. And that may have accounted for some of the lack of sales for the first album.

PAUL V.: They put out "Mountain Song" and "Had a Dad" like the official singles from the album. It got played on alternative and college, but even on college radio, the other side of the coin, there was some resistance because the band to them sounded too rock 'n' roll, too metal. Either way, it was an uphill struggle during *Nothing's Shocking* to say, like, "Don't listen to it with those ears, listen to the whole palette of sounds." And the lyrics, just listen to the lyrics.

PERRY FARRELL: The success of R.E.M. really helped what they now call "modern rock."

CHARLEY BROWN: Suddenly, organized college radio became a new marketing outlet for major labels after R.E.M. broke. Somebody started calling Jane's "alternative" and then, fuck it, it became a whole genre. After Jane's all the labels had to do to qualify for college airplay was call it "alternative.". . .

NOTHING'S SHOCKING: THE CRITICAL REACTION

BRIAN WARNER (aka Marilyn Manson, rock singer-showman): My first article in my college (Broward Community College) newspaper, the *Observer,* was a review of that [Jane's Addiction] show [at Woody's on the Beach], headlined "Jane's Addiction Returns to Shock Crowd at Woody's." Little did I know that there was a word in that headline that would go on to be used several thousand times to describe my music, and it wasn't "woody."[72]

DAVE JERDEN: When the record [*Nothing's Shocking*] came out, the mainstream rock press just trashed it. *Rolling Stone* said, "this record is unlistenable."[73]

TRENT REZNOR (leader, composer, producer, Nine Inch Nails): I really liked *Nothing's Shocking*. I sampled a little of "Had a Dad" . . . the scream and the drum fill. And there's also a guitar loop of that pattern going through the song.[74]

FLEA: I remember the first time I heard *Nothing's Shocking*. Perry had just finished up recording and we were on our way to a friend's house to watch the big Tyson–Spinks fight. On the way there Perry was like, "Oh, this is my new record, listen to it." And then I realized what a great, great band they were. It was just a big, weird day. I heard Jane's music for the first time, Tyson knocked Spinks out in the first round, and then I came home and got the call that Hillel [Slovak] was dead.

DAVE JERDEN: I went into a record store and asked this guy with glasses and a ponytail behind the counter if he had *Nothing's Shocking*. And he looked at me and said, "Are you kiddin? I wouldn't carry that piece of crap in this store." I knew then we were either going to make a big belly-flop or we were really gonna do something.[75]

STEVEN BAKER: There were some limitations on the first Jane's album. We didn't have a video on MTV and it was not exactly what KROQ was playing at the time. There weren't that many [alternative] stations across the United States. They didn't mean as much. They didn't have as good of numbers as they do now. *Nothing's Shocking* did about 200–250,000 the first year.

DAVE JERDEN: *Nothing's Shocking* was not a mainstream record, although eventually it found an audience all right [more than a million copies sold]. There's not one person I talk to today who's in their early thirties who didn't listen to that record in college. *Nevermind* was a fucking classic record, and the press has marked that as the beginning of this big change in alternative becoming mainstream. But it wasn't. *Nothing's Shocking* was. It didn't have the same sales, but it made the same cultural mark and it made it first.[76]

FLEA: [Jane's music] is just massive and epic and deep and original with a bottomless groove and it's ferociously violent, yet beautiful and relaxing, and the lyrics are great. Perry's singing is great. The whole band is incredible. It's just a moment in time that could never happen again.

CHRIS CUFFARO (photographer): Jane's were [probably] the first band to ever have a full-on mosh pit at Madison Square Garden [since the Violent Femmes circa '82, '83 who had kids stage-diving into the pit]. They were so nervous about the pit getting out of hand. There were all these little mosh pits all over the place. Kids going nuts.

TED GARDNER: Jane's Addiction was pre-barricade. Pre-security in front of the stage. So Cal-style punk stage diving and death metal mosh pit action were merging, like a new extreme sport for jocks coming into its own in a big way nationally. There was an interaction musically and physically between band and audience. We never had bodyguards. Just me and my guitar roadie.[77]

PERRY FARRELL [onstage at The Cotton Club, Atlanta, GA, 2.8.89]: Ya know, that, uh, bullshit about being thrown out of here for stage-diving is just merely bullshit. My bouncers won't fuck with you if you don't fuck with us, that's the way it goes.

TED GARDNER: The kids that came to see Jane's Addiction knew that if you got on stage you could dance, you could dive, you could do whatever, but you could never touch the musicians. And everyone respected that and that enabled the band to do what they were doing, which was to perform.[78]

AXL ROSE WANTING DAVE BAD

Circa April 1989

JOSH RICHMAN: Axl Rose became obsessed with Jane's Addiction and wanting to get Dave in his band. Axl always wanted Navarro in the band. And never ended up getting him.

JOHNNY NAVARRO: Dave and I really liked Guns N' Roses. We thought they were really great. We loved the way Slash played. He was the only guitar player in town as good as Dave. No one knew about Frusciante yet. Axl was also a really big Jane's fan.

PERRY FARRELL: I hung out with Axl one night, he came to our show when we did the seven-night stand at John Anson Ford Theater.

DAVE NAVARRO: Axl called me up and said, "Dude, I had a dream, you and me were rocking on stage together."[79]

JOHNNY NAVARRO: Axl was shy, quiet, and polite. He'd come backstage and say hi to Dave. He seemed to like him as a person, as much as he said he liked his guitar playing. We used to call Axl like "The Stalker."

He was calling Dave just about every single day and leaving messages on his machine. He would play a few of them for me.

DAVE NAVARRO: I wanted to take the job but I was afraid of looking foolish and being judged a sellout.[80]

DAN NAVARRO: Dave's comment was, "I don't want to go on the road and be Guns N' Roses guitar player and play someone else's parts and someone else's songs. But if they want to make a record, that's another thing."

JOHNNY NAVARRO: Axl wanted Dave to take Izzy's place. Dave, unfortunately, was strung out at the time and didn't have a whole hell of a lot going on. He was like, "Dude, should I do it?" I said, "Go for it! It's fucking Guns N' Roses, who gives a shit?" Finally, he said, "OK, I'll do it." They announced it on MTV, showed Dave's picture and everything, but when the time came to start the tour, Dave just did a no show, he just bowed out. He was concerned about going on the road strung out with Guns N' Roses, not knowing where to score. Dave just didn't want to be the guy always going to his road manager, "Dude, get me some dope . . . now!"

SEVEN NIGHTS IN APRIL

LEON BING (journalist, writing in L.A. Weekly): There were bare midriffs and leopard prints; there were fishnet, fringe, rubber, leather, 'jams, stiletto heels, and bright red winklepickers; there were pink bustiers and jackboots and peaked military hats cocked to one side in a 1989 update of 1939 Berlin. (June 16, 1989)

DAN NAVARRO: The Anson Ford shows were family affairs all right. Dave's dad would be there, Eric's family, Steve's parents, too. . . .

KARYN CANTOR: Perry wanted every show to be a special event.

MARC GEIGER: Whether it started small and they did an acoustic set with balloons and a couple of dancers in the earliest days at the Variety Arts Center and Scream, Perry always had a flair for the theatrical. As

Jane's got bigger and bigger, he had more and more thoughts about how to not be conventional in a rock-show format.

BRYAN RABIN: Even though it was so theatrical and so arty, you still related to them. They were art tarts *and* rock gods combined, but somehow they were still normal guys. It wasn't like seeing Poison or Great White, or Ratt or the other bozo hair bands.

KARYN CANTOR: Danusha [Kibby] and I were, like, the initial dancers before the strippers came into Jane's Addiction's set. We created costumes. One time we made these outfits out of colored cellophane. We'd strut onstage in these elaborate outfits with big hair bows carrying these huge silver trays. When they played at the John Anson Ford Theater for seven nights in a row Danusha and I were the tortilla tossers. We came out in these sexy Spanish señorita outfits we had made carrying these huge trays and then threw tortillas at the audience . . . that was so fun.

THE BEST OF THE WEST

Circa July 1989

DAN NAVARRO: The creative antecedents for Jane's were people like Fishbone, Thelonious Monster, Chili Peppers. The Chili Peppers were already the grandfathers of the scene because they'd been around since like '83. They already got their record deals, the socks on their dicks, lots of touring, the Full Monty.

ERIC AVERY: The Peppers, Fishbone and Thelonious Monster, L7, there was always such a scene around them. They were more popular than us because they moved in such circles that was related to everybody who worked at the *L.A. Weekly*. They were just so much hipper than we were, more social and sociable than us.

FLEA: Dave told me they used to take the piss out of us at Jane's rehearsals. They did this thing were they'd go like "Chili Peppers!" and Eric would start slapping his bass, and Steve would play a funk beat, and Perry would run around in circles around the microphone.

Red Hot Chili Peppers as fresh-from-high-school kids who worked their way up through the local underground. Around the time (if not the actual night) of the socks-on-dicks episode. (Lynda Burdick)

ERIC AVERY: Fishbone were always the band with real musicians. We were all friends, but they were certainly intimidating as musicians.

JOHNNY NAVARRO: All those guys loved Fishbone, they respected them as the most accomplished musicians out of all that group. Perry and Flea and Bob Forrest and even Anthony would all be going, "We're fucking great, but look at Fishbone." There was this amazing level of musicianship, poetry, and performance art that Angelo Moore brought. That whole band had an amazing amount of skills.

FLEA: The Chili Peppers and Jane's Addiction ended up playing this unforgettable show together—a Fathers' Rights benefit for [Fishbone bassist] Norwood, who was having a hard time getting his kid from his ex.

DANUSHA KIBBY: She took off with the baby and he had to find her. She was worried they were going to take the baby away from her. She just up and left and Norwood had no idea where she was. He was trying to hire some private detectives.

WALT KIBBY, JR.: She was trying to cut him out of his rights to see his son but she still wanted him to pay. We decided to have a Fathers' Rights benefit. Norwood wanted custody or at least shared custody. He got together a lot of bands: Jane's was one of them, Chili Peppers, too. . . .

JOHN FRUSCIANTE: There was an argument on who was going to headline. Should it be the Chili Peppers or Jane's Addiction? *Mother's Milk* hadn't come out yet, I think it was like coming any day now, but their album *[Nothing's Shocking]* was already out and doing really well. That was the main reason they won that argument. They deserved to headline but we were real egocentric and headstrong. Once I saw that show I realized we weren't shit. We would have made total idiots out of ourselves if we had headlined. Those guys were like kings on stage. This was the first time I'd ever seen them live and they scared the crap out of me. . . .

FLEA: I remember thinking, just from the energy in the room, like "God they're a much more together rock band than I thought." There was just a vibe in the room. And I thought, "Oh shit, we better rock tonight; they're serious." And when they came out, sure enough, the crowd went crazy.

JOHN FRUSCIANTE: Musically, it was like really dark, tense . . . up to that point music for me was just like something that was fun, like with my band, which was about being crazy and jumping around, but Jane's was at this whole other level. I was scared shitless by how intense they were, how good it was. I'll never forget Perry looking into the audience. It looked like there were lights shooting out of his eyes. He looked at me at the side of the stage with this really scary look and then he looks at the audience and, like, this light comes from his eyes. Wherever he would look there would be this huge burst of energy.

JOHNNY NAVARRO: We're talking about Thelonious Monster and Fishbone and Jane's Addiction and Red Hot Chili Peppers all playing the same night in Hollywood at small clubs, That's a fuckin' rich heritage that we all got to experience. We just don't have that anymore.

ERIC AVERY: The entire bill was filled with our peers and our closest friends and stuff. There was definitely a focus of energy that evening because of that.

JOHN FRUSCIANTE: Jane's Addiction was so far beyond anything I thought a rock band could be. It was so scary it just seemed like they were a bunch of murderers on stage! I just didn't think rock music could be that powerful. There was this darkness and this magical glow that had nothing to do with the music; this whole other energy that had nothing to do with human beings on stage playing music. I can only imagine that would be the same kind of energy that would be around Jesus Christ.

WALT KIBBY, JR.: Remember John was kind of young then, too, he was still a teenager . . . he hadn't really grown his fighting teeth yet. He might have been a little fearsome. Hillel [Slovak] was still the man to most people and Jane's Addiction was in peak shape, at the top of their game. It was a hell of a night. I wish I had a video of that show. That was a serious night of great music.

JOHN FRUSCIANTE: I remember going home after that show and just being so freaked out . . . that somebody had opened up the door to this world of darkness and madness that I didn't even know existed. It took a while for me to change enough to feel like I could be a part of the energy of something like that. They became my favorite band and I saw them every chance I got. Without Perry Farrell's influence, without the inspiration I got from him I would have never been able to do all the shit I had to do to get where I am now in my life where I'm pretty much set with everything.

WALT KIBBY, JR.: That night seemed like the beginning of the explosion of those bands, where they just took off and there was no coming back to the club scene per se.

"JUANA'S ADDICIONE" (1989–90)
The Making of *Ritual de lo Habitual*

PERRY FARRELL (from the Ritual de lo Habitual booklet): Blessed is "Ritual de lo Habitual," a love story between three people.

CINDY LAIR: "Señores y Señoras . . . nosotros tenemos mas influencia con sus hijos que tu tiene. Pero los queremos. Creado y regalo de Los Angeles, Juana's Addicion."

["Ladies and gentlemen, we have more influence over your children than you do. But we love them. Born and raised in Los Angeles, Jane's Addiction."]

PERRY FARRELL: Cindy Lair was a Latin Marilyn Monroe. I met her in rehab. She was a video queen for one of these one hit wonder rap cats of the 80s. She wore a pair of short hot pants that said "Stop" on her rear end. I thought, Holy Mother, this girl is just gorgeous. You can see her at the beginning of *Gift*. I wrote out the spoken introduction for her, but I didn't know how to speak Spanish fluently. We liked the piece so much, for *Gift*, that we put it on the record.

DAVE JERDEN: It's a ballsy way to open an album. It's like, "We have your kids."[81]

PERRY FARRELL: We were having a lot of sex. I would run away to hang out with my partner—a partner or two and have some fun. The *Ritual* album was a reflection of that. I like to build things on the run. It's a certain time of your life, and you're in a certain state of mind, and if you can grab the things around you and place them together, they start to tell a story. That was the story of my life right there.

JOHN FRUSCIANTE: When we were writing *Blood Sugar Sex Magick* I'd hear all these things about the goings-on with Jane's Addiction . . . a girl would come over to my house and tell me she'd had an orgy with Perry and Casey. . . .

PETE WEISS: You don't write songs about three-ways and stuff expecting to be mainstream.

"THREE DAYS"

"I'm either going to be a famous artist or a famous waitress."

—XIOLA BLUE (FROM *BEN IS DEAD* MAGAZINE)

CASEY NICCOLI: Perry wrote a song called "Xiola" for the Psi Com album. She was his girlfriend before we met. She was maybe thirteen or fourteen when Perry met her. She was this really colorful, crazy, risk-taking, artsy girl who was a lot of fun to be around. She was a good artist, a painter. She was like a rich girl from Malibu or Newport Beach, or something.

PERRY FARRELL: The word for Xiola is "precocious." When I first met her she was wearing a chartreuse and yellow dress and her hair was green—in dreadlocks. And I think she was wearing yellow lipstick, yellow tights, and she had very light freckles and a very pale face. She was the kind of girl who looked like a 1920s cigarette ad, except in vivid ultra color.

CASEY NICCOLI: Perry told me all about her. He said, "She's a friend, I went out with her, but she's too young for me. I'm in love with you, but I really want you to meet her. She's fun, she's really cool. She's coming to town.' So I met her and we became friends, although she ended up moving to New York to go to art school so we didn't see her a lot.

JENNIFER BRANNON (friend of Xiola Blue): Xiola was so young when she dated Perry. They fed off each other's energy and creativity. They even looked alike. They moved and danced in the same ways. Xiola loved him so much. She was ecstatic after he told her he had written a song about her.[82]

JANE BAINTER: Xiola Blue was another huge influence on Perry. More like an inspiration than an influence. She came out from the East Coast to visit Casey and Perry, and they had a long weekend together of sex and drugs, which the song "Three Days" is all about.

CASEY NICCOLI: Xiola was another person that we did drugs with occasionally. It was only playing around [for us]. It wasn't a daily thing. She had a little friend with her, whose drug habit she also supported. They were both just tore up. Emaciated. Her friend was just open sores all over her body. They were speedballing, like shooting coke and heroin and stuff. I really loved her so much. I really cared about her a lot, but I didn't love her more than Perry. I used to send her packages and presents. I'd send her a box full of blue things . . . blue lingerie, blue candy, and blue whatever I could find . . . because she was named Xiola Blue. . . .

PERRY FARRELL: When she died [June 1987], it was just kind of a jolt. An electric jolt.

Ritual de lo Habitual album cover.

CASEY NICCOLI: We all had a physical relationship, me, Perry, and Xiola. She spent three days with us, hence the song "Three Days." We just got high and danced with each other and made love and listened to beautiful music. We had a room we called "the love garden." It was decorated with plants and tapestries and candles. It was really romantic. There were like three small rooms, and the bedroom part was actually a patio. When it rained, you got wet. When you slept on the bed you got wet because it wasn't really insulated. . . .

JANE BAINTER: Perry was devastated. It was like the first wake-up call—"Oh maybe all this fun with drugs just isn't all it's cracked up to be."

CASEY NICCOLI: Xiola was a really neat, really smart girl. She was like a tragic Edie Sedgwick character. So colorful and creative, but she's also a hardcore heroin addict. She was a trust-fund baby and had tons of money which she would just *spend*. Her father had died and left her a bundle. Friends found her overdosed in her apartment in New York. She was like, only nineteen years. Xiola's real name was Lisa Chester and her family is so opposed to anything about Jane's Addiction. Her mom especially felt betrayed by Perry because he made her famous for being a drug addict.

JENNIFER BRANNON: Xiola died of a heroin overdose and Perry immortalized her on *Ritual de lo Habitual* via sculpture, song, and photos. I hate Perry Farrell for making my friend famous for nothing else but being a junkie. That makes me so crazy, to see this incredible girl reduced to nothing but her demise. Someone in Perry's position could have made her famous for all the things she wanted to be famous for. He could have taken her art and turned it into the most beautiful eulogy ever. He could've made all of her dreams come true. I feel like I have to defend her honor, but at the same time I'm not really sure if she'd want me to.

PERRY FARRELL: We were experimenting with different lovers and having a good time. Xiola was one of our lovers. The image on the *Ritual* cover is of Xiola. I love both of those girls. To love two women at the same time is a pretty amazing moment in any personal history.

JENNIFER BRANNON: Life was a big dance party to Xiola and the littlest thing could be fun—when she was clean. When she was clean she was a princess. Her makeup was impeccable. She'd take two hours to get ready to go anywhere and wouldn't go until you told her she looked beautiful. When she wasn't clean she'd stay locked in the bathroom with her makeup running down her face as she tried to make herself feel beautiful in other ways.

CASEY NICCOLI: Perry talked up the *Ritual* album cover [in interviews] where he's in bed with two lovers at the same time, and one of them is her daughter, who's dead. It really made [her mom] angry. We did the sculpture for the *Ritual de lo Habitual* cover in honor of Xiola. It's Perry, me, and Xiola, like we're these abstract bodies lying on a bed.

JENNIFER BRANNON: I can't decide if I hold Perry responsible for my dear friend's death in some warped way or if I should be kissing his feet for doing for her in death what she didn't have the time to do in life.[83]

EARLY RITUAL SESSIONS

Circa mid-1989

DAVE JERDEN: We were supposed to start recording the *Ritual* record in June or July, but because of his rift with Eric, Perry just didn't show up for weeks. We started recording without him.[84]

ERIC AVERY: Casey tried to bridge the increasing gap between me and Perry—like some kind of emissary.

DAVE JERDEN: Eventually Eric and Perry talked and decided they would just come in at different times to do their stuff.

STEVEN BAKER: They played as a band on the first record. With the second record, it was more like they were laying down their parts separately.

DAVE JERDEN: But there was one magical day when I got them all together and we cut "Three Days." I set the whole band up, they played it, and that version is what's on the record, note for note.[85]

PERRY FARRELL: We came up with the title when we were doing seven nights at the Anson Ford Theatre. Casey and I came up with "Ritual of the Habitual" for that particular event. I thought it was funny.

STEPHEN PERKINS: We started a few songs for *Ritual* with Dave Jerden producing again, and then decided we needed to get away from each other, and then took like a two- to three-month break.

DAVE NAVARRO: I found out recently that we were in such poor condition that we had to stop and take a break for several months.

PERRY FARRELL: Was it from drugs? Did anybody mention that it might be from drugs? Was it me that time-out had to be taken for? Or was it somebody else? Casey was really sick and had to be taken to rehab and she wouldn't go unless I went with her. I didn't want to go into rehab, but Casey was going to drop dead within a week. She just didn't want to be alone. I hate rehabs. I never want to be in another one. Maybe that's where this break comes from.

JOHNNY NAVARRO: They took a break. Everyone was fucked up. There were times that Dave didn't even remember what he did. I would come to the studio where he was supposed to be recording his leads and bring dope.

STEPHEN PERKINS: We'd try to pull [it] together and Dave would call and say, "Oh, I can't make it." Perry would show up two hours late. Because of drugs. They were just more into getting high than working.[86]

DAVE NAVARRO: I have absolutely no recollection. I couldn't even tell you who was in bad shape, but I'm certain I was one of the culprits.

PERRY FARRELL: Me, too.

TOM ATENCIO: Dave was in and out of rehab during the recording of *Ritual*. Nobody was visiting him. Nobody talked to him when he was in rehab. I was the only person who went to see him. They were totally dismissive.

DAVE NAVARRO: My memory of recording *Ritual* lasts about five minutes. In my head, we spent five minutes in the studio.

JOHNNY NAVARRO: There were nights where Dave threw up all the time. I used to go to work on heroin, so did Dave. As soon as you mainline you'll never go back. Now this was fun because I'm a mainline junkie and Dave's a mainline junkie and we're just fucking junkies. When *Ritual* was made, Dave and I were full-blown mainline heroin addicts shooting dope every single day. Dave was also going to the methadone clinic. He was trying to maintain his intense level of usage, but it was all about do you have any? Yes. We started hanging out with this guy in a trailer park in Northridge, the dude was a sick hardcore junkie. We're not talking about like weekend chippers, not people you meet after a show, not people that you'd go to their nice house in the Hollywood Hills to do a little dope. We're talking about mainlining like every single morning 7 A.M., first thing you do when you wake up is get your fix, shoot it up and then figure out your day after that.

PERRY FARRELL: Much has just been erased from my memory because I was loaded all the time . . . those days I don't remember that well.

ERIC AVERY: At the time I was clean and so I was kind of like what the fuck is this? What am I doing here? At the time we were doing *Ritual* I was taking astronomy courses at Santa Monica College.

BAD MANAGEMENT WOES

Circa January 1990

CHARLEY BROWN: While the booking agency side was solid with Marc and Don, band management was a whole other pit of snakes. I could always tell when Perry was changing management. Whenever anyone said no to him he tried to fire them. We [Triple X] lasted the longest. Three years.

MARC GEIGER: They went through seven managers in my lifespan, which is definitely a story unto itself.

PERRY FARRELL: Gary Kurfirst managed the Ramones, Blondie, Talking Heads, and Bob Marley. We wanted to be with his company because, once again, I wasn't sure about the man, but I was sure about the artists.

CHARLEY BROWN: Geiger said this was a once-in-a-lifetime band . . . right before he screwed us and set the band up with Gary Kurfirst.

CASEY NICCOLI: Gary did absolutely nothing. He didn't have to. So they had to fire him. . . .

PERRY FARRELL: Here's a guy on the East Coast and we're on the West strung out and running wild. We don't even know when the next paycheck is coming. We obviously badly needed help, and it's our own damn fault I'll admit, but if you're taking ten percent for keeping us together then, goddammit, earn your ten percent.

TED GARDNER: I was the original tour manager for Jane's Addiction on the *Nothing's Shocking* tour [when] the band's current manager Gary Kurfirst was fired. Then Ron Lafitte came in for a couple of weeks and was fired.[87]

STEVEN BAKER: It wasn't well advised. Gary Kurfirst was the manager and all of a sudden it was Rob Kahane and Ron Lafitte.

PERRY FARRELL: Ron was connected to a company by the name of Lippman-Kahane who saw that we were hurting. They said, "Look, we're going to pick you up, clean you up." I wasn't interested in being clean. Next thing they knew I fled from rehab and I'm running around talking up my next big adventure, a movie in Peru, but their ambition was just to get me to piss in a cup weekly. Somebody wasn't going to get their way, and I did not end up pissing in any cups. They were in the picture for maybe three weeks or . . . it could have been a year, I don't remember them being around that long.

STEVEN BAKER: They were finished with Gary in their minds [though not contractually], and they were moving on to Ron [Lafitte]. Ron was very involved with the band at that time, especially with Perry. Gary certainly had a lawsuit. You can't just up and leave . . . he has a deal with the band. Gary was like, "Hey, I have a contract with you, I'm going to continue managing you. You can have that guy over there manage you . . . fine, if that's what you want, but I'm going to continue getting what I'm supposed to get."

CASEY NICCOLI: And then they hired Tom Atencio. Tom had a couple of big English bands, like New Order, Echo and the Bunnymen.

TOM ATENCIO: Kurfirst had New York arbitration in his contracts, so he proceeded to haul Perry's ass in front of a labor arbitration court, where he played out the drama of the victim sayin' in effect, "This fuckin' kid is a junkie and a liar. I'm a New York businessman, I've done this and this and this, I'm a square shooter with ethics, your honor . . . exercising my rights to protect my interests . . . and this jack-off dope freak over here is just trying to weasel out of a very clear contract!" The labor board awarded Kurfirst full rights to his contract. Fortunately, I was able to cut a reasonable deal with him to let me have enough of a percentage so that Perry wouldn't have to pay more than he should for management.

ERIC AVERY: I wasn't in on the legal proceedings surrounding the attempted canning of Gary Kurfirst. We sent Perry off full of vim and vigor. He was going to New York to show those litigators; instead he got his ass handed back to him tied in a bow. . . .

STEVEN BAKER: We heard that Perry wept in court, that he broke down in tears during the arbitration hearing. . . .

REBECCA AVERY: They were paying him [Kurfirst] a percentage for a long time. That was another episode where the whole band ended up having to pay for Perry's mistakes.

PERRY FARRELL: I hate the motherfucker [Kurfirst]. It's very easy to point a finger at somebody who uses drugs—everybody frowns upon it—like calling someone a flag-burner. At the time I *was* using drugs way too much, but the reason was I was completely overworked. I was playing my ass off, more shows than we should have. I had a fractured rib, a broken ankle, a busted-up eye. We're real physical live and need to be worked like an athletics club—a massage from time to time, a Jacuzzi, a day off. How's your throat, how're your calluses? The guy wasn't around to take care of us. When I got off the road I was wrecked.[88]

ROLLING STONE "IN BRIEF": EX-MANAGER SUES

Circa April 1990

Gary Kurfirst, the former manager of Jane's Addiction is suing the band, claiming it dumped him in violation of a three-year contract that wasn't due to expire until August 1991. Kurfirst, who also manages

Talking Heads, says in a suit filed in Manhattan's State Supreme Court that he took the band from playing $1,000-a-night stands to gigs playing ten times as much. He also alleges that some band members have drug problems that resulted in "clouded judgement" when they began looking for new management. Kurfirst alleges that as of the suit's January 25th filing date, lead singer Perry Farrell was enrolled in a Beverly Hills drug-rehab center and lead guitarist Dave Navarro was in a methadone program. Alan Mintz, the Los Angeles lawyer for Jane's Addiction, says the band has "decided not to finalize any arrangement with a third party until we reach an amicable settlement with Gary."[89]

CASEY NICCOLI: Both sides knew Tom just wasn't compatible either . . . both sides wanted out.

STEVEN BAKER: And then Tom Atencio was gone and so finally Ted became manager and he continued right through the first Porno for Pyros record. . . .

TED GARDNER: At the beginning of the *Ritual* record Perry said, "You're now the manager."[90]

CASEY NICCOLI: Ted Gardner was Perry's tour manager and sidekick. He was on every tour and Perry trusted him. He's this big Australian guy. Perry just asked him to be his manager.

PERRY FARRELL: I met Ted on the back of my tour bus. He had a cold, a running nose, a hangover, and a three-day growth on his chin, and I liked him because he looked like he was a salt-of-the-earth guy, good-humored, not afraid to punch a man out if he thought somebody was going to give him trouble, and for a number of years we had a great run of it. We'd drink champagne and talk about tomorrow on tour.

REBECCA AVERY: Ted was a crazy guy. It was a tough job for him trying to keep these nuts somewhat in order.

⚜

PERRY FARRELL: [The cover art] was made with chicken wire, papier-mâché, and we were living in neighborhoods that had these little Santerian curio shops. Bright on the eyes. Earthy. It hit me deep spiritually because of the beauty of the artistry.

MODI FRANK: It was like Santería meets Mary Magdalen and Our Lady of Guadalupe. Catholic Mexican art meets Santería art. They would make a rosary around Mary surrounded by piñatas.

PERRY FARRELL: I enjoy the way they gather things to make the shrines and fetishes they have in their homes. There's a certain primal power there, even if you don't understand it.[91]

DAVE NAVARRO: The Santerian imagery was Perry's idea. Whether or not he practiced it I don't know; I certainly did not. But I was a fan of the imagery, and our stage ended up being very ornamental because of it.

PERRY FARRELL: I was just drawn to the colors and the sly joke of it all. I also responded to the pageantry. I wanted to concentrate on things of value, the necessities of life, the things that make you cry in a film. These people used Christian symbols to goof on their captors because they didn't want to get flagellated. They posed as Christians without giving up their true beliefs.[92]

MODI FRANK: Exene [Cervenka of X] was more elaborate in her lyric sheets and inner sleeves with the Catholic imagery, which is half of Santería . . . basically Haitian voodoo with heavy Catholic iconography thrown in, right? Perry was more elaborate on stage. X would just bring a wooden cross and put it up there, but Perry had candles every-where. There were never any conversations like, X used to do this or that. He was just coming from his own zone. He just reminded me of Exene in how much he controlled and executed his art.

PERRY FARRELL: We loved Exene and her aesthetic.

DAVE JERDEN: After we finally finished *Nothing's Shocking,* I got a call from Warner Bros. saying, "We're very concerned about this record." And I'll be damned if I didn't get the same call after the second record.[93]

PAUL V.: I remember everyone at Warners freaking out over the cover of *Ritual.* It was just laughable: three-way sex made out of papier-mâché? The second version had the freedom of expression clause from the Constitution.

PERRY FARRELL: I turned in the cover artwork, and they said, "Oh, boy, here we go again!" [Warner-Reprise Records CEO] Mo Ostin and

[Warner Bros. Records president] Lenny [Waronker] said people were getting arrested for selling albums that any local law-enforcement type decided was "pornographic." They said retailers were so cautious that the record could wind up selling 1,000 copies. But I refused to budge when they wanted to airbrush out the male genitals. It's laughable by today's standards, but it was a scary time.

STEVEN BAKER: Who wanted to end up like 2 Live Crew? Their records were vanishing overnight from the chains. Clerks were getting busted for selling them to minors. For Perry it was the worst thing ever. How could we not use his artwork?

TOM ATENCIO: When we delivered the record, the sales department was aghast. They knew they couldn't get it into the major stores, especially their big crosshair target: the mega-mall outlets. I said to Perry, "You're going to have to change the cover."

STEVEN BAKER: I remember this really emotional meeting in Mo's office. Our sales guy says, "You know that you're not going to be able to get in all the stores?"

PAUL V.: I remember going through that with them. You're really not approaching this right. You're approaching it from a greed level. The controversy will help sell more records because now people will know that there's a cover they can't see so they're just going to want it all the more. Work it to your advantage.

STEVEN BAKER: We finally decided on two covers. Let people who want to buy the original cover buy that, and people who were frightened can buy the other. We came up with this idea of putting the First Amendment on the cover just as this bland document. Very few people bought it. Most people bought Perry's version.

TOM ATENCIO: Perry took the record and wrapped it in the First Amendment and told me, "This will be a collector's item because when the kids find out what my artwork really is, they'll return these fuckers and they'll go and get my original. Everybody that's stopping this is going to get stiffed." And he was right. Everybody ended up carrying the original artwork by popular demand. The fucking Constitution copies became collector's items.

PERRY FARRELL: I only agreed to do a second cover if they'd guarantee to run the original uncensored. Having two different album covers started off as a compromise, but I ended up liking it. I could verbally abuse those people who stopped growing up at the age when you first start dealing with your genitals.[94]

DAVID J: I've always felt a psychic link with Perry. One time when I was in New York, during the time of Jane's third album, I got this mad urge to call Perry. It was like 4 A.M. I thought, "There's something about this bird, I've just got to ask him what he's doing. I think there's some connection." So I called him up and asked, "Hey, Perry what are you doing?" And he said, "I'm designing the cover of the next album." I said, "Does it involve a bird?" There's silence and he said, "Man, I just put a bird into the picture!" Then I told him why I called. When the album came out, sure enough, there's a bird and you see three of them in bed. There's also a tribute to Love & Rockets in the same artwork . . . a heart and a rocket. We went to see Jane's play in London at the Brixton Academy and he had the original piece of work—this enormous life-sized thing—suspended above the stage. It was all there: the bird, the heart, and the rocket.

DAVE JERDEN: I went to this WEA convention and Mo Ostin gets up to the podium and says something to the effect of the whole world has changed. Mo Ostin is like the Wizard of Oz, he's like God in the record industry, and he's saying, "You guys have made a record that has changed everything."[95]

TOM ATENCIO: The first single from *Ritual* was already out when I came on. Warners was marketing it as a hard-rock record. I said to them, "Look, this is not a typical hard rock band. This is really an alternative thing. The station who should be playing it isn't KLOS. It should be KROQ with the new emerging format that is alternative radio." We fired everybody around it, fired the publicist, fired everyone. Brought in Heidi Robinson to do publicity. I rethought what the record company was doing. I said Perry had to do a lot of press, which he hadn't done much of before. Perry was completely cooperative with me.

TED GARDNER: *Ritual de lo Habitual* was recorded and delivered, and then the band was unhappy for various reasons and it was decided that they would tour and then break up and go their separate ways. That was between the band and myself. No one else knew. We all picked the places we wanted to go—Australia, New Zealand, Yugoslavia, Austria, Vienna. We played Rome at Easter and stayed in this quaint, beautiful hotel two blocks from the Vatican and in the café next door they were selling espresso and heroin. . . .[96]

THE MAKING OF *GIFT*

Circa 1990–93

CASEY NICCOLI: *Gift* was meant to be a full-length feature film. It was like our *Gift* to the fans or whatever. We had no script. We just had an idea of what we wanted to do. It was going to be reality documentary and fantasy mixed together. Perry and I costarred and codirected it.

STEVEN BAKER: We [Warner Bros.] funded *Gift*. We got a video or so out of that. And so it paid for itself. We went half with the band's management.

TOM ATENCIO: The record company was a way for him to finance recording and the making of his home videos. The band consequently became terribly in debt to the label. To cover the advances for the filming, Perry even mortgaged their mechanical royalties from the publishing side. The band was making nothing from the record company or their publishing, but they were making good money on the road. They really didn't give a shit as long as they were playing and had something coming in.

PERRY FARRELL: I told Warners I'd give them six or seven videos if they'd let me make a film. They said, it's a bargain. My ambition was to go to Peru, to film and surf down there and of course get into all kinds of trouble, but they wouldn't allow us to go [there]. And I think they probably made the right decision! If I was trying to make a living with a group of fellows or ladies I wanted to work with, I sure wouldn't have chosen us.

ALLAN WACHS (filmmaker, videographer, producer of *Gift*): I was brought on board by Warners as producer of *Gift*. I was the pragmatist whose job was to ensure Perry and Casey's creative vision was realized as much as possible within the bounds of reality. Almost from the get-go there was a kind of antagonism where they looked to me as some kind of formidable, repressive authority figure. I was the eyes and ears of the record company, the people signing the checks. There were major head trips. They had their own scenario as to who I was and what I was trying to do.

CASEY NICCOLI: We'd already hired these two goons who presented themselves as seasoned filmmakers but they were just fans who really hadn't done anything. We weren't involved in the film world enough to know that until it was too late. It ended up a nightmare, because we didn't really get along with them. They kept trying to say that it was their movie.

PERRY FARRELL: They gave us a gang of cameras, and a van full of camera equipment, and these two crazy young filmmakers who were making videos at the time were eager to jump into the fun that we were up for.

ALLAN WACHS: They just struck me as hanger-on types with their own ambitions who were using Perry for their own ends. Maybe they were good for shooting second camera . . .

PERRY FARRELL: We wanted to do it *Spinal Tap*-style, and we'd sew the whole thing together as we went. We figured we knew enough trippy people that it was gonna be a hoot.

ALLAN WACHS: Perry and Casey gave me an outline and ran down what the story was. It was pretty loose, but it definitely wasn't random either. Many scenes were improv'd, although they did have set goals for what each scenario would accomplish. The shooting concept was mostly setting up in some interesting environment, documentary style, with minimal lighting, no huge crew, and just allowing things to happen.

CASEY NICCOLI: Perry and I had moved into our own place in Venice, this little two-bedroom house, and we filmed most of it there. It was intended to be very intimate and personal, to do with what happens to people who are under the influence of a lot of drugs.

ALLAN WACHS: The basic story is about a couple who have a death pact with each other and then the guy comes home and finds his wife OD'd and goes through a major quandary of whether he wants to honor that pact. To live on or to die alongside her? In doing that he goes through the backstory of the relationship, traveling around Mexico, scoring drugs on the street and all the rest of it.

PERRY FARRELL: We were able to go to Mexico. We got a show down there for Jane's to cover our travel costs.

ALLAN WACHS: My main concern was that I didn't want to take drug addicts to Mexico. They'd keep saying, "Oh no, we're clean, we just got off rehab, we're fine." It was quite dangerous being an unconnected junkie down there, and I just didn't want to be put in that situation. It also wasn't safe for the people I was going to be bringing down.

"CLASSIC GIRL" GOES TO MEXICO

STEVEN BAKER: We got a video for "Classic Girl" out of *Gift*, the wedding scene with Perry.

PERRY FARRELL: Mexico is wild. The people are hot-blooded, the weather is hot, the food is hot. The art is great, too.[97]

CASEY NICCOLI: We went to Mexico and filmed our wedding in Catemaco, Veracruz. It's a big witchcraft town, a very mystical place. We got married there by a Santerian priestess. We had to be cleansed before she would agree to it. They roll the egg over your body. And then they break the egg open and if it's black, it means there's evil in you.

ALLAN WACHS: In the jungle, two hours south of Veracruz, just a little village on this lake was a real witchcraft center on this remote *ranchera*. The Santerian priestess, Isabelle Aderi, did the egg test on both of them. When she opened the egg, I saw a bloody mess, which means a lot of toxins. She said, "You guys have to clean your act up if I'm going to marry you." We were planning to come back in three or four weeks for the wedding and she did a cleansing of them. Her son was a qualified medical doctor, MD-equivalent, but also this kind of psychic doctor. Her father, Oscar Aderi, was a well-known psychic healer.

PERRY FARRELL: The Warners people were scared shitless. The movie cost $500,000. Or $450,000 and going upwards fast. Considering the shape we were in, that was a lot of dough when promo video clips were made for just $80,000.

ALLAN WACHS: Casey almost died in Mexico City. She was drinking beer and shooting tequila with the guys and she went into convulsions and had to be rushed to hospital. The emergency room nurse came out and said, "I can't find a vein anywhere on her entire body!" Casey was just like totally shot up everywhere. Everything was collapsed. Her arms and face were just oozing with pus-filled scratches and bruises. . . .

CASEY NICCOLI: I was on drugs and was not in my right mind. Neither was Perry.

ALLAN WACHS: They were so lucky to have the crew that they did. I got really good people for them. I don't think they realized any of it. I was basically dealing with inexperienced people trying to get a finished product that could potentially be shown to a mass market, further complicated by the fact that Perry and Casey weren't always totally forthcoming about what they wanted to do and some of their hangers-on would do weird things like try to steal the film package from the production office.

PERRY FARRELL: At one point we were literally on the lam with the cameras. They were sending people to repo them, so we just hijacked the gear and took off in a biplane to this island off the coast of Mexico. We were basically filming on the road to get all the ideas we needed before they finally caught up with us and took the cameras away.

ALLAN WACHS: The higher-ups at Warners weren't sending out cops to repo their cameras. It was basically me trying to keep tabs on the production. People would come around our production office and try to break in to steal the cameras. We knew some of the equipment was in the hands of drug addicts and people who didn't really know how to use it. One camera just didn't come back. One of my favorite moments during the concert in Mexico City was watching these two joker hanger-on guys shooting B cameras onstage. We'd have runners giving them mags when they'd run out of film and you'd be watching to see how they were doing. You'd be tapping these guys on the shoulder and they'd be looking at Perry and they'd say, "Get away, get away . . . I'm shooting!" But there was no film in the camera.

PERRY FARRELL: We just kept on filming it, [until] . . . WB finally says, cut these guys off, end this nightmare now . . . they'd even assigned an additional camera team to us, to make sure that we got something.

<hr/>

ALLAN WACHS: When I came back from Mexico, I was done. I didn't want to have anything more to do with it. Jonathan and Valerie took over postproduction. . . .

JONATHAN DAYTON (filmmaker, videographer): On some level, *Gift* was a little bit like *Apocalypse Now*. They went into the jungle and they made this movie. They came out of the jungle and had all this footage but they were fed up with each other.

VALERIE FARIS (filmmaker, videographer): Perry hated the producer that Warner Brothers had hired so much. There was such bad blood they said there's no way he can finish this, maybe Jonathan and Valerie should come in.

JONATHAN DAYTON: The producer didn't like them and they didn't like him.

ALLAN WACHS: After they came back from Mexico, they shot *Been Caught Stealing* and the concert at the Hollywood Palladium with Jonathan and Valerie. We were already so far behind schedule as far as having anything to coincide with the release of their album that deadlines didn't matter anymore. I would have loved to see it come out a couple of years earlier when it was more timely, but overall, I think the film came out as good as it could, amazing considering all the adversity!

CASEY NICCOLI: It took forever to get it out.

ALLAN WACHS: There was a lot of footage. . . .

PERRY FARRELL: Now we were left to edit it.

VALERIE FARIS: Once Perry saw that we were benign and weren't going to try to take it over, that we just wanted to help them, things got more relaxed.

JONATHAN DAYTON: They just needed somebody to help them get it together. We set them up at the Holiday Inn in Santa Monica where they were living. We bought them a deck and a TV so they could log the footage . . . we were basically just assisting.

ERIC ZUMBRUNNEN (film editor, edited *Gift*): I got pulled into working with Perry and Casey when they were transferring the film to video. We would work a little bit on *Gift*, intermittently, between the videos and touring. It was very sporadic. I'd go to their hotel in Santa Monica and work for a week or so there and then at other random places all over town, whenever they were off the road I remember one time waiting eight hours for them to show up. With *Been Caught Stealing* Casey didn't even show up for the first three days.

PERRY FARRELL: We installed one of those Avids into the tour bus, and every night we'd be editing the tapes on the highway to the next city. *That's* why it took so long.

ERIC ZUMBRUNNEN: Perry and Casey would work on stuff while they were away. They'd just send the tape to me and I'd put it together, basically following what they did and then finishing it up. They did the *Classic Girl* video that way.

ALLAN WACHS: It took three years to complete *Gift* because they'd keep losing the offline tapes.

VALERIE FARIS: We never experienced the fuck-up part of Perry, really. For the most part, he was just so full of incredible ideas and so much fun, always sharply focused knowing for the most part exactly what he wanted to do.

ERIC ZUMBRUNNEN: Perry was a really nice guy. Casey was really nice and during that whole process I could see their relationship deteriorating. They might be having an argument or something that would throw our whole workday out of whack. There certainly were times when people were passed out or not showing up and maybe not the most lucid they could have been. They would have creative differences, too, but it wasn't at all a horrible experience from my perspective. It was mostly something really fun to work on.

JONATHAN DAYTON: Allan Wachs was the overall producer, and Eric Zumbrunnen's genius as an editor was that it all flowed and made sense in the end.

ERIC ZUMBRUNNEN: People I know that had never done hard drugs, were fairly repulsed by the explicit drug usage parts. Perry's cooking it up and talking on a voice-over about how he could write a whole album in a night. Then there's blood in the syringe and the other gross-out stuff with Casey shooting up while she's talking on the phone. It's just unabashed. They didn't hide anything. They seemed to be living it and were completely fine with representing it on film, adamant about it even. Some people would ask if *Gift* was glamorizing drug use and I would say, "No way!" It certainly didn't try to make it seem exciting and cool and rock 'n' roll. It made it all seem so very mundane, so banal . . . and very, very dirty, which, as any junkie will tell you, is what addiction is really all about. Look at how scuzzy their place was, how messed up their health was. It didn't romanticize it like *Drugstore Cowboy* did, but they did seem to have a sense of humor about it; it doesn't seem like they're trying too hard to be serious or overly arty, even though there are some very serious things about it.

ALLAN WACHS: Perry possibly intended *Gift* as some kind of bizarre morality tale. Rather than saying, "Go out and get high and shoot up drugs," Casey dies in the story, and he gets hauled off by cops. It's not like there's no adverse consequences to their lifestyle. Some of it was pretty brutal. *Gift* de-glamorizes the whole dope-shooting trip, making it the nauseating ritual it really is. They were slipping back and forth between their own addictions throughout, but credit them with trying hard to say something real about it. I wasn't there as a censor or some sort of moral judge. People will figure that out for themselves. They'll want to see it or they won't want to see it. They'll want to release it or they won't want to release it.

CASEY NICCOLI: We wanted it released in art theaters. In the end, the Warners guys decided to put it out on video without even releasing it.

ERIC ZUMBRUNNEN: The record company's point of view was always that it was going straight to video, but Perry and Casey really lobbied hard for a theatrical release . . . they got a week at Sunset 5.

CASEY NICCOLI: By the time that film was finished, we weren't together anymore. It took so much out of us.

PERRY FARRELL: I wouldn't call the movie the reason that we broke up, but it puts a very, very undue stress on a person to come through with art guaranteed on a deadline. . . .

JOHN FRUSCIANTE: I saw a rough cut of *Gift* in the early days, like a few scenes from this work in progress. I told Perry I had some music that's the same vibe as his movie and he said you should bring it over to the studio. We listened and it went perfectly with this other scene I hadn't seen yet that had no music—the scene with the crawling ants. It looked like I had scored the music to this movie, but the weird thing was I'd already written it and it just fit perfect. Somehow we were on the same wavelength again. There was another part where I play a typical rock 'n' roll kind of bend and that's right where you see the poster that says, rock 'n' roll will *kill* you. . . .

THE *RITUAL* TOUR

August 1990–September 1991

ERIC AVERY: *I was clean at this point. I felt so apart from the rest of them. I just had this sense of why am I even in this band anymore? What's the point?*

TED GARDNER: At the beginning of the [Ritual] tour Eric was definitely going to get clean and he was going to stay clean. Everyone else was still using their brains out—not Stephen—Stephen never did heroin.[98]

ERICA PAIGE: There were times where David and Eric were really close, and there were times where no one wanted to talk to anybody. Who was hanging out with who would keep switching. Eric was sincerely trying to make some better changes in his life . . . and if you're planning on getting clean and staying that way, you reassess every area that is around you, the band being one of them.

ERIC AVERY: Perry still always thought I was trying to sabotage him in ways that just didn't cross my mind. I was talking to some guy in a

Drinkin' Wine Spodee Odee. Pass that bottle o'er here. (Chris Cuffaro)

bookstore who asked me about the new record, and he said, "What do you think of it?" And I said, "Well, I think it's a little overproduced actually. I prefer *Nothing's Shocking.*" And it turned out that guy was the fucking gossip columnist for *BAM* magazine, or something, and he goes and quotes me. Then I get this cryptic weird call where Perry's saying, "We're gonna have a meeting to see if you're still in the band." I was really scared and upset. When I get there Dave and Stephen have no idea what's going on.

STEPHEN PERKINS: The *Ritual* tour lasted thirteen months, ending in Lollapalooza, and that was the end of the band, basically. Communication between Perry and Eric was gone.

TOM ATENCIO: Perry and Eric were just never going to patch it up.

PERRY FARRELL: The thirteen-month tour behind *Ritual* was half the reason we wound up unable to stand each other.

ERIC AVERY: Casey was always trying to build bridges. I remember talking to her solo and she was sort of doing the "You know, he really respects you" spiel. And I was like, "I respect him, too."

Eric Avery on epic bass. (Chris Cuffaro)

She was really trying to get us each to see the other's side of things, the other part where we still had affection and respect for each other.

REBECCA AVERY: It was getting pretty clear that they weren't going to be able to stay together. They were going to have to get a divorce. It was like a marriage of convenience. Especially at the end. The closest of us knew that this was it. They weren't announcing it, but it was like let's just do these last dates and just agree to do that and part ways.

BOB FORREST: I saw their last gig at Irvine Meadows at the end of Lollapalooza. They were just *awesome*. And they weren't even talking to each other anymore. I love things about bands like that! Eric was standing over one way and Perry walked on another way and Dave was already on the other side. Three humans that don't talk to each other, but as soon as they hit the opening chords of "Three Days" it was magic, just unbelievable.

REBECCA AVERY: The Universal Amphitheatre was near the end. I just remember that they were great shows but that something was different. Everyone seemed unhappy. It just wasn't the same. They weren't having fun on stage anymore.

STEPHEN PERKINS: We'd come to L.A. to do shows, but wouldn't sleep here for more than a week. We did three nights at the Palladium and kept touring. Came back and did four more at Universal Amphitheater. More touring. Came back and did three at Irvine for Lollapalooza. All in support of *Ritual*. It may have broken the band in a great way recognition-wise, but it may have also broken the band's spirit.

"ALTERNATIVE NATION"
READING, THE GATHERING OF THE TRIBES
THE PROTO-LOLLAPALOOZAS

Circa August 1990

PAUL V.: *Jane's Addiction never really got their due as the impetus for "alternative" music coming to the mainstream. Perry Farrell, Jane's Addiction, and Lollapalooza finally found a key that unlocked that door and cracked it open a hair and Kurt Cobain stuck his boot through it. He couldn't have without Jane's Addiction and Lollapalooza. Who knows what it would have taken for that music to finally break through without them?*

MARC GEIGER: We went to England for Jane's first festival run at Reading during August 1990. Reading and the other European open-air music festivals were the templates for what would become Lollapalooza. . . .

TED GARDNER: We were due to play the Reading Festival. But Perry lost his voice and we couldn't play but Perkins and myself still went to the site to hang out and we met up with Geiger. We were sitting around talking and we were lamenting that America did not have a music festival along the lines of a Reading or a Glastonbury. . . .[99]

PERRY FARRELL: I lost my voice the night before. . . . I got too fucked up. So I didn't make it to Reading. My voice was just shot. When you're on heroin, you can't really sing, your voice kind of clamps down.

MARC GEIGER: Not only did those festivals put on a lot of bands but they had a lot of exhibits and they demonstrated other performance pieces with an all-day carnival atmosphere. Perry never made it down to the festival grounds, he got a sore throat. It was Stephen, myself, and Ted.

TED GARDNER: Marc brought the idea up of why don't we invite a bunch of our friends to play on the American leg of the tour and try to create something like a Reading Festival, but taking it on the road? The inspiration was a number of people, but Geiger was really the seed-planter. I thought it was a good idea and took it to Perry who watered the seed and came up with the name Lollapalooza.[100]

PERRY FARRELL: Marc Geiger encouraged me to be creative. He said, do whatever you want on this summer tour, get whoever you want to open for you. I just went to him with this wish list of groups that I liked . . . and came up with a name. . . . I think I got it thumbing through the dictionary. Lollapalooza is someone or something very striking or exceptional, number one. And number two, it's a giant swirling lollipop.

MARC GEIGER: It wasn't truly European, because Europe is more like Coachella where you just go to it, versus a traveling thing. We felt we could book multiple bands across multiple genres. Whether you're talking about the Cocteau Twins and Metallica . . . or Nick Cave and George Clinton on the same bill, that diversity was sadly missing from this country.

TOM ATENCIO: There were lots of other precursors for Lollapalooza in North America. It wasn't just about replicating Reading as a traveling tour. It's a huge myth that this idea just popped out of nowhere in Perry's head with no precedent. Geiger knows that very well. He and I had already done touring packages with New Order and other alternative acts back in '87 and '89. Quite big venues. Amphitheaters across the country. That really was the beginnings of the idea that Marc took up with, now reinforced by his experience at Reading. We'd already done Echo and the Bunnymen, co-headlining with New Order and Gene Loves Jezebel. Two years later we did New Order, PIL, and Sugarcubes, which was even much more successful.

TED GARDNER: The U.S. festival planted the seed for all of it.[101]

TOM ATENCIO: Ian Astbury from the Cult did the Gathering of the Tribes pre-Lollapalooza. Ian certainly put alternative rock and rap together on

the same big stage first. The Gathering of the Tribes had Ice-T, Queen
Latifah *and* Soundgarden, Iggy Pop, the Cramps, the Indigo Girls . . .
experimentation with the diverse bill concept was already well under
way. . . .

> Dubbed "A Gathering of the Tribes," the all-day pop smorgasbord at
> the Pacific Amphitheatre on Sunday attracted 9,000 to 10,000 people.
> This gathering sprang from British rocker Ian Astbury's idea of creating
> a festival of contrasting stylists ranging from hard rockers to folkies to
> rappers. While at least 95% of the audience was white, listeners' enthu-
> siastic embrace of the lineup's two rap acts, and their willingness to
> sample and enjoy the 10-hour day's full range of performers, showed
> that diversity has a constituency. Queen Latifah, Michelle Shocked, the
> American Indian Dance Theatre, Ice-T, Soundgarden, Public Enemy
> (no-show), Tower of Power, The Indigo Girls, Crash Vegas, Charlatans
> U.K., The Cramps, Mission U.K., Steve Jones, Iggy Pop.
> —*Los Angeles Times*, October 9, 1990

IAN ASTBURY: During 1990 I was hanging out with bands like Mother
Love Bone, before they became Pearl Jam, and Soundgarden. I knew
the scene in Seattle was going to happen. Nobody believed me. I did the
Gathering of the Tribes festival in 1990, which became Lollapalooza
the next year. All my energy went into it. I probably lost $50,000 of my
own money. Hip-hop's going to explode as well. I saw this coming, too.
There was a bit of an agency war over the bands who wanted to be involved. Oddly enough, the guy who wouldn't let his groups be on our
bill was at the forefront of Lollapalooza.[102] A premiere alternative rock
agency got wind of the festival and they had so much envy because they
weren't involved, that they tried to destroy it. I had Iggy Pop calling me
at home saying, "I can't do the festival." I said, "Why not?" He said,
"People have said it's going to be a failure, it's not going to be good for
my career." I said, "We need you, don't listen to their shit." I was ripped
off. I never got the credit. We didn't do it for the money, we did it for the
community.[103]

TOM ATENCIO: Lollapalooza became the business codification, it was a
consolidation, a new collective brand name for many new marketing and
promotional opportunities that were already out there. They just needed
a credible spokesperson, a PR figurehead to front the package. . . .

PETE WEISS: An agent came up with this, but they needed someone for people to believe. Who would be the perfect mouthpiece for it? They got Perry Farrell, who influenced almost everyone he met.

TOM ATENCIO: What really set Lollapalooza apart was that it *expanded* on the idea with more bands and the second stage concept, a much more complex set of logistics. Nobody had ever tried to build a stage that could accommodate that many bands. Nobody had ever toured that many bands. Lollapalooza was such a major undertaking. There was no existing infrastructure. When you have eight or nine bands, coordinating between seven different record companies, that's a lot of information.

ADAM SCHNEIDER (agent, manager Porno for Pyros, producer of the ENIT festival, another former Jane's Addiction manager): The blueprint for many future touring festivals was the second stage, touring performance artists, touring social and political activist groups, artwork vendors.

MARC GEIGER: We proposed that Jane's Addiction's last tour become a traveling Reading festival and Perry's piece of that was to explore the pleasing of the senses and to add more than just the music. Don and I were the programmers in terms of the artists and the mechanics, and the business structure, but Perry and his band members were also directly involved in the selection process for which bands participated.

TED GARDNER: We all put our heads together to assemble this package and it was up to Don Muller to sell it to promoters. Muller, myself, Geiger, Stuart Roth [Jane's road accountant], and Perry.

We had Siouxsie and the Banshees, one of Dave's favorite bands. NIN Perry knew about. Ice-T because we knew him and his band Body Count as a labelmate at Warners. Henry Rollins was a friend of mine. Convincing regional promoters was slow. Everyone at first was a little like, "We don't know. What does this mean?" Those that got it right away were Jam Productions, Chicago, and Bill Graham Presents in San Francisco. Others were skeptical, but they saw potential. We naively thought this would be cool as a one-off. We had no intention of doing it again.[104]

TOM ATENCIO: Perry was over in Europe during Desert Storm '91. He called me up and said, "Tom, it's incredible because we're being lied to so much. The news over here is very different to what we're getting in

America." I said, "Perry, we're planning this Lollapalooza thing; you have all these feelings about politics and welfare. Now you have a platform. We used it on MTV, let's use it on Lollapalooza, too. The homeless, the political aspects, bring it all in. Let's do Greenpeace. Let's do Heal the Bay, gun control, and all the shit you're concerned about. Make MTV deal with it."

PERRY FARRELL: I want to see what happens with a major exchange of information. I don't like the idea of the world being controlled by the news media. We need to exchange ideas somewhere else, another forum. The cafes aren't being used anymore, so let's try it at a festival. Everybody's all of a sudden aware at a different level.[105]

PAUL V: Perry thought, "OK, if my name and my band can get 20,000 people here, maybe I can inspire a hundred of them to go vote or twenty of them to join Greenpeace or whatever it was that he believed in. He invited both gun control activists *and* the NRA people to come down and set up their booths. . . .

PERRY FARRELL: I'm not declaring myself left wing or right wing, I'm actually bringing both sides into it. It would be way too easy for me to take everything that's obviously politically correct and have this hip, left-wing event. But I don't want to make out I have the answers, all I want to do is pose the questions.[106]

PETE WEISS: Perry and his business people knew there was a large group of people out there—living like us—who were not represented by mass media. There was this huge swollen underbelly, this underground scene that had been fermenting for a decade since the early punk days that was already living like that. What Perry did with Lollapalooza was say, "You stick your flag up and say 'Here we are'" and everyone comes and rallies around the flag. Then they realized there's this huge number of people willing to participate. That was culturally where Lollapalooza really hit the chord.

ERIC AVERY: We didn't know if the concept was even going to work; having this eclectic mix of bands and people coming together like NIN and Ice-T with the Butthole Surfers, Henry Rollins. . .

MARC GEIGER: Over the next seven years some of the pairings and some of the groups that played were historic milestones in the careers of a bunch of extremely diverse artists.

DAYLE GLORIA: Perry approached me and Mike Stewart about doing Lollapalooza with him—when he'd just had the idea. We had dinner at Tommy Tang's, and me and Mike were looking at him like he's a total nut. Of course, millions of dollars later. . . .

STEVEN BAKER: Perry very luckily had people around him like Don and Marc on the agency side who so totally loved and believed in him.

JON SIDEL: Perry called me one day strung out of his brain. He was going on and on, super high talk. He was editing *Gift* and he was like "Dude I wanna meet with you. I got this idea and it's kinda like Powertools, and I'm calling it Lollapalooza, and it's like I wanna do this fucking circus review thing, and I want you to do it with me." I thought he was out of his tree, but I guess he obviously wasn't. I was like, "Perry, call me back later."

MARC GEIGER: At Lollapalooza Don and I were flat salaried employees with no share of profits.

PERRY FARRELL: I cut Ted Gardner in because I wanted to work with him because I liked him.

MARC GEIGER: The first tour was Jane's Addiction's tour. They made so much more money than they ever had made before as a group. But everybody was very cognizant of ticket price. Did anybody gouge consumers? No. Tickets were, like, twenty, twenty-five bucks for seven bands, and then ultimately seven bands on the side stage over time, that's cheap by today's prices. . . .

ERIC AVERY: Lollapalooza was able to transcend the sum of its parts. That was the idea. When you look at that lineup, nobody was a stadium draw at that point. We certainly couldn't have done the kind of draw that Lollapalooza did.

DAVE NAVARRO: I think of Perry as the godfather of alternative rock. I call him "The Don."

MARC GEIGER: Perry was the front man, the spokesperson, as well as the guy we all tried to please in terms of creative ideas. Perry would come up with 10 ideas of which the mechanics could only produce three. . . .

CHARLEY BROWN: Perry was a showman and a great Barnum and Bailey ringmaster. He loved putting on parties and special events, from the earliest club days onwards. Lollapalooza was just the perfect gig for him. . . .

MIKE WATT: Perry is just one of the all-time best frontmen. He's the bridge between the kids and the stage. They become him. He becomes them. He makes the thing human, not like fusion or the 'lectronic thing watching too-cool nerds operating machines and laptops. He is the flesh and blood of it. He'd sing and dance with them. Perry excels in this role.

JOHNNY NAVARRO: Perry doing his thing, the fucking shaman, guy's a madman. He's not afraid to say whatever he wants to say or do whatever he wants to do. And he's got this wail. It was pretty intense and pretty awesome. It was an amazing time to live in Los Angeles if you loved music to be around those guys.

PERRY FARRELL: I enjoy loving people. I enjoy bonding. I enjoy amalgamations. I enjoy attraction. I like having a good time and being flamboyant and I like to throw parties, that's my forte.

STEVEN BAKER: Perry is a guy with a big heart who believes in himself and actually loves people.

PERRY FARRELL: The Lollapalooza concept . . . just throwing a party with you as the host. So what are you going to have for the people there? You have one day of their time. And you have a field or some place that will allow you to rent it. It's really no different from any of the other parties we would throw in Los Angeles, except it's now a macrocosm of them. Same attitude. I liked walking the grounds of Lolla. Passing through the art gallery and seeing the chair that was made out of nails. Then I'd go through the film tent or watch people listen to poetry. I remember bungee-jumping while Soundgarden was on. And, of course, having sex during the day is always exciting.

HENRY ROLLINS: My band was asked to be on the bill while we were on a string of dates opening for Jane's Addiction. We gratefully accepted. I didn't know if the shows would work but there was no pressure on us other than to play well. If the tour tanked, it was more Perry's thing to deal with. I had a great time.

Circa October 1990

ERIC AVERY: Inger Lorre was the anima to Perry's animus. The female version of Perry. She was very theatrical, a real show person. They were cut from the same mould . . . magician, shaman, that kind of witch doctor ability for live performing.

INGER LORRE: Me and Dave and Eric Avery used to hang out. It was definitely a drug thing first before I even knew their music. Eric was well-read and one of the smartest people I ever met. We'd just get super-high and lie around his apartment discussing dark art and all this macabre, dopefiend literature that he'd boned up on. We talked constantly about Burroughs, who wrote about drugs. We were just kids making excuses for our own drug use because people like him, these amazingly talented, literate people used drugs to get to other levels for their art. The Nymphs were sort of like Jane's little sister band and they let us open these humungous shows like John Anson Ford Theatre and Universal Amphitheatre, and that really gave us a core audience because our music was similar in some ways, although very, very different in others. Jane's audience instantly got it. Voilà, we had a huge number of fans.

PERRY FARRELL: There was "a particular girl in a particular band" and I'd rather not mention her by name, if you'd do me the favor, because she's apparently been diagnosed. Said "particular little diagnosed girl" was excluded from this Halloween party we were playing up at this fellow's house in Bel-Air by the name of the Colonel.

INGER LORRE: Josh Richman introduced the Colonel to Jane's Addiction and they ended up playing a party at his house. It was really surreal; it was a kitschy 70s *Shampoo* movie scene, this huge mansion, and all these beautiful cro-people there. Our friend the Colonel was a ragin' freak on fire with a saggin' butt mid-life crisis. He had all the money, the big mansion, the cocaine, the champagne . . . oh, and this testo red Ferrari . . . and now's he's King of Cool Hill with Jane's Addiction playing his birthday party.

JOHN FRUSCIANTE: There was this Halloween show at the Colonel's, which was just after *Ritual*. Me and Anthony and Flea showed up wearing dildos. We were just hanging out at the party and Jane's played and then they asked us if we wanted to play a song at the end. We played "Search and Destroy" by the Stooges. . . .

INGER LORRE: The Colonel was just livin' it *large*, just pissin' that cash away like water. He had the best coke, the best drugs, the coolest-looking people at his parties. He'd say, "What do you want?" You'd tell him, "This much heroin, this much coke, and this many hits of Ecstasy." And he would just get it. No problem. When I started dating Rodney Eastman I had no idea Josh [Richman] was one of his friends. Josh just freaked out and tried to get me blacklisted from my own freakin' friend's party. He called the Colonel threatening to blacklist his name among all the top cool people; he would never speak to him again if I came to the party. . . .

PERRY FARRELL: She was really pissed because the Colonel specifically didn't want her to come. She'd gone up there plenty. We'd all gone up there plenty. This guy was like fifty years old, hanging out with the likes of us. For some reason, she took it out on me and broke into my home. She smashed this guitar into smithereens that I had written many songs on and the cover for *Ritual* was beheaded, as was the cover for *Nothing's Shocking*.

JOHN FRUSCIANTE: Inger Lorre called me up once and said she wanted to do a project with me and Dave on guitars. She wanted me on acoustic and him on electric or the other way around, or something. She asked if we'd record a couple of songs and I liked the idea, and Dave and I talked about it on the phone. I was really looking forward to it and then during some late-night party session Perry and I were talking and he said, "Don't do it." I'm trying to remember the word he referred to her as. Something got destroyed when somebody broke into Perry's house. They left a note behind that said something like, "We came for you." He thought for sure she had done it.

INGER LORRE: Somebody broke in and smashed Perry's artwork. We'd had a falling out and he thought it was me. I didn't know why he was so mad at me for the longest time until Dave finally told me, and it really, really hurt my feelings. First of all, he lived on the fifth floor. I was like, "Hey, P . . . be real, mister, how do you think I got in there?" That was after the peeing-on-Tom Zutaut's desk episode so maybe he thought I had supernatural powers. He said, "You climbed in the window. I know you got in here."

PERRY FARRELL: OK. It was circumstantial. No hard evidence. The culprit was never found. Lyrics and a poem were left. Whoever did it knew me very well. This same person broke the windows of my home on several occasions but the Number One Suspect was always like an innocent little angel when I'd see her. Wanting to be tight and partying with us.

INGER LORRE: As an artist myself I would never, ever hurt somebody's artwork. That's the last thing I would do. I'm the type who'd smash your windshield or kick a door in. I had a bad temper, no doubt, but I swear on my father's grave, who is my favorite person ever, it wasn't fucking me who fucked up the art, OK?

PERRY FARRELL: A brick would go through your window and you'd see the back of the little angel's head, piling into a car and jettin' off real fast. Once in a while I'll still see her lurking and hovering around the country and it's the scariest thing.

"BEEN CAUGHT STEALING" BECOMES A RADIO AND MTV HIT

Circa November 1990–July 1991

PAUL V.: "Been Caught Stealing" did not get worked to rock radio at first because the guy in charge of the format thought, "Well, we can't really get behind a song that might encourage shoplifting and the video encourages shoplifting." I thought he was just kidding around. I'm standing there with my mouth on the floor, like, "This is a joke, right?" At this point, I just threw my hands up. This is what we're dealing with. It's going to take a miracle or a brick on this guy's head. That was the beginning of my demise at Warners.

DAVE JERDEN: Our A&R person Roberta Petersen said, "'Been Caught Stealing' . . . that's going to be the single." We were taken by surprise. It had never occurred to us [to think of it as a single]. I hate to classify it as a novelty song, but we just considered it a fun track. We were adding some vocals to it one day and Perry's dog Annie was trying to get into the vocal booth with him, because one of her toys was in there. She happened to bark on cue and we kept it.[107]

TOM ATENCIO: Eric was absolutely appalled that it was going to be a single.

TED GARDNER: The commercial success [of *Ritual*] stemmed from "Been Caught Stealing," the single. That was the only [Jane's] single that made it to radio in any mainstream daytime airplay. It was one of those quirky little songs. No one really took any notice of it until Perry said, "Hey, let's do a video for this song." It was timing.[108]

CASEY NICCOLI: I copped a lot negativity when I was doing the "Been Caught Stealing" video. Perry told me straight out that it sucked and would ruin his career. I didn't want to go [to the MTV Video Music Awards, July 1991] any more than Perry did. He hated the idea of awards shows, but their asshole manager was supposedly going to accept the award [for Best Alternative Video] on their behalf. Why should someone else get an award for something I did?

CHARLEY BROWN: Billy Idol was set to announce that Jane's Addiction had won Best Alternative Video and so he tears away at the envelope and goes, "And the winner is . . . Jane's Addiction . . . 'Been Caught Wanking'," and then he sticks the statuette thing down between his legs and was thrusting his hips out . . . and jerking off the statue.

DEAN NALEWAY: Casey came on behind Dave, who stumbled onto the stage completely out of his tree wearing some crazy boa and feathers outfit and these huge crazy Sly Stone sunglasses.

DAVE NAVARRO: Casey was in quite a state. She seemed to be speaking nonsense.

CASEY NICCOLI: I was in a total blackout. Dave was pretty out of it himself.

PERRY FARRELL: She went up there pretty loaded.

DEAN NALEWAY: Casey was trying to make some kind of acceptance speech . . . but she was too wasted to be coherent . . . she was going on and on about what a genius Perry was . . . then Dave grabbed her and was trying to stick his tongue down her throat. . . .

PAUL V.: I was like, "Oh my god, somebody get that mic out of her hand!" She went on this tirade, basically that Perry Farrell is a genius, a God who created the universe and we should all bow down to his feet.

CASEY NICCOLI: Perry disappeared the day before the show with some chick he'd picked up at the 7-Eleven. He saw the show sitting in her bed. That's why I made such a fool out of myself. I was so drunk and sad about Perry. I don't remember Dave kissing me. I'm still really embarrassed about the things I said on camera, but, oh well, it's only rock 'n' roll!

PAUL V.: Even though she directed the video and it was her privilege to say whatever she wanted to say, I was real upset because it made the band and Perry and everything they'd stood for look really stupid. A little embarrassing, but it was a rock 'n' roll moment, I guess.

PERRY FARRELL: I was nice and high. I just didn't feel like getting out of the house; it wasn't that important to me, the whole attitude of MTV and what it stood for. Casey wanted to go, so I said, "Have a good time." I didn't watch the show, but eventually I saw a clip.

STEPHEN PERKINS: We should've been together in one place at one time, and gone up as a band. But there were communication failures, no focus, no sharp intention. It was scattered, and it was shown right there on national TV.

ERIC AVERY: To us, MTV was never anything that could be taken seriously. I didn't watch the MTV Awards. It was of absolutely no interest to me whatsoever. I heard about it afterwards.

JOHN FRUSCIANTE: I was seeing Perry resisting success, not so much spitting in its face, just not jumping right into this huge success without looking, because if you go blindly jumping into the arms of success it will crush you. Resisting success I feel is an important thing for people to do, like when I see these bands today and they're just chasing success and they'd just do anything for it, it's really unexciting and transparent. When I was in my teens I was confused all the time. I also resisted success and I'm glad I did. In the short run it made my life hard and it made a lot of people around me really confused, but in the long run I feel good about it. The way he dealt with it, even if he has regrets about it now, it was really inspiring to me at the time.

PERRY FARRELL: I don't necessarily want to be popular. I did [want to be popular] when I wasn't, but now that I've had a taste of it, I realize it's not that exciting. Public opinion is usually the most ignorant opinion you can gather. It's like the architecture of a 7-Eleven. When you have to duplicate it too many times, it starts to suck. When you mass-produce pancakes, sooner or later, twigs will start to show up in them. Mass communication tends to reduce things to their lowest level. You're forced to boil things down so everyone understands. I know for a fact not everybody likes me, but, to me, that's healthy.[109]

PF'S "CHILDLIKE INNOCENCE"

DAVE JERDEN: Perry was always talking directly to the minds of the children, the kids, teenagers, whatever. And he thinks that way. He's very childlike. And that's the side of Perry I love so much. He picks up on things, the little edges of the fractal, that most people wouldn't even notice.[110]

MIKE WATT: Perr once told me, "Having the child's eye is not the same thing as being naïve or infantile." He was talking about keeping a sense of wonder. He said, "You don't get cynical because you think you've got it all figured out or you think like everything's fucked up and lame . . . so you just take to scamming and burning whoever you can." Perr's got a real street sense. This guy isn't a neophyte. On the other side he's a dreamer. It's a weird kind of marriage. He's a very interesting cat.

PAUL V.: When you're in the room with him and you look at his eyes he looks like a little kid. He's still wide-eyed and innocent about a lot of things.

ERIC AVERY: There was something infectiously childlike about Perry which is totally linked to his power and his charm. Marshall McLuhan talked about the amateur eclipsing the innovator since the expert is often too bounded by science and other institutes of limitation, thus stunting unbounded creative possibility. Some might call it naïveté, but Perry seemed to have this natural fiery procreative force. He just didn't think about the consequences.

BOB FORREST: Perry had this idea to have a big rave on the West Bank, this huge love fest that was going to solve the Israeli-Palestinian conflict!

ERIC AVERY: Once he thought it would be cool to fly a helicopter over impoverished areas and drop money on them. It's a sweet, positive idea, but it doesn't take into account that it could create riots or that people might get violent with each other. And I think that's totally connected to his creativity. It's the kind of childlike imp that he is.

JON SIDEL: Perry's genius is that he's such a tremendous front man, an entertainer whose character walks the tight wire between absurd cheesiness and overgrown juvenile . . . who's also capable of intellectual and musical brilliance. It's very childlike and sometimes what he's saying if you really look at it closely is very corny. At certain points you want to go, "Come on Perry, you're being ridiculous."

MARC GEIGER: There was conflict in nearly everything Perry thought. The best artists are nearly always the most out-of-touch with business reality, because it is polluting. I think it's very difficult for somebody as creatively pure as Perry. The reality of what one can and can't do, one's liabilities; the intrusion of consequence was always an impediment to Perry's artistic muse. . . .

MODI FRANK: People from management and the record company were always trying to put the brakes on him.

CHRIS CUFFARO: Perry always does his thing. In a sense he's like a spoiled brat. His ego is pretty big and he is what he is. It's about treating people with respect. Some people, Perry or whoever, don't do that. They just don't.

STEVEN BAKER: Perry always had fifty ideas. You'd listen to all of his incredible schemes and then pluck stuff out you felt you could actually help him with. Before the first album came out he wanted to do a Jane's

Addiction culture magazine about the band and their friends and artists. It was The World of Perry all the way. . . .

MARC GEIGER: We'd have to discuss a lot of issues to figure out which were reality. Perry wanted a full-on marching band on every show. Now he was saying his perfect evening touched all the senses: ears, nose, throat. He became less interested in the music and more interested in the culture and the other senses—whether it was smell, taste, or touch, and other pleasing experiences that were tangential to music.

JON SIDEL: Perry had this crazy idea where he wanted to feed 10,000 people a meal, like how the Krishnas do, with all this different food and stuff. I was like "Perry you're out of your mind, 10,000 plates, how are you going to do this?"

PERRY FARRELL: I've been told that I don't always exactly see straight. . . .

MARC GEIGER: Perry wanted to create aromatherapy for the masses. He wanted 30,000 people to have a variety of smells battering them as they entered, and then they'd go to different parts of the venue, and there would be all these different kinds of scents, a different one for each corner of the venue. We'd tell him, "Look, Perry, this is *outside*, they're just going to dissipate!"

PAUL V.: Most of the time Perry was saying something, I felt like I understood him 100 percent, but there were times he would say something and you would either like not pay attention because you knew it was like, What? Huh? If you stripped it away, beneath it there was always something cool and mystical or whatever. . . . I looked at Perry as sort of a pied piper. He was a guy that people wanted to hear what he had to say. He had some off-kilter views of the world and was going to say something that you certainly wouldn't hear anyone else in a rock band say.

FLEA: Perry has a childlike enthusiasm for what he's doing. When something intrigues him he gets really excited and happy and he loves it.

JANE BAINTER: The innocent, sort of child . . . is another side of him. These many different faces of Perry don't really go together too well. It's easier for him to switch from one into the next than combining them all, but he can play all the roles well at different times.

PAUL V.: Perry would rather look at the good in people and not think about the evil. He would rather know that people are capable of really good energy and of doing good things.

LOLLAPALOOZA FIRST NIGHT

July 18, 1991

PERRY FARRELL: The first day of Lollapalooza, in Phoenix, Arizona. It must have been 110 degrees out there.

TOM ATENCIO: The tension was unbelievable because the band was ending, Ted and I weren't getting along. Dave was so tender, fresh out of rehab, but we had no fucking concept of keeping people straight . . . he was flung headlong from rehab, straight into this grueling, vigorous tour.

CHRIS CUFFARO: Everybody backstage was in a bad mood and pissed off. The heat was just nasty. It was just too damned hot.

TOM ATENCIO: We were getting in fistfights amongst ourselves on how to treat the audience. Should there be misting tents? Should there not be misting tents? Because it's 114 fucking degrees in the middle of the desert. Some people said that misting tents would make people go into shock. Others were saying, "Are you fucking nuts. . . . of course you've got to get water and shelter!"

JOHNNY NAVARRO: Come Lollapalooza time, Dave's with this girl Tania . . . She looked a lot like a young, thin Siouxsie Sioux. When he got together with her he was with another girl. He cheated with Tania and brought her over to my house and like I met her the first night he met her.

DAVE NAVARRO: Perry had been working very hard at putting together this Lollapalooza tour, getting all the bands together, and on the very first night in Phoenix, Arizona, I was in no shape to perform.

TOM ATENCIO: It was incredibly stressful because we didn't know how the revolving stage was going to work, we didn't know about all the coordinating between the bands and the managers and the record labels, a fucking lot of people were involved.

JOHNNY NAVARRO: The day of the show, Dave goes, "Do you have any shit?" I'm like, "Well, yeah—" I was trying to hoard for myself. I was like, "Yeah, aren't you hooked up?" Now we need to go score downtown on the fucking street just so he can make it to the show. Otherwise there's no fucking Jane's Addiction at Lollapalooza.

PERRY FARRELL: I was in a testy mood. Dave was sick and wanted to bail. He just didn't wanna play anymore.

JOHNNY NAVARRO: Somehow he'd bailed out on the bus and all the transportation people that were going to go to Irvine Meadows. So he calls me, he's like, "This is Dave . . . dude, I've got a little situation." He's like, "Can you and Arty pick us up?" Sure. My friend Arty Nelson who's only got sixty days of new sobriety picks me up in his Jeep Wrangler. We drive to Westwood to pick up Dave and Tania. Dave comes out wearing a cape with a hood over his dreadlocks and Tania with her fucking PVC pants and her boots and her huge fucking dreads. As we're driving from Westwood to Irvine I break it down to Arty that we have to make a stop; so all four of us drive into Pico-Union and score some shit there on the street, and Dave fixes and I fix and Tania fixes, not Arty.

PETE WEISS: Perry was like "Dave's too sick to go on, how are you guys holding over there?" I brought him a little bit of Persian to get him on. I said, "Dave, you know you gotta cut it with lemon?" So he has someone bring up twenty cut lemons. I said, "No, Dave . . . just a little teeny bit." I was like, "Dude . . . how can you know you're going to be on tour and not have it together?"

JOHNNY NAVARRO: Dave was doing three or four grams a day, sometimes more. We're talking up to 700 dollars of dope in one day. I didn't have the resources or the time to be able to do that. Dave would just shoot nonstop. He was addicted to bangin' as much as he was to getting loaded. He really liked—any junkie does—the fucking ritual of fixing. He liked it so much that he would fix and then he would go smoke a cigarette and then he would come back and fix again. He'd end up with these incredible fucking tracks down his arm. "Your arm's like hamburger," I'd say. "Dude, what are you doing? You can't get any more high." He'd say, "I just like the fix." There was always the risk that he would OD and he did a bunch of times.

DAVE NAVARRO: Ultimately I had to leave during our performance, and I don't remember who got physical with whom first, but I've since apologized to Perry because I feel that I was responsible for shattering something that he'd worked so hard on. The opening night was a rough night for me to behave so irresponsibly. . . .

ERIC AVERY: Perry and David got into a fight onstage and it cut short our set. Dave was out of his mind on Valium and shit and one of the two bumped into the other one and the other got upset and so then they started taking runs bumping into each other. Then it turned into literally them entangled falling off the side of the stage fighting.

CHRIS CUFFARO: Toward the end of the set, Dave just snapped and threw his guitar into the audience and stormed off, knocking over stacks. Perry walked off after the song was finished and they just started wailing on each other, punching each other out. Ted finally jumped in and broke it up. We didn't know if they were going to come out for an encore. The crew reset the stuff back up and they came out again and started playing, but then Dave started body-slamming Perry while he was trying to sing. Dave knocked over his stacks again, took his guitar, and launched it into space . . . again.

TOM ATENCIO: Ted was weeping like a baby. He was blubbering, "It's all blown up in smoke, everything that I've been working for, for two years. The whole fucking tour is going into the shitter."

PERRY FARRELL: I don't think there's anything wrong with losing your temper, you can always make up.

ERIC AVERY: I was nearly clean and I was like, "This is the first night?"

❦

HENRY ROLLINS: It was so wonderful to play and then get to see the Butthole Surfers and Ice-T back to back, and then later on, see Jane's Addiction—*every night.*

ERIC AVERY: I had a blast because I would go out and play on the encore of "Head Like a Hole" with NIN, and I'd play one song with the Rollins band earlier in the day, sometimes I played drums with the Buttholes.

HENRY ROLLINS: The highlight [of the first Lollapalooza] for me was Jane's on the second night in Dallas, it was one of the greatest nights of live music in the last century. Ask anyone who was there.

TOM ATENCIO: The only real Lollapalooza was the first one. I think that was the genius one where you had a really eclectic mix of countercul-ture. Not a single cheesy band on the bill. There was no crass commer-cialism then. It was fun. Thankfully, we also made a shitload of money.

INGER LORRE: Dave always liked older women. He had a thing about Siouxsie Sioux. . . .

ERICA PAIGE: Dave was hanging out mostly with Siouxsie and Budgie on that tour. He looked like death. As a friend I was really worried. It was like watching someone dying, literally. He had a lack of regard for life and was having no joy anywhere. Dave's a really smart, funny guy and it was like looking at this empty, hollow person in the body of this amazing, vibrant guy I once knew.

CHRIS CUFFARO: Dave was always in his closed dark world behind sun-glasses. They were all in their separate little worlds. Stephen's energy was the glue that kept it all together. Eric just came and did the shows and left. He didn't want to be around. If you're trying to stay clean, the last place you want to be is hanging around Jane's Addiction backstage before a show!

ERICA PAIGE: [Dave's fully blown addiction] wasn't anything that was se-cretive. Once I was house-sitting for him and went to pull out a box of ce-real and syringes fell on my head. In the van driving to the show, it wasn't being hidden at all. Someone was sent out to buy bleach. It had reached the point that everybody knew it was happening. When I walked into this hotel room [in Seattle] everybody was racing to get ice to revive him.

TOM ATENCIO: About a third of the way through Lollapalooza it wasn't just about the bands, it was this whole countercultural event that was coming to fucking Des Moines, Iowa. We were being interviewed by the morning news on television, the evening news, major TV network stuff. It wasn't *Rolling Stone*. It wasn't fucking Podunk radio. Lolla-palooza became a national news event about getting a tattoo and piercing and talking about gay rights.

PETE WEISS: Every night Perry would come out there with his bottle of wine, the place was always electric.

TOM ATENCIO: That mix of smack, coke, and red wine was a little volatile. You never knew where it was going to go.

PERRY FARRELL: The only way I can see that excess is against nature is that maybe when you get intoxicated, you can get sick. Decadence and the back-to-nature impulse are about freedom. You feel free when you hit the great outdoors, and you feel free when you get intoxicated.

STOP!

Circa Fall 1991

PERRY FARRELL (Head shaved to black stubble . . . to a Dutch audience in Amsterdam): *I am a Jew by birth! Thanks for hiding my ancestors during the war! No, really, if it weren't for you people, I wouldn't be here right now. The folks back home asked me to say thanks. Hey, this is not a Nazi look. This is how we looked in the concentration camps. [Utter silence]. That's a joke! My name is Perry and I'm into Satanism and sports. That's another joke—I don't like sports! I guess you don't understand my sense of humor. Hey! Do something up there! It either comes out of your asshole, or it gives you cancer. You might as well laugh it out, right? Oh, another joke. I think it's funny. But then, I'm dying. . . .*

ERIC AVERY: I was so fed up I decided to split. I told Dave first because he was my best friend in the band.

DAVE NAVARRO: We were very, very close in the band. I still consider Eric a friend.

ERIC AVERY: I said, "Dave, I'm splitting after this leg." And he went, "Oh, okay, cool. Me, too." And then we ran down the hallway and told our tour manager. So the guy says, "I want to talk to you about doing Japan before you split." I said, "I don't need to talk to you about it. I'm out. I'm not interested in doing Japan or anything else. I'm done." We just did one last show in Honolulu, Hawaii [September 27, 1991].

DAVE NAVARRO: It's gone too far. Our singer is somebody that I don't get along with or agree with. I respect his right to believe what he believes, it's just not what I'm into, creatively. There's a lot of people working with us and for us, and I don't want to screw them over. We've been doing it for five years and it's gotten to where my heart's not in it anymore. I'm leaving and I'm going to do my own thing. I [told my tour manager] I'm out of here at the end of Lollapalooza.[111]

PERRY FARRELL: I didn't know Dave and Eric were bailing, but I sure knew that I was.

STEPHEN PERKINS: I knew the band was coming to an end, so I just kind of accepted it. We planned on doing Lollapalooza and then breaking up in Seattle, but we were contracted to finish the tour in Australia and Hawaii. The hardest thing was going to Australia and playing small clubs right after Lolla. It would have been much cooler to break up in Seattle in front of 30,000 people. But we did it, 'cause we never break agreements.

PERRY FARRELL: We weren't brothers, we weren't tight, we weren't a team. I felt that to stay in a situation like that was bullshit. It would be doing it for the money and for the fame and glory. And believe it or not, it ain't worth that much to me. I want to be working with people that I get off on.

CHRIS CUFFARO: When we were in Hawaii for the last show Tanya [Goddard, Dave's then-current girlfriend] came down to the bar where I was hanging out with some people. We were like, "Where's Dave?" She said, "Ah, you know, he's in his room, he doesn't want to come out. It's too bright." There's Eric out on the beach with his girlfriend swimming and snorkeling. Tanya was tired of being with an addict all the time who never wanted to do anything else. I think she left Dave and got clean soon after that. . . .

TED GARDNER: Jane's broke up between tours, last show in Hawaii. We played on the Port Authority in this building without air conditioning.

Perry did the whole set naked. Stephen was naked. Only Dave and Eric still had their clothes on. . . .[112]

CHRIS CUFFARO: After the first song Perry took his pants off backstage and came back out butt naked. We were all just sitting there waiting for cops to stop this. We're all like, going, "Any minute, any minute now . . ." and then another song goes by, "They're going to come now!" Still nothing. It was so hot Eric was standing in this pool of sweat, Stephen got naked, too, behind his drums.

PAUL V.: Perry got totally naked and it was just the right moment. It was the most honest naked moment. It was like, "This is it folks, here it is, The End."

Perry shows all during Jane's final night in Hawaii. (Chris Cuffaro)

CHRIS CUFFARO: After they did "Trip Away," the house lights came on and Perry came back out and went on this tirade about making a difference and then he jumped into the audience. For me, that was like the last breath of the original Jane's Addiction we knew and loved. (Chris Cuffaro)

ERIC AVERY: That last night [in Hawaii] was the closest that Perry and I got to a fistfight.

PERRY FARRELL: We just didn't take care of each other.

PAUL V.: That was a very hard night. It was very bizarre. It was sort of like, OK, when the curtain goes down I'm not going to be able to see my favorite band again. I'm not going to be able to hear these amazing songs booming out of a sound stage again. I didn't talk to the band. I just sort of watched the show because I knew what they must have been going through. As a fan it was one thing, for the band I'm sure it was a whole other.

DAVE NAVARRO: There were times when Perry and I literally hated each other. We got into fistfights offstage. We once got into a fight on stage during a performance in Australia. But even with that much animosity and hatred flowing between and around us, I still felt really connected to him and everybody else when we were playing music.[113]

YOKO ONO [summer 2004]: I was exposed to Perry Farrell and his incredible talent by my son, Sean, who brought me Jane's Addiction and made me listen to it. My bones relaxed immediately. It was my kind of music, totally. It was genius. The next thing I knew Jane's Addiction was over. Oh, well. Something that was so magical could never be repeated. One night, he graced my show in L.A. and jammed with me and the band. I felt honored. He turned out to be a very nice guy as well. I'm still addicted to the memory of Jane's Addiction. Go back and listen. It's one power house. Rocking Schoenberg . . . that's what it is. (Heide Foley, courtesy RU Sirius, *Mondo 2000* magazine)

PERRY FARRELL: I [became] the hero and this scapegoat at the same time. I was hated for breaking up Jane's Addiction, although I was the one who created it. It's something I had to do.[114]

MARC GEIGER: Perry did much more contemplation after the band broke up. There was so much in the short life of Jane's Addiction which was also clouded by heavy drug use, constant change of management, and all these other things. There was never time for Perry to sit down and reflect while Jane's was alive.

PERRY FARRELL: The last night I went off the deepest end a fella can go. We're talking about a ravishing, young hottie showing up with a doctor's bag in her hands and a wink in her eye, who wasn't really a doctor, if you know what I mean . . . nudge, nudge. And so I spent, I don't know how many ecstatic days on the paradise island of Hawaii getting high and feasting on her beauty. [Afterwards] I remember getting off the plane and feeling really light and free. I felt like, man, all that big swirl of energy and attention and work, there's nothing to it anymore. And there I was on the curb, just waiting for a cab . . . thinking man, that was some chapter, you know. Hell of a chapter.

EPILOGUE: THE JANE'S AFTERMATH LOLLA '92 (THE SECOND YEAR)

Circa Spring 1992

TED GARDNER: It was Geiger who said, "Hey, why don't we do this again?" And everyone went, "OK, whatever." '91 was the risk, '92 was the juggernaut. In '92, this big-time promoter said, "Play my venue and I'll get you all Corvettes."[115]

JEFF AMENT: We [Pearl Jam] had already toured for like a year and they approached us and asked if we wanted to do it. We found out that Soundgarden was doing it and the Chili Peppers were doing it, too, who we had been on tour with. It sounded like a total blast. Lollapalooza at that point was still a brand-new thing for America, the big festival thing. It was an exciting time.

TED GARDNER: We didn't know Pearl Jam, but we liked the music. We didn't know Soundgarden, but we liked the band. Seattle scene bands were exploding everywhere, it was a no-brainer to book 'em on there. . . .[116]

CHRIS CORNELL: A lot of people bought tickets to Lollapalooza '92 because it was Lollapalooza, not necessarily because Pearl Jam or

Soundgarden were on the bill, or Ministry, or Ice Cube, or the Chili Peppers, although it was a moment when Pearl Jam was really blowing up, and Ministry was having their biggest record ever. It's hard to say. Would the numbers have suffered if we weren't on it? I'm sure it wouldn't have been as strong. The idea was to have these vital new bands, but at the same time bands that had a draw, and there just happened to be a bunch of 'em at that time that had roots in the Seattle band scene.

TED GARDNER: In '92 Lollapalooza really blew up. We put more thought into the music. Five of us were doing A&R. We were looking at young bands that had solid local followings. The Chili Peppers who'd left EMI for Warner Bros. had known Perry for many years and now they were starting to happen. They had a very strong following in L.A. and other parts of California and now they were starting to break out nationally in bigger heartland markets. It was all starting to come together with radio.[117]

CHRIS CORNELL: Lolla '92 was one of my favorite tours ever. It was very fraternal. We knew a lot of people on the bill. We knew most of the Chili Peppers, of course we knew Pearl Jam, and we knew Al Jorgensen, whose band is Ministry. Almost all of the Ministry guys were in The Blackouts, which is a Seattle band, which was a huge influence on our scene for a long time.

ANTHONY KIEDIS: The '92 lineup was way too male, way too guitar-oriented [for my tastes]. I wanted [the all female band] L7 on the bill, and everybody in the agency just scoffed. They said, "They don't mean anything." What do you mean? They rock, and they're girls. It was upsetting to me.

❦

MARC GEIGER: There just wasn't that much greed at the beginning. There was never any corporate sponsorship in terms of maximizing the dollars. And so the band split the money the first year because they were a group. During the ongoing years of Lollapalooza Perry made a lot of money, but the group didn't, and that may have been another reason Eric was so alienated. He was also a person who was becoming clean and starting to see things with a bit more clarity.

TED GARDNER: There was a sense of elitism. We felt that we could do what we wanted and have the bands that we wanted and we weren't going to be dictated to by anybody. We never took corporate sponsorship. It was a case of let's sink or swim on what we believe to be good bands, not what we think is going to be commercially successful. We never sat down and said can we sell more tickets? How can we make more money? Let's put another dollar on the ticket. We were very much about the music and bringing it to the attention of a lot of people. Radio started to change. MTV started to change.[118]

LOLLA '95

LEE RANALDO: In some ways, the tour [Sonic Youth] headlined in '95 killed Lollapalooza because I don't think it was as full as some of the others. We had a lot to do with who was on it. We were really happy with the bill, the Jesus Lizard, Pavement, and Beck. Maybe it got to be too much to sustain it. Maybe Perry got tired of dealing with it.[119]

TED GARDNER: We made money every year. Some years we made more than others, but we never lost. Never stiffed a promoter. Every band got paid, all the crew got paid, and I cashed a check at the end of the tour, as did Perry, as did William Morris.[120]

PERRY FARRELL: Finally Ted just stopped caring. Or I just stopped caring by my behavior. The worst thing that happened for me was that I lost the respect of the people who worked around me. And they decided to make all the decisions without me in mind. I had no chance to balance the show out. That's when the art got lost.

MARC GEIGER: We also had different views on Lollapalooza's historic importance. Perry saw it as a creative outcropping of Jane's being able to put on their best carnival experience. Lollapalooza had a lot to do with the ending of Jane's. Don and myself just thought Lollapalooza was something much bigger than Perry's "carnival" experience.

TED GARDNER: After the seventh year I was going, "Enough already, I don't want to do this anymore." And Perry had also reached that point. Marc was gone already, the dynamic had changed. We got lazy, we got fat. We forgot what the core of Lollapalooza was. We started to look at how can we make it bigger? "Can we get The Beatles to headline? Oh no, one of them's dead." We had gotten very, very good at seeing what kids wanted and liked, but we had stopped doing that. Things like Ozzfest and H.O.R.D.E. came along, and Lilith Fair, and Warped. They took the traveling circus concept, and fine-tuned it to a specific demographic.[121]

LOLLA '96

ADAM SCHNEIDER: Perry left William Morris [Agency] and Lollapalooza in a very public dispute over the booking of Metallica to headline Lollapalooza in 1996.

TED GARDNER: Metallica was one of those moves where everyone howled, "That's so wrong!" Geiger set that one up.[122]

CHRIS CORNELL: [Booking Metallica] ended up a really bad idea for two reasons. One, it had a pretty big effect on the fraternal aspect. Metallica had a large entourage that were used to touring all over the world as Metallica; where everything's always about Metallica, and that was the way that they ran their show at Lollapalooza. There was a lot of tension with their crew. It was one of those situations where you're so huge that there's this machine that's just rolling and rolling beyond your control. The band was always trying to hang out and get things going on, but their crew was putting police tape across their trailer so you couldn't just walk in and say, "Hey, how's it going?" because it's fucking police taped off! Even though I had a pass as a singer in the band that played before them, the guys wouldn't let me go on stage and watch them.

ADAM SCHNEIDER: We had the opportunity of booking other bands that I won't name that would have made it a slam dunk. It was with total respect to Metallica. Metallica is its own thing. It just wasn't tailored to the Lollapalooza aesthetic now defined by Perry. He just wouldn't do it. He wanted a show that he could stand behind and look back and go those were the artists that I wanted to work with at that moment in time. Perry is always very aware, he's always taken the long view of how this will look in history. How is this going to look in the books?

CHRIS CORNELL: Number two, it was a bad idea because of the audience. There were a lot of Metallica fans obviously. With Soundgarden, there was a fairly good crossover. We did very well with their audience. But there was also a percentage of the Lollapalooza audience which would tolerate Soundgarden, but not Metallica. And so there was this huge division.

PLEASANT GEHMAN: Lollapalooza quickly became corporately co-opted. It was good for what it was, but it was a cheap carbon copy of what had been going on at the beginning. Eventually it became like a parody. It was literally parodied by *The Simpsons*—Homerpalooza.[123]

PERRY FARRELL: I wish I'd have been one of the cartoons. They didn't even get me in the episode.

DON WALLER (veteran rock journalist): Lollapalooza came back in 2003 after five years with Jane's Addiction headlining, and grossed $13.7 million from 25 shows, according to Billboard. High production costs and/or low ticket sales—depending on whichever spin you wanna put on it—led to the cancellation of a few shows, but most dates apparently performed well. The lineup was Jane's, Queens of the Stone Age, Incubus, Audioslave, the Donnas, and A Perfect Circle. The 2004 lineup didn't have a chance; it was scrapped to avoid a total financial bloodbath.

PF'S POST-LOLLA MAKEOVER

PERRY FARRELL: I used to whip my dreads around for all the solos. I cut them off when the war broke out, the Desert Storm War in 1991. Dreads can weigh you down, and it's never a bad idea to shave your hair. It can feel really lightening and enlightening. You really don't know what to do when war breaks out. There's a real feeling of helplessness. Some people go on a corner and hold up a sign, some people dance on a corner, some people honk. I chose to shave my dreads off.

JOHN FRUSCIANTE: Perry cut all his dreadlocks off. Now he had blond short hair and was wearing like these sharp tailored suits with vests

and stuff, a whole new look, like Bowie, Freddie Mercury, or somebody
. . . no more crazy, eccentric outfits, he had gotten rid of the ring
through the nose, the dreads and stuff because it was such an easy
thing for the public to reduce him to.

PERRY FARRELL: It was a tough thing at first. The first time I went out
there without that [dreadlocks], I had to reconfigurate my body to
move right . . . consider a palm tree when it sways in Miami Beach. It
has this sense of balance and weight that was now just gone.

JOHN FRUSCIANTE: A lot of people feel they have to keep this same image to retain that kind of popularity because that's what got them
there, but Perry just went completely against the grain of how a
person normally responds to his success by getting rid of his image
completely.

DECONSTRUCTION

Circa February 1993

*DAVE NAVARRO: I was not only self-destructive, but destructive of every-
thing around me. I regret my attitudes and my behavior back then, but I
don't regret the outcome so much because that was in '91–'92. Everything
happens for a reason. Perry and Stephen got to do* Porno for Pyros *and
Eric and I went on to do* Deconstruction, *which was a very experimental
album, a lot of non-sequitur pieces of music. . . .*

JOHNNY NAVARRO: The only ramifications were you might die, which
[at one point] he might have considered a welcome alternative. Dave
had never gone to jail. Never lived on the streets or in poverty. Born
and raised rich, Dave had become a successful rock star anyway.

ERIC AVERY: Before I decided to split from Jane's, Dave and I had talked
about making a record together. We started to do it, then it started to
kind of turn into a band [project], but then as we got closer to finishing it, Dave wasn't really into it and didn't like what we were doing. He
specifically didn't like me as a singer and kind of got cold feet and

pulled out and didn't want to have much to do with it, so it turned into a minor side project record, just what it started out as. Rick Rubin was just kind of like, just put it out . . . but didn't want to promote it.

STEPHEN PERKINS: I was actually gonna play on the *Deconstruction* record. But when Warners found out that it was everybody but Perry making a record they didn't want me to do it. It was on Rick Rubin's label, which WB was financing. They said, "We don't want three members of Jane's Addiction making a record without Perry. We want you to make a Jane's record—or not."

ERIC AVERY: Dave got turned off to the whole record and didn't talk about it for a long time. Later, he said some guy started going on about how great the *Deconstruction* record was. It was Taylor Hawkins. Years later Taylor told me about coming up to Dave and trying to talk about the *Deconstruction* record. Taylor at the time was playing drums for Alanis Morrisette.

STEPHEN PERKINS: No one was really brave enough to get us in a room, to try to make us work it out. It was sad. Maybe if a manager had said, take a year off then make a Jane's record, *Porno* and *Deconstruction* could have merged somehow to become Jane's next record.

DAVE JOINS THE RHCP'S AS THEIR FOURTH/FIFTH LEAD GUITARIST

Circa 1994

DAVE NAVARRO: After that [the *Deconstruction* record], I joined the Chili Peppers.

JOHNNY NAVARRO: There were always wild times in Dave's life until the Peppers, when he really got clean and started to go in this new direction.

JOHN FRUSCIANTE: Once Jane's Addiction stopped, it seemed like I was around Perry a lot in partying-type situations . . . especially right after I quit the Chili Peppers. Perry said, "I understand where you're coming

Dave during his days with the Red Hot Chili Peppers. (John Eder)

from because I did the same thing with Jane's Addiction. You can't just do something because you're successful at it. You have to go to the next step and make it part of yourself." It felt like the healthy thing to do. I don't know how to explain it but I still think I was right. The worst thing psychologically for people who are screwed up in the way we are screwed up is jumping into the arms of success for its own sake without looking.

FLEA: We had this massive audition [after John quit] and we saw a million people and it didn't work out. Then Dave made himself available. He came in and he was just ready to go. He was ready to be in a big rock band and play.

JOHN FRUSCIANTE: The night of Jane's Addiction last California show was the first time I did heroin. I was so depressed after I quit the Chili Peppers and I had so many things going on in my mind that I couldn't resolve. The world just seemed like this ugly place. My whole perception of things was completely flipped around where everything that was once beautiful was now ugly. I couldn't get any enjoyment about being alive anymore. Being on heroin and cocaine all the time, I felt like myself again.

JOHNNY NAVARRO: The Peppers had already asked Dave once to just come down and play. They jammed and played covers and he told me, "I have a sense they're going to ask me to join the band."

JOHN FRUSCIANTE: I'd made this decision to be a drug addict after I'd been doing dope for a few months and all these people were trying to get me to stop. I would always say, 'Give me one good reason not to do it,' and nobody could, except for Perry, who I respected so much. He came over to my house in the middle of a crack run. He'd been on a binge for days. He sat in his car and explained, "You've got to take drugs and not take drugs. . . . once you do it for a while it's that much harder to stop and the longer you wait the harder it becomes . . . like if you try to stop now you should be able to do it in a few days, but if you stop in four years or something, it's going to take a really long time."

DAVE NAVARRO: Flea called me out of the blue asking if I wanted to try out and I initially declined because I was still recording with Eric, but when the record was done I wanted to tour more than Eric did. Then Flea called me back again to see if I wanted to jam, and I was much more open to it.

JOHN FRUSCIANTE: Perry completely convinced me to stop and then he said, "OK, let's get you to the hospital right now." I had this bag of about an ounce of Persian heroin and about an ounce of cocaine and I was just doing as much as I could in the hospital parking lot. Finally we go in and Perry was like . . . saying to the nurses, "Listen, I'm going to be really honest with you, he's really on a lot of drugs right now so why don't you wait on giving him any medication."

JOHNNY NAVARRO: After *Deconstruction* didn't do what he wanted it to do, we were driving around one day and Dave goes, "Dude, I hate to say this, but I want to be a fucking rock star. I want all that that entails." I was like, "Dude, if you feel good about saying it, then do it, go for it." He said, "All right, I'm supposed to jam with the Peppers again. If they ask me, I'm gonna do it."

DAVE NAVARRO: We were in similar overlapping circles, yet I didn't really cross paths with the Peppers until like '89. I always loved to go watch them, because they were such an entertaining act. I don't remember liking their records so much, but they were always amazing live. That's how they'd built their whole rep.

JOHN FRUSCIANTE: I once called Perry at like seven in the morning and said, "How do you get snakes out of your eyes?" He said, "What?" I said, "There are snakes in my eyes, how do I get rid of them?" I'd be looking in my bathroom mirror at these little snakes in my eyes. I'd even hear them talk, they'd make weird little noises and stuff. A snake would poke his head out and I'd try to grab it. I'd be reaching in my eyes trying to pull 'em out. I fucked with my eyes so much doing this. I'd sit in the bathroom doing it for hours at a time. My eyes were just shutting on their own and I'd struggle to pull 'em open. No use. I called Perry and told him, "The snakes have shut my eyes." Perry told me I was off balance, something about too much yin and not enough yang. Perry gave me goggles after that. That was my outfit when I would go up on the roof to wage war against the ghosts. I would have my goggles on and my ski mask and every part of my body covered. No holes. I'd wear sweatpants tucked into socks. You couldn't get into me on any level anywhere. It made a lot of sense at the time!

JOHNNY NAVARRO: Dave stayed with the Peppers for four years and that really propelled him to another level. They already had *Under the Bridge* and the *Blood Sugar* album, which John Frusciante had a huge hand in creating. . . . John and Rick Rubin together put the Chili Peppers over on this whole other musical level . . . as well as their popularity with the masses. . . .

DAVE NAVARRO: I came from Jane's Addiction, and had a bit of history, and some people had heard of me, but the Chili Peppers were so much more enormous and were such a fine-tuned machine to step into. I had to learn how to bring my style into the Chili Peppers. I learned so much from those guys about friendship and musicianship and brotherhood and just doing it right. The Peppers have a great work ethic and they're spiritually minded, healthy fellas. The Chili Peppers are less of a one-man show than Jane's Addiction was. No slag to either band. It's just a fact. Perry Farrell is a very charismatic performer, and a lot of people who went to see Jane's Addiction primarily went to see Perry. With the Chili Peppers, the attention is distributed a little more evenly on stage. In Jane's I felt a little more connection between band members, as a foursome. Which is ironic, because I feel like I'm better friends with the

Chili Peppers than I was with Jane's Addiction. I felt completely bonded with them—even if I wasn't getting along with them off stage.[124]

JOHNNY NAVARRO: Dave had never had that level of celebrity, being that recognizable, traveling all over the country, all over the world. It also gave him wealth and power that he's never been lacking since. When you have someone make a cartoon of you, like when Dave was in the Beavis and Butthead movie doing "Rollercoaster" with the Peppers, he achieved a different level of status in the rock world. There was a lot of weird dynamics in the original Jane's and the way that Perry foisted his creativity on Dave, which mirrored a lot of the domineering nature that his father had. Perry was like a second father to Dave, and Dave got into rock to rebel from that. As soon as he walked into the Peppers, that didn't happen anymore, and as soon as he walked out of the Peppers that didn't happen anymore.

DAVE NAVARRO: I got a call from Flea: "Dave, in order to continue to make music, we feel it would be better with another guitar player. You've started using drugs again. We've already lost one guitar player to a drug overdose, and Anthony's had his struggles and is trying to live in health."[125]

FLEA: I felt like we were adequate during the time Dave was with us. We were doing the job, but we didn't really connect a lot. What made the Chili Peppers great for me was the fact that we just improvised like crazy . . . we'd get together and sometimes just jam for three hours without even playing any songs. That's really the force of our band . . . that feeling that we could do that whenever we want because there's so much music just floating around in the air, but Dave wasn't into it. He wanted to play songs. He didn't wanna jam.

DAVE NAVARRO: It was really awkward at first to join a pre-existing band like that. I tried to make that clear to them, and they tried to understand, but it wasn't until Flea joined Jane's Addiction [the Relapse Tour] in '97 that he took me aside and said, "How on earth did you handle joining the Chili Peppers? This is so stressful."

FLEA: I just don't think Dave ever really felt comfortable in the Chili Peppers. He just didn't really feel that he could be himself and be completely happy with us.

DAVE NAVARRO: I got a lot of online hate mail from [Chili Peppers'] fans. Those were the most fun to respond to. Like, I'd say, "Don't forget who hired me! If you have a problem, take it up with Anthony, Flea, and Chad. Talk to my employers."

JOHNNY NAVARRO: [*One Hot Minute*] is really a great record but it didn't catch on with a lot of the Peppers' fans. I think over the long haul it will be rediscovered, reappraised artistically and finally recognized.

DAVE NAVARRO: I've been asked, "How do you feel about making one of the least successful Chili Peppers records?" [1995's *One Hot Minute*] And my answer has always been, "Not only do I love that record, but it is, to this day, the most successful record that I have ever been a part of, commercial-wise." When I listen to that record, I hear myself growing as a musician and I couldn't have had a better group of guys to learn from.

JOHNNY NAVARRO: When Dave walks out and John comes back in and they sell more records than they've ever sold in their life, that sets up a certain dynamic with Dave's head. All he wanted to do was sell more copies than fucking *Blood Sugar* did and that just didn't happen. Dave thinks about that stuff. It weighs upon him.

DAVE NAVARRO: We had finished an album, we'd finished the touring cycle, and we had just finished a Jane's Addiction tour with Flea taking Eric's place. If there was ever a time to part ways, that was the time. Flea had never seen that kind of chaos coming from me. I don't think I was in a position to go back and I don't think they were in a position to have me back.[126]

FLEA: We were playing at the Olympic Auditorium [in Los Angeles] when I was playing bass in Jane's a few years later, and all of a sudden, I felt this amazing energy coming out of Dave. He was on fire. Just going crazy and playing his ass off. Completely putting his whole heart and soul into it, and I realized I never felt that from him in the Chili Peppers. He couldn't let loose with us because Jane's was really his home.

DAVE NAVARRO: Stephen and Eric are such a different rhythm section than Flea and Chad. Eric and Stephen are like a combination of Led Zeppelin and Joy Division. And the Chili Peppers are more hard-edged funk rock, Funkadelic goes Bad Brains. We were very fluctuating in our timing in Jane's Addiction, but the Chili Peppers are very precise.

FLEA: I consider Stephen Perkins and Chad two of the best rock drummers in the world. Both are phenomenal, but so different. Stephen is more ornate and precious—more involved in beautiful, pretty little things. Chad is stronger. Hits a lot harder. His meter is steadier. Stephen has a tendency to speed up and slow down in really great ways [that] make you breathe with the music. Stephen's a vegetarian pothead and Chad's a beer-drinking steak eater. Chad is more John Bonham–style smashing with a more simple setup, Stephen has all these little drums, bells and chimes and zingers and ziggers and African testicle-skin pebbly things. I have to think a little more with Steve.[127]

DAVE MARRIES RHIAN GITTINS ON AN IMPULSE

Circa September–October 1994

RHIAN GITTINS: Dave had just joined the Chili Peppers when we were introduced through a mutual friend at the Whisky in Los Angeles. We went on a date a few days later and three weeks later we were married. He swept me off my feet. [Our courting] was like a chess game. He would make a move and I'd match it. It was like pushing the envelope and pushing boundaries.

JOHNNY NAVARRO: Dave was two years clean when he married Rhian Gittins [October 15, 1994]. They married legally in Las Vegas and he called me that day and said, "Dude, I just got married."

RHIAN GITTINS: I was going to Vegas to see Nine Inch Nails and Dave said, "We're going to get married if we go to Vegas" and I said, "That's fine by me" so we went to Vegas and got married. I had a cubic zirconium gold-plated ring. I still have it somewhere. It was very passionate, quick . . . very romantic, especially for a young girl from Canada with a sparkle in her eyes. I was twenty-four then, or had just turned twenty-five. He was twenty-six or twenty-seven.

The honeymoon couple. Dave and Rhian Gittins.
(Courtesy Rhian Gittins)

JOHNNY NAVARRO: I was having a barbecue at my house and Dave's ex-girlfriend Pinky who he was supposed to marry is also at that barbecue. I'm looking at her outside my bedroom window while I'm talking on the phone. I knew she'd be devastated. He calls to tell me he'd married someone he'd known for like one week. He goes, "You're not saying anything, what do you think?" And I go, "To be honest, dude, I'm getting sick to my stomach." I wish I could have just rolled with it, but at that moment I was so close to Pinky because he had been with her for so long and we just all loved her so much. I just thought he belonged with Pinky. She was perfect for him.

RHIAN GITTINS: The summer before I met him was when he went to testify against his mother's killer. It was a really tough time. It affected him very deeply. I couldn't even begin to talk about it because I would never know what it was like. It was a fantastic amount of hurt, just endless grand canyons of pain.

JOHNNY NAVARRO: Rhian was very impulsive. Dave was very impulsive. Their whole relationship was like that. If Dave's really into you or into something like an idea or something, that's it. He will convince you. Dave could score heroin in the middle of a snowstorm. He was with her almost every day. When he gets this drive, you cannot divert him from his goal. He went after her with that appetite and she kind of matched that.

RHIAN GITTINS: We didn't live together. I loved him 100 percent. It was a crazy, silly thing to do and it had repercussions that neither of us realized at the time. His managers and lawyers freaked out the next day. They thought I wanted his money. I never wanted his money. I never took any when we got divorced. We broke up after a few months and I asked Dave for a divorce and he said, "OK" and sent me over the papers. I signed them and that was that. I didn't want anything. That wasn't what it was for. It was all for love and passion.

JOHNNY NAVARRO: After Dave and Rhian broke up, but they were still legally married, she hooked up with this guy Christian Stone from the band Campfire Girls who'd become buds with Dave. Dave had a lot of bad feeling toward that. When Christian ended up fucking Dave's wife, that caused this major rift between everybody in that circle. Dave freaked out and cut everybody off and felt horribly betrayed. They'd [already] officially split. He just didn't expect one of his closest friends would fuck his wife. It really hurt.

RHIAN GITTINS: My father is extremely angry about it to this day for not involving him [in my wedding] and he was angry at Dave for hurting me. He was obviously put out because he didn't get to walk me down the aisle. When a fire burns so brightly, so quickly, of course it's going to burn out just as fast. . . .

JOHNNY NAVARRO: Dave ended up producing a record around it, a solo effort called *Rhimorse*. Some of the songs eventually ended up on his solo album. This horrible pain he experienced, he ended up putting into the music. That record never got released, he just did it on his own and cut like 1,000 CDs.

RHIAN GITTINS: He recorded the *Rhimorse* record after our breakup.

ALAN DI PERNA (journalist, biographer): He explained [during an interview I did with him for *Guitar World* magazine] that he'd made the record in his home studio and that it was very personal and painful.

Kind of a catharsis or therapy. His way of talking about it was very strange, like he was reluctant to discuss something so "private" but at the same time he needed to "confess." He had a bunch of copies in a cardboard box with the cover art depicting his ex-wife's hand carving her name into his chest, with blood dripping from the letters. On the inside, there was a photo of the blood-splattered marriage certificate. I assumed he was giving me a copy, but he quickly took the disc out of my hand and said "Oh, no . . . you can't keep that."

DAVE NAVARRO: That record's filled with a lot of hate and bitterness. Not a very positive energy to put out there. My initial intent was to leave stacks of them for free at record stores. Just put them up at the register, and if anybody was interested, they could have it.[128]

RHIAN GITTINS: Some of the lyrics and even the title were bizarre. It was a pun on my name, spelled *Rhimorse*. Dave's a very funny person, but I don't think he meant it to be funny.

DAVE NAVARRO: It was potentially very hurtful to my ex-wife. And it gives away some pretty heavy secrets of mine. By the time I had the discs printed up, I'd decided I didn't want them out there.[129]

JOHNNY NAVARRO: There was a lot of spiteful shit in there. In the end he just kept them and never released them. Later on, he made peace with Rhian and Christian. Years later, they all made peace.

RHIAN GITTINS: I hold him very fondly in my heart and we're friendly now.

JOHNNY NAVARRO: Dave's not a mean guy, he's not spiteful. He finally came around [to thinking] "Hey, I had already broken up with her and I was probably banging three or four other girls at the same time anyway, so why should I care?" [He thought] if you're a guy's friend, you usually don't sleep with either his girlfriend, his ex-girlfriend or his ex-wife, unless you're clear with him first. That's kind of the unwritten code and Christian did not adhere to that code.

ALAN DI PERNA: My assignment for *Guitar World* magazine was to discuss Dave's role in the Red Hot Chili Peppers' *One Hot Minute* album and so an interview and photo shoot was set up at Dave's house in Hollywood.

TWIGGY RAMIREZ (musician, member of Marilyn Manson, A Perfect Circle): Dave was still in the Peppers when I first met him. We became friends afterward. We never really hung out too much because he was on the straight and narrow. That was the '90s and at the time I sure as hell wasn't. Our friendship really blossomed after we spent a straight summer together—we would play a lot in his house.

ALAN DI PERNA: Dave's pad was macabre all right, but also still and beautiful, with lots of heavy velvet drapery in burgundy, magenta, black . . . heaps of religious artifacts, crucifixes and Pagan icons were everywhere, way before that goth rococo bordello look became such a big design cliché. There was also a prie-dieu from a Catholic church with a cushion for kneeling, and a rail to rest your arms, and a big silver cross facing it with statuettes of Pan and skulls all over the mantelpiece. A Warhol *Electric Chair* print was hanging over the mantel. The living room coffee table was a real coffin; the entire wall of the dining room was covered in a huge blow-up of that famous photograph from the Vietnam War, where a prisoner is about to be executed. The gun is right up to the guy's head and he looks terrified. I asked him what was inside the coffin and he said, "Nothing. But a lot of stuff took place inside it. I can tell you that."

TWIGGY RAMIREZ: It sounds creepier and crazier than it really was. I guess I was desensitized to it after you see it for the first time. It was just a coffee table to me. I saw so much weird shit with Manson that something like that was no big deal.

ALAN DI PERNA: The bedroom downstairs was also lots of velvet. This divan had a human skeleton on it. Another skeleton was hanging by the bed. It was all so carefully and painstakingly arranged. Like an art installation. There was a photographer and many female assistants. Dave had a house full of women, so he was definitely "on" peacocking around shirtless in leather pants, showing off the "nipple rings and buff pecs" thing. He was also wearing quite a bit of makeup. When you're interviewing a male, presumably hetero, or bisexual rock star, the presence of women is a mixed blessing. On one hand it brings out this demonstrative, flirtatious "rooster" behavior on the guy's part, which can lend a lot of color to the piece you're writing, but at the same time it distracts your subject from focusing on the interview.

TWIGGY RAMIREZ: Dave had a shotgun. There were some accidents a few times that it went off when people were there. There was a hole blown into his wall. We're all just lucky to be alive.

DAVE NAVARRO: My shotgun went off and I shot a hole in the floor. I was really fucked up. I could have killed myself.[130]

ALAN DI PERNA: Dave appeared with this huge shotgun and started waving it around. He opened it up to show it wasn't loaded. But it was still disturbing when he pointed it right at me. He wanted to be photographed with it, along with his guitar, but the photographer was concerned that the magazine wouldn't dig something like that—that the shotgun would send the wrong message to *Guitar World's* impressionable, adolescent, metalhead readers. But Dave insisted. I can't remember if the photos were used or not.

TEETH

PERRY FARRELL: I started this website called TEETH. Initially we were asking people for money. So they wanted to read exactly what we were going to do. Thank God, it didn't work out. I just said I'd rather spend my own money and not know what I'm going to do. It's so much more fun with a person on the street, say, who asks, "Can I have five bucks?" And I say, "Well, I'll give you five bucks, but I want you to come into my website and tell me about life and do something on the computer—even though you've never worked with it. Do something artistic." And I'll put that up for the day. I could never have storyboarded that, because I didn't know there would be a man waiting for me asking for five dollars. Presupposition . . . forget about it. I'm not interested. It's a bore. There's no room for miracles.[131]

PAUL V.: TEETH was the beginning of the end of my working with Perry. They had an office set up in Venice where a lot of talking took place and I went there a few times. Lots of money was spent, lots of talking, but no concrete results really came of it. Perry was constantly hallucinating people. He was in total panic one time, yelling, "Get a gun! There's people on my roof! Stop them! They're trying to break in!" Perry would often spend a month at a hotel. One time he knocked a hole in the wall because he thought people were inside the wall of his room at the Mondrian. So he kicked the wall in to get at them. When cops came up they found a gun on him. This was also the Kim Leung period, his girlfriend Kim of the time, this Asian girl who had a child named Donovan, not by Perry. Perry loved that kid. Kim when she was sort of sober was nice and sweet but, oh my god, what a tragic mess on drugs, what a casualty. . . .

PORNO FOR PYROS

Circa Spring–Summer 1992

PERRY FARRELL: *The industry was constantly changing during the Porno for Pyros era. It was the end of the classic epoch era for the record business. Our beloved WB—the class act of the industry was crumbling around us. Mo Ostin and Lenny Waronker were eventually let go, which symbolized to many the ethnic cleansing of music people from the corporate music world which was hijacked by lawyers, accountants, and various other manicured Wall Street criminals during the 80s and 90s. It was great fun to watch if you were a fan of trainwreck mega-corporate blundering. But, unfortunately, I was standing right underneath this . . . my ass was roarin' in the thick of it.*

PETER DI STEFANO: I met Perry through Eric's friend Greg Lampkin. We went on a surf trip to Mexico and I shared a cabana with Perry and he heard me play some classical guitar, finger pickings and he was like wow, that's great, you should jam with me and Perk when we get back.

STEPHEN PERKINS: The first Porno for Pyros record was the result of three months of jamming in my garage. We thought, "Should we get a major producer? No, let's just use what we got, like the Jane's Triple X record."

PETER DI STEFANO: I kept saying no to Perry at first, not because I wasn't into it, anything but. It was because I knew the whole world was going to hate me. Jane's Addiction was everybody's favorite band and I knew that Perry wanted to do something different and I knew that I wasn't going to get a fair chance. They were going to compare me to a band that broke up at their peak. In the end I did it, put my head down and plowed through.

STEPHEN PERKINS: There are some great songs on that record, but it wasn't the next Jane's Addiction. It wasn't even supposed to be.

PETER DI STEFANO: There were a bunch of guitar players at this audition and everybody was going crazy trying their hardest to impress and I thought, "This is lame," so I packed up and left and that caught his attention. He goes, "Do you want to jam with Skate Master Tate and I?" So we got together and did "Orgasm," "Thick Meija," and "Blood Rag."

PETE WEISS: The day Martyn [Le Noble] got into Porno for Pyros they were having open auditions for a bass player. Casey was at the sign-in table, and if you looked cool enough—then they'd see if you could play.

MARTYN LE NOBLE (musician-songwriter, member Thelonious Monster, Porno for Pyros, Jane's Addiction, The Cult): I had already quit Thelonious Monster. Perry wanted to make sure that he wasn't pulling a bass player out of another band. So he called Pete and Bob and asked them. I guess I was the last guy to come in.

PETE WEISS: The Monster was a farm club for other bands, you know . . . like with [John] Frusciante and Chad [Smith] going into the Chili Peppers, and now Martyn's going into Porno for Pyros. Guys who hung out with us until something better came along.

PETER DI STEFANO: We were smoking crack cocaine and shooting heroin. Stephen didn't do any of the heavy stuff. He'd just smoke his weed. When you first start with that serious hard narcotics shit, it works for a second.

PERRY FARRELL: In Jane's I would wait until after the show [to get high]. In Porno I couldn't even sing if I wasn't on the pipe. I couldn't get out of bed, I couldn't move without it.

PETER DI STEFANO: I'm one of those guys, the only way you stop is if you put me in jail or hospital. I'm like Scott Weiland or Robert

Downey, Jr. You've got to lock me up or I won't stop. I'll lie for it, die for it, steal for it. It's just too powerful for me.

MARTYN LE NOBLE: Perry would say, OK, on Monday the tour starts—this on a Wednesday—so let's party until Friday, then we kick and on Monday we go on the road clean, which kind of worked for him, but not for me. Monday would come around and they'd be banging on my door and I would be passed out, strung out to the gills still. Perry would get clean, I would be loaded and then I would get clean and he would be loaded, so it was always a really unproductive, crazy, really miserable world which just got worse and worse.

PERRY FARRELL: In Jane's I'd see that we were off on tour in two weeks and I'd kick . . . it was important for me to be good onstage 'cause heroin cuts your notes out. Your throat can't open up. Even though everybody thought I was a junkie in Jane's Addiction, which I was, I was still able to pick my spots so I'd be able to sing good.

PETER DI STEFANO: We were partying with Kurt Cobain, smoking rock backstage at The Palace in Hollywood right before a Nirvana show. I remember him saying to Perry, "Who's this guy?" Perry goes, "This is my new guitar player." We were all talking about how great smoking coke was. We smoked it with him and then he went out and played his ass off.

PERRY FARRELL: You'll have to ask [Courtney Love] why she made [after-midnight] calls asking me to talk to Kurt about his continued depressed state. She might have admired the fact that I could break away from what I was doing, and take care of my business. I [always] had a way of getting out of bed and of going to work when I had to. She called me up for two reasons, one she was looking for him, and I don't know, you never really know what's in Courtney's head. She also asked me if I'd talk to him and I didn't really feel I had the right to. That's a very personal conversation. I had met Kurt a couple of times, but I didn't think I knew him that well that I could take him to the side and put my arm around him.

JOEY ALTRUDA: Perry asked me to play bass at a session for Porno for Pyros after my regular gig [Jump with Joey] at the King King. So I show up after two in the morning to Crystal Studios, what an aptly named place! Perry and Peter were doing heroin and crack.

PETER DI STEFANO: We wrote the first record in Venice and recorded it in Hollywood at Crystal Studios.

JOEY ALTRUDA: It was fun to just hang out and chill, but after awhile I got tired of screwing around and just wanted to play the song and go home. Perry was showing us how this thing would go on the guitar. We'd say, "Just show us the basic idea." We'd get it right away, but then he'd change it and do it differently. Or, he would miss it. Or he wouldn't be able to play the thing. It was 6:30, 7:30 in the morning and we were still dicking around with this really simple lick, but he'd keep changing it. The sun was up when I finally got out of there. . . .

MARTYN LE NOBLE: I cowrote pretty much all of the stuff, including "Pets" but never got proper credit. Perry had a very interesting structure. We went into the studio and recorded the whole record. Then Eric Greenspan, the attorney, came in and said, "We'll structure it like this. I suggest you get your own attorney." After Eric Greenspan left, Perry said, "When Dave and Eric got their own attorney, that's when I broke up Jane's Addiction." He was like, "You can get your own attorney, but if you do, this band will probably not exist."

JOHN FRUSCIANTE: Jane's music reminds me more of heroin and Porno reminds me more of crack. I know firsthand that Porno for Pyros was on crack all the time. . . .

PETER DI STEFANO: The first record it worked perfect, smoking rock and shooting heroin. . . . Matt Hyde and Perry co-produced the record. It took a couple of weeks of writing and two weeks of recording. That was it. The songs were all written coming off drugs. During drugs we never wrote.

<hr />

Circa April 1992

JOHN FRUSCIANTE: In Porno for Pyros . . . there was always drama going on around them. Martyn was always scoring drugs in weird places and getting into fights, getting into trouble.

MARTYN LE NOBLE: I take a lot of responsibility because I was a complete asshole. I was a junkie. I was unreliable, I was selfish, I was a jerk, just like everyone else, out of control.

JOHN FRUSCIANTE: Porno for Pyros had a much more street energy to it, like Martyn lived in a house with some Crips and stuff. . . .

MIKE WATT: The name Porno for Pyros comes out of the Rodney King riots in L.A. . . .

PERRY FARRELL: We [Martyn, Peter, and myself, not Stephen] went out and did our thing and rioted as well. We wanted to feel the street and the rush of what was going on. So we headed over toward Crenshaw. We were toting guns, that was like the years when I thought it was cool to carry a gun.

MARTYN LE NOBLE: We all got guns. I was in my own world of insanity. I was putting out fires with a garden hose and toting a gun at the same time. . . .

PETER DI STEFANO: That was the excitement during the L.A. riots. We went to South Central. We drove up the 10 to Crenshaw, got off, made a right, and just started partying right after the Rodney King verdict went down. I used to always carry a 25 anyway, and Perry also got a hold of a gat, I can't remember what.

PERRY FARRELL: We'd watch each other's backs and bust into stores along with the other locals. That's where I got all the furniture and bric-a-brac in my house. I don't have it anymore.

PETER DI STEFANO: We drove to this bank building [name omitted] and shot it all up. No one was in there. They'd closed it up and left so we didn't hurt anyone. No cops anywhere in sight. Then we shot up this electrical plant and when we were done with that we just looted all these stores.

MARTYN LE NOBLE: Palm trees were on fire, the liquor store on the corner was on fire.

PETER DI STEFANO: Fire and smoke everywhere. It was a crazy drug rush, total adrenalin. Perry decorated his whole house with looted stuff like couches and tables. It was a wicked time and a wicked record came out of it.

April 4, 1992

PETER DI STEFANO: The first official [Porno for Pyros] gig was the Magic Johnson AIDS Benefit at the Hollywood Palladium. The Chili Peppers played, The Beastie Boys and Fishbone played. . . .

JOHN FRUSCIANTE: Perry had this vest on with no shirt underneath and a chain in his pocket and suit pants and he looked really great. I thought Porno for Pyros was going to be this real sort of mellow thing. He was playing that harmonica type thing he plays and the music had this kind of ethnic feeling to it. I was blown away. It was my favorite Porno for Pyros show of all of them.

MARTYN LE NOBLE: The tour for the first record was great. "Pets" was on the national CMJ charts. It was fun, and it was miserable at the same time. It's hard to tour when you're a junkie. The music is not that important. Everything comes secondary to getting high, having to get well, which is a full-time job and nothing else gets done. There were wonderful moments, great shows, but also horrible shows and just misery.

Circa 1993

PETER DI STEFANO: The first Porno for Pyros single was "Pets," but the record company didn't pick it. They said "Pets"? No way, because the first line is "Children are innocent and teenagers are fucked up in the head/adults are even more fucked up" . . . but after Jed the Fish [DJ at K-ROQ] played the record in its entirety and everybody was calling in for "Pets" they very quickly changed their tune. The success of "Pets" helped the first album go gold.

MARTYN LE NOBLE: After we finished the record, we took a trip to Bali and I'd been awake for almost two weeks. I was so out of it I was seeing things crawling on the floor. I spent a day and a half on the floor. I couldn't move the left side of my body. It was completely paralyzed, my face, my legs, too. On the way to the airport Ted Gardner had a stack of contracts and said, "You've got to sign these."

I said, "I don't want to sign them. Can I sign them when I get back?" He started yelling at me, "Do you want to stop the release of this record for another six months? Do you want to make sure this record doesn't come out on time?" I was so high I couldn't even read. I'd been awake

for so long that I just sat in the back of the limo while he was flipping
the pages and signed everything.

GOOD GOD'S URGE

Circa 1996

PAUL V.: John Eder the photographer always wanted to work with
Perry. We said OK, we'll do some press shots. Maybe he can come up
with something great for the album cover. So of course the photo shoot
was an excuse to have a party at Shangri-La at night and everybody
was on hash and mushrooms and he came up with this great concept
of making a skirt out of the oranges, this sort of ethereal feel.

JOHN EDER: The first suggestion was that they all take mushrooms and
go out and look for flying saucers in the hills down by Zuma or something, which was a ridiculous idea for a photo shoot. Then they
wanted to throw a party at Shangri-La with weird costumes and stuff.
The house was really chaotic because they were moving out. It was the
last night they were supposed to be there and some other band was
coming in the next day. These girls came dressed as brides but they
were so fucked up they were absolutely undirectable. Juan Manuel,
this really fabulous designer from Argentina who'd worked with them
on clothing and stage sets throughout their Porno for Pyros career,
made that dress out of oranges that's on the cover. That cover shot with
Christina Cagle was one of the last shots of the whole night. We had to
beg her to get into that thing because she just wanted to lie down. As
soon as the guy with the mushrooms arrived, things started to get in-
creasingly chaotic and weird. People were getting really, really wasted.
One of the girls was seeing monsters and had locked herself in the
room where the makeup girl's stuff was. They had to crawl through the
window. At the peak of pandemonium we had all these people in crazy
South Seas outfits, sort of Fellini meets Sergeant Pepper's gone Tahiti
kind of feeling. Everybody's screaming and yelling and going wild and
I'm trying to direct them and the main light suddenly falls on my head.
It gets knocked over by this pizza guy, who'd wandered in and gone
back out to his car and got his Happy Snap, so we had to kick him out
and go back to shooting. Suddenly there's a tap on the window and it's

JOHN EDER: The cover with Christina Cagle was one of the last shots of the whole night. We had to beg her to get into that thing because she just wanted to lie down. (John Eder)

the cops. The sheriff of Malibu is out there. They said there's a guy in the hospital who said he was up here and he said he took some stuff called GHB—and we're not going to arrest anybody (because it wasn't illegal at the time) but we need a sample to take to the doctor. The party went to like 2:00/3:00 in the morning. Somebody else had to get carried out and rushed to the hospital from the same stuff. I guess if you drink on top of it, it will wipe you out.

PAUL V.: Working with Porno for Pyros was literally like holding a stick of dynamite and pinching a fuse three quarters of an inch before it goes off in your hand, but even on his worst, most drugged-out day, Perry was still one thousand times more creative and more real than someone else who is put up on this place of being the artist. He doesn't have to try. That really flows from his brain through him. It's a real energy that's inside him.

PETER DI STEFANO: The second record the drugs turned on us. We were tore up and trying to find God and health and going to islands and that's what that record is about.

PERRY FARRELL: With Porno, it all just caught up with me. I needed a lot before I could even go on. I never left my house without crack and some dope.

MARTYN LE NOBLE: I was so messed up. I was suicidal, I was miserable, I couldn't get clean. I wanted to get clean.

JOHN FRUSCIANTE: Porno for Pyros time . . . was just like this huge crack binge. Perry would get real close to overdosing on cocaine . . . he was smoking rock all the time.

MARTYN LE NOBLE: The second record took forever. I didn't stay around until the end. I accept responsibility for my share of being a fuckup, I'd be gone missing for weeks at a time. I'd say I had an errand to run, I'd say, "I'll be right back" in the middle of recording, but I was just going to cop. Three weeks later they'd get a phone call that I was in jail. From jail I ended up in rehab, from rehab I ended up in a psych ward, back into rehab.

STEPHEN PERKINS: The second record had all the songs written in Tahiti, in Fiji, in Mexico, all those songs and experiences came into the new record, that's why it's more exotic folkie and island-sounding. Less hard rock, 'cause it was written in Tahiti on an acoustic guitar.

MARTYN LE NOBLE: I didn't want to go to Fiji. They were going there to clean up, and [at one point] I was already clean. The last thing I wanted to do was watch two guys detox on the island. The really sad thing was the day they got back clean from that trip, I went and copped and did my disappearing act again.

PETER DI STEFANO: Fiji was another detox, buff and shine, another way to go and get off of dope without facing what we really had to do. It was always another excuse to get another surf trip. We spent a lot of money

They're all laughing and asking why I'm shooting them in the garage with stars in some backdrop when there were real stars in the sky outside. (John Eder)

In the thick of it all. (John Eder)

on these trips. They worked but only temporary. They'd help clean us up, we'd get strong, come back and then start partying and getting stuff done, but then we'd crumble in three or four weeks. We'd go out on another trip for a week, come back, work another week, crash again.

PAUL V.: I would think that if they could just come back one time and stay in that creative mode long enough to finish this record . . . but it was always just like putting a Band-Aid on a gunshot wound. They would soon have to go away again.

PETER DI STEFANO: We went to Porto Escotino, G-Land in Indonesia. We went to Java, we went to Sumatra, and we lived on a boat for a week in the Indonesian islands. We went to Bali two times. We'd been to Taberil, which is a small island off of Fiji. We'd been to Samoa. We'd been to Costa Rica, and then we'd been to San Blas, Santa Cruz, Puerto Vallarta, Mexico a lot. We went on probably ten to fifteen trips.

PAUL V.: *Good God's Urge* was basically all about a two-year surf trip with a little bit of intermittent recording occasionally going on. I couldn't get any help from Roger to reel them in because Roger was a surfer. Roger got to surf in Bali and Hawaii and whatever. He was like a pal that got to go play.

MARTYN LE NOBLE: We began recording the second album at Shangri-La Studios in Malibu where The Band filmed some scenes for *The Last Waltz*, the in-between-concert footage. Eric Clapton tracked a record there called "Shangri-La" and it's got a picture of him in the pool room looking extremely skinny and unhappy. Clapton was out of his mind there, the worst time of his life. The guy in The Band hung himself a few years later. We were the most unproductive ever there. Skinny Puppy the band there before us were never able to finish their record. They said Elvis used to stay there when he was shooting movies before he completely lost his mind. Some blues guy shot his dog there because he thought there were people outside or something. It seemed like the house had a curse—everyone who recorded or hung out there eventually lost their minds.

PAUL V.: I came in for the second Porno for Pyros album that took two years to make, and it probably took two years off my life! I thought, "This is such a cool move" because there was going to be two of us co-managing the band—myself and Roger Leonard. My role was more like the record company liaison guy because I had the background in radio, marketing, and promotion, while Roger would babysit the band and deal with their day-to-day drug-related dramas. Perry thought it would be good to have somebody from the inside who understood the band and all the problems and quirks to be the buffer between them and the label. It all very quickly turned into a nightmare. It was an extremely difficult, impossible situation for me. While Roger had 24/7 access to the band—he was like their surf buddy and always got to be the cool cop—I was stuck playing the party-pooper bad guy. Kind of like opposing parental roles; like, with Roger playing mom, we get to go surfing, we get to stay high, we get to go out to play all the time, but with Paul, it was like, boo, it's mean old man time! Here he comes now, dad the big drag, the buzzkiller, just bummin' everybody out . . . he's gonna make us do a video, he's gonna make us talk to some journalist for *Spin*, he's gonna make us go shake hands at some doofus radio station. He's gonna want to hear the tapes. I had to enforce all the business side of it that they just didn't want to do. Perry didn't want to do anything,

**Perry, Peter, and Stephen outside Shangri La. Warners publicity shot.
(John Eder)**

although on some other level if I wasn't bound by this job, I can't really
blame him [from being resentful about] having to deal with these
people, sort of like kissing babies and shaking reptilian hands when
you're trying your best to be creative with the music and you're out of
your mind on all manner of narcotics. . . .

MARTYN LE NOBLE: We paid all the expenses out equally, but if you look
at the publishing contracts you see that Porno for Pyros is all Perry Far-

rell; so when it says on the records, "All Songs Written by Porno for Pyros," it means it's Perry Farrell's company, he's the sole owner, and so he doles out the publishing as he sees fit. Basically, he screwed everybody out of their publishing. I was the only one that quit and so they settled with me, a pretty small settlement. Perry was really eager to settle because he didn't want Peter and Stephen to find out that this was how the business structure was set up. Basically, the longer you stayed in Porno for Pyros, the more money you owed the record company.

DAVID J: They were really stretching creatively on the second Porno for Pyros album. They were recording at this place where the band lived, some bungalows that once belonged to Elvis Presley in Malibu.

PAUL V.: It was a long drive to Shangri-La in Malibu from my HQ in Silverlake. Roger would be like, "Oh yeah, they're working on something very cool, it's a good day to come up," so I'd drive all the way up the coast and either Perry's door was locked shut or there's no one there. I'd talk to TJ, the guy who was co-producing the album with Perry. I'd be like, "Can you please, please play me something, anything?" He'd play me these little dribs and drabs of stuff, but remember I'm the one that's got the record company breathing down my back. What's going on up there? I really could not give them any tangible information or progress report because there was nothing to report. It was all very quickly making me look stupid. Peter used to drive me crazy because he had no spine. Great person, a fun guy to be with, but Perry sort of had him wrapped around his finger. Peter would worship at the feet of Perry, his idol. Because of the drugs Peter wasn't about to get sober when his hero wasn't. It was an endless cycle of everybody whacked out of their mind.

DAVE NAVARRO: Flea and I played on the second Porno for Pyros record. We're still friends with all those guys. It was great to see and play with Perry and Stephen again. I'd met Peter Di Stefano before, but this was the first time we played together. Peter comes up with great ideas as a guitarist, and it was great to jam with Steve again. Everything was fluid and loose. When Perry sang, I got the chills. There's something about playing with him that's magical. It's like playing with nobody else in the world.

DANIEL ASH: I got a call from Perry's manager or somebody, saying hey, Perry wants you to come down and do some guitar for the Porno for

Pyros record so I said great, fine, I'm there. Then I told the other two, David and Kevin, about it and they said we want to come as well, let's all go. So we all went down and we all ended up playing on the track.

DAVID J: The track was "Porpoise Head" and it was a documentation of one of Perry's extreme wigouts. He was living life very much on the edge at that time.

DANIEL ASH: I don't know what went on behind closed doors. We were recording with them one minute and the next minute we looked around and the whole band had disappeared.

PAUL V.: When we needed a video for the first song "Tahitian Moon," Perry's like I'll direct it. We're going to be in Tahiti so we'll just get footage from that. It was a total mess. They were high all the time. They had a film crew that cost a ridiculous amount of money, but we were barely able to pull together the kind of video MTV was demanding if they were going to play you in heavy rotation. It didn't need to be a million dollar video but it needed to not look like a home movie. Roger had literally saved Perry's life when they were in Tahiti. Perry was so high one night he drifted too far out into the ocean and just couldn't get back in. Thank God, Roger was able to rescue him. The lyrics to "Tahitian Moon" are all about that episode.

MARTYN LE NOBLE: I ended up playing on about eight songs. They're beautiful songs. Mike Watt played on some of it and it's amazing. David J. played on it, too. It's a great record, really beautiful. It's really a shame that no one gave it the attention it deserved.

PAUL V.: Kimberly Austin is a wonderful artist. She has one arm and Perry loved her work. . . .

DAVID J: We were recording the *Sweet F.A.* album and I had a song partly inspired by him . . . "Clean" that I wanted Perry to sing vocals on. It's about drug addiction and the chorus is "When are you clean?" He agreed to do it and the night of the session he didn't turn up. Stephen played percussion and I ended up doing the vocal myself. We heard later he had gone on a bender and was howling at the moon.

BOB FORREST: I went to visit Perry when Porno for Pyros were making the second album in this big house in Malibu. Since I was the homeless person crashing there, I was nominated to go with him to look under the house to see if anybody's there in the crawlspace!

MARTYN LE NOBLE: I remember that night! It was right before I quit. Bob and I got arrested the next day. Perry was so paranoid, so freaked out that you couldn't communicate with him anymore. I would constantly tell him that he was just seeing things. There are no people in the bushes, there's no one here trying to kill you, but Bob was playing along with that and crawling under the house. In Malibu the power goes off a lot and one time my alarm clock was flashing and I remembered that I'd put batteries in there so I opened it up to see a little wireless microphone in my alarm clock. It just sounds insane, but that's how it was. Another night I'm sleeping in bed and I wake up suddenly and Perry is standing over me with a knife, his hand shaking, and he had these crazy eyes and he goes, "Hide this for me," and he put the knife under my pillow. I was like, "Oh my god, he was going to *kill* me if I hadn't woken up right at that moment. . . "

JOHN FRUSCIANTE: Perry was so paranoid he had cameras everywhere in the house. Martyn said Perry had some bizarre dream, something to do with a little kid getting raped, and he was in such a state he couldn't distinguish reality from the dream. He was always thinking there were people lurking around. Martyn always thought there were cops outside. "Cocaine psychosis" we used to call it.

MARTYN LE NOBLE: We had armed bodyguards with submachine guns and shoulder holsters in this tree house and Perry was running around naked with a gun one night. These two hired goons were just laughing their asses off at us, milking it for all they could get. They'd be like snickering, "Hey, Perry, you know, I think we saw something last night—" that would be, like, another five grand . . . or whatever, and Perry would be just oblivious.

JOHN FRUSCIANTE: Martyn and I were hanging out all the time together. We'd be shooting up all day long in a room together, not a very glamorous life, but we were serious drug addicts who had to be doing heroin all the time just to feel normal.

MARTYN LE NOBLE: During one of my MIA episodes I drove back to the Shangri-La house, but was too embarrassed to go in because I was so high and out of it. I went into the garage and heard them walking into the kitchen, Peter, Stephen, and Perry, and they were talking about this asshole and what were they going to do with him. I decided that I should hang myself in the garage. I found some guitar cords and made a noose and tested it, but I was so fucked up that I lost my balance and fell.

JOHN FRUSCIANTE: We were just not healthy; they sent someone over to the house and they sent back a report that Martyn's not good, John's not good.

MARTYN LE NOBLE: I had one hand still in the noose and I just hung there suffocating and trying to scream for help. They walked back into the kitchen, but no one could hear me. It was the worst way to die. I ended up swinging with my hand between the noose and my neck until I was finally able to pull it far enough from my neck and to swing my feet on top of this old refrigerator in the corner. I didn't want to quite hang myself yet because I still had a bunch of drugs to do first! I was so embarrassed after I'd heard them talking about me that I just snuck out and disappeared again for a few more weeks and ended up in psych wards.

PETER DI STEFANO: We didn't even get a fair chance to tour behind the second record to promote it. So sad, such a great record gets neglected, abandoned. . . .

STEPHEN PERKINS: Unfortunately, we never toured real hard, we never got involved with pushing the record and trying to break it. I thought the songs were wonderful but we never spent the time and energy pushing it.

PETER DI STEFANO: We never even made it to a third record. The third record would be a cross between the first and the second. I don't know if we'll ever get to do it. We have a third record written. It's in my head. I have ten songs written, Perry's got the words and everything.

TED GARDNER: Porno was not given the opportunity to grow by critics and audience, because of the magnitude of Lollapalooza and the success of *Ritual*.[132]

MIKE WATT: People really had a negative view on these cats, outsiders. All this lame-o pre-opinion, pre-judge shit.

PAUL V.: When *Good God's Urge* came out it just landed with a thud. First of all it was sort of a mellow record. I personally think that five years from now, people will go back and listen and hear how genius that record is and how beautiful it is. It was way ahead of its time.

PERRY FARRELL: Musically I feel like we [Porno for Pyros] were extremely underappreciated.

WOODSTOCK '94

PAUL V.: It was like two days away from Woodstock '94 where Porno was booked to play the second day. We all got on the flights to New York we were supposed to get on. We wanted to be in on the Thursday just to be there a couple of days early, but Perry didn't take the flight. This was when Perry was really deep into the drug stuff. . . . So Friday we thought, OK, no big deal, Perry will take another flight. Perry doesn't take a flight on Friday. Saturday comes around and we think, OK, Perry will take the flight today, but he still doesn't show up. Turns out he's in San Francisco. Doesn't know how he got up there or why he was there but there he was. We were flipping out. What the hell were we supposed to do now? We were all like this is it, we're going to get sued. Porno's not playing, we're off the bill. We're fucked. Roger got him a limo or a car, or something, and got them to the airport, then we had to charter a special flight from San Francisco to New York, which cost another ten, twenty grand, at least. He finally arrives at like three in the morning. Then we had to shell out for a helicopter to take us upstate New York and it was raining the whole time. Woodstock '94 was this slithering mudfest and it was one of the worst sets they had ever played. Perry had been up for like five days straight doing drugs. Peter I think was high. I don't know about Martyn. We had to rent stage suits so we went to Western Costumers. Martyn was wearing this real cool green and yellow zoot thing and Peter got some wild suit on, too . . . Perry got this beautiful fluorescent purple number. Peter and Martyn never returned the suits. When you rent from a costumer they charge like $5,000. Poor Perry, if you watch the Woodstock footage, you can just see in his face like tension and exhaustion. It was all just bad, negative energy. They were playing some new songs from the new album that weren't really done yet. There were a few really great moments, but for the most part it was really sad. It was like this band should be on top of their game and they're barely grasping for air.

NOT GAY

Circa 1994

BRYAN RABIN: I eventually got to know Dave Navarro personally through clubs of mine and mutual friends. The Cherry Club. It was a mixed crowd . . . gay/straight/bi/tri/transgender . . . whatever . . . it was rich and famous, it was poor gutter kids with style, all of it brought together and we played alt. rock 'n' roll on Friday nights at several locations. Some glam stuff, some punk stuff, a really good mix of hard rock. The only people willing to dance to rock 'n' roll at that time were gays and drag queens . . . and . . . Perry Farrell . . . whose star pull during the early days helped boost Cherry's cachet. Perry was one of our club's first VIPs.

JOSEPH BROOKS: At Cherry we were playing retro rock in what had been the Backlot At Studio One (L.A.'s iconic first all-gay mega disco in the 70s), but this was '94, the straight club community in Los Angeles was really busy with hip-hop while we were playing "Been Caught Stealing."

BRYAN RABIN: Dave and Perry came to Cherry a lot during that period because it really embraced everything that they were and are still about . . . being provocative through dressing in a very androgynous way, and flirting with iconic homosexual imagery, classic rock 'n' roll things. Visually Perry and Dave tried to one-up each other. Perry would come down and dance to his own songs and have a great time. He came like three weeks in a row. Being around Perry was like watching a cult leader at work. He's an electric charismatic person when he walks into the room. People are drawn to him and are sexually attracted to him. They just want to be part of what he's doing. I've seen straight men get these weird crushes on him.

INGER LORRE: My boyfriend was always saying, "I'm not gay, but if there was any guy I'd like to be with, it would be Perry." One time [we were] partying at my place on Commonwealth Avenue with Perry. We just got really, really high. Perry was bugging me all night. A lot of girls think he's really hot, but he just wasn't my type so I kind of threw my boyfriend at him instead. He was one of the prettiest boys I ever dated, he might as well have been a girl . . . and that night . . . he just dropped jaw right there in front of me and gave Perry a blowjob on my couch. I was only mildly interested in watching my boyfriend getting skull-fucked by Perry Farrell. I was much more interested in my drugs and getting away from Perry. After the boyfriend did that, I broke up with him.

PERRY FARRELL: This guy gave me head. I'm not gay, I just wanted to see what it felt like. I thought, it's gonna be good because he's a guy. And he stunk. He went at it like he was eating corn on the cob.

BRYAN RABIN: By most standards Perry shouldn't even be a front man. He's a big, tall, skinny Jewish guy . . . but he's got that X factor, that thing that you can't quantify, that you can't put your finger on. He can make you feel like you're the only person in the room. That's an obvious classic sort of leader mentality, but he has an electricity that draws you to him in the first place.

ENIT FESTIVAL (1996)

PERRY FARRELL: *You know I lost a million dollars with that? Yeah, my money. I don't think I'll do that again. I was saying, "Screw you all, I'll put my own money up." There was no sponsorship. I was happy to do it, I don't regret it for a minute. So much good talent and such a good time. . . .*

ADAM SCHNEIDER: The ENIT Festival was an early attempt at merging alternative rock with the electronic acts that same year with Porno for Pyros and Love & Rockets co-headlining with the Orb, the Sun Ra Arkestra, and others.

PERRY FARRELL: A lot of those anonymous electronic producers are extremely talented people. . . .

DANIEL ASH: We had a meeting with Perry and he had all these fantastic ideas, bring in circus acts and really open it all out and introduce dance music and alternative artists to the rock 'n' roll artists, and vice versa, if you like, leaning heavily toward the whole dance culture that had been going on in England for quite some time.

DAVID J: I remember Perry coming up with the idea for ENIT when we were at Timothy Leary's house. Perry was going off . . . it wasn't just a music festival, ENIT was going to attract *extraterrestrials!* These ENIT festivals would be staged simultaneously on other planets and would all be hooked up via satellite. He was going right out there. Tim was up there with him. No limit to his imagination. So far-reaching, wildly adventurous, reaching in all directions. In that way, Perry was a true son of Leary and Sun Ra. I think sometimes, just as with Tim, the drugs got in the way. They were constructive to a degree but then they became detrimental.

MIKE WATT: He was always looking at it like someone in the crowd who thinks, "Hey, I want to see something that I don't see with the other bands." Perr's whole thing about ENIT was not to have them at regular same old, same old venues. Get out in the woods and stuff. Go anywhere but the norm. He ran into a lot of problems with that. A lot of promoters didn't want to do it.

DANIEL ASH: Originally there was going to be between twenty and thirty gigs but it eventually got condensed down to five or six, because of screwups with management and organization.

ADAM SCHNEIDER: All of the money Perry made on Lollapalooza '96 he poured into his own festival. [Love & Rockets, as well as Black Grape and Buju Banton later pulled out of ENIT; and due to poor ticket sales, many of the dates were canceled.]

PAUL V.: ENIT crumbled pretty steadily where a lot of people who were supposed to be in it changed their mind and it fell apart and Perry had to foot the bill. ENIT was a great idea and Perry could have made it something better. He did what he could with the situation because he was still with Kim Leung at that point. As long as Kim was in the picture not a lot was going to get done.

MIKE WATT: I did three tours [playing bass] with Porno: the ENIT tour, a U.S. tour, and an Australia/New Zealand tour. I had never played the sideman role before. Some of these guys were famous so there was a lot of hype associated with them that I never had to deal with before. In the music media world it turned into this huge hyped-up thing, an "alternative super group." I hated the whole idea of that "alternative" shtick as a way of selling things in the early 90s.

PAUL V.: Perry Farrell is an artist in every sense of the word. He's a visual artist, he's a musician, he's a singer, but he doesn't create hoping to line his pockets. He creates in the hopes of turning people on and bringing them in to his ideas. Very few people can say that and back it up for real.

MIKE WATT: What hurt Perr real bad was the last ENIT tour. It cost him a lot of bones. He put his fucking heart and soul, even his own cash into it. We were in Miami. His dad was dying, and he tells his pop I'm putting up my own moolah into this. It was a heavy time. People try to disrespect him as superfluous, but the dude is pretty real. Coming from the Minutemen I see almost everything as a splurge. I don't use hotels. I conk at peoples' houses still. I was like, "Hey, I'm on the deck. You can put me on the fucking deck of the bus and save some bones." It was a privilege to play the music. I didn't need all that shit. I'm not used to it. That shit adds up real quick and then he's bringing in the dancers because he wants a spectacle.

PETER DI STEFANO: If I tanked my life's savings, I would be devastated. I didn't hear about that until after. Everything came out of his pocket. Perry's very generous. I just showed up at the end and partied. That was all Perry's doing.

MIKE WATT: That was one of the big heartbreaks for me. I just didn't dig the idea of everybody partying with Perr's money. Perr took all the risk. But then you hear the bitching and the moaning. I'll stand behind him 100 percent. There was a lot of expectation put on it. He was really going to have fun and really blow it up and maybe change the business of rock a little bit.

JOSH RICHMAN: Perry would put his own cash into anything he believed in. Lollapalooza made him money, but Perry felt that Lollapalooza was no more important or valuable an idea than ENIT. He's succeeded, he's failed, but he's always had the balls to put himself out there. . . .

DANIEL ASH: Money wasn't everything for Perry. That's why he's successful. He's an optimist.

PERRY FARRELL: I'm not interested in the money, I prefer to draw from the spirit world. . . .

❧

MIKE WATT: The ENIT show at Big Bear was great in every way, the production, the sounds, the lights. Flawless. Spot on. It was a ski lodge out in the woods, which was neat.

DANIEL ASH: That was a crazy night, a hell of a good time. I got totally plastered on lots of different things. I remember seeing Perry and thinking, "Jesus, how skinny is this guy?" He looked like he was under a lot of stress. He was like skin and bone, but having a great time still.

PERRY FARRELL: That was the longest I've ever French-kissed a guy. Daniel holds the record.

DANIEL ASH: I was in a good mood. I was high and I went to the front of the stage and started acting like a fan and waving my arms and everything just as a joke. Then somebody pulled me up on stage—I can't remember who—and we were dancing around. I sort of jumped on Perry, wrestled him to the floor, we were both laughing and joking and that's all I remember. . . .

PETER DI STEFANO: Daniel Ash just came out at the end, drunk as a skunk and had some fun. It was just a joke. He came out and sang with us and slapped Perry on the ears. It was all great fun. He got caught up in the moment. He wanted to jump on stage. I was on ecstasy and heroin. That show was the best, and the one in New York.

MIKE WATT: Perry hears everything. He's like a conductor with a baton except with his hands. I'd watch his hands. I could always tell when I was too loud or too bassy. He ran us tight. [Some thought] the guy was out of his fucking mind and oblivious. Bullshit, I was on stage with him. He had that shit down. He could hear the smallest clam, when one single note was sour ass. He told me one time about knocking

Dave Navarro out [after he wouldn't stop playing in between songs]. He was like, "Dude, the song finished already!" BAM!

✦ ⌁⌁⌁⌁⌁ ✦

JOHN FRUSCIANTE: Martyn had been out of the public eye for about six months when Perry called him up about playing in Porno again.

MARTYN LE NOBLE: I had already been out of the band for nine months, or something, and Mike Watt had been touring with them in my place. I was still living with John [Frusciante] and we were both still in horrible shape, just the worst shape. I got a phone call from Perry. They were playing at the American Legion Hall. He asked me if I wanted to play a show with them and join Porno for Pyros again. I said sure. Perry sent over these food baskets in preparation for the show to get us healthy.

JOHN FRUSCIANTE: It seemed like this big offer was coming out of heaven or something. Martyn was going to play a song or two at the end. . . .

MARTYN LE NOBLE: Mike was going to do the first part of the show and halfway through I was going to finish it or play a couple of songs. Showtime I'm standing on the side of the stage with John, Christina Applegate—she was kind of watching me at the time, trying to save my life—and then it's my turn to go on. I walked out and Mike unplugs his bass and hands me the cable and suddenly Perry goes, "No, no, no . . . get off, get him off, get him outta here!" he shoo'd me off like an animal, like a dog, like in front of all these people. I was like, "Oh my god. What's happening to me?"

JOHN FRUSCIANTE: That fucking hurt Martyn's feelings. Watt was crying afterwards because he felt so bad about being put in the middle of this weird dispute. I'm not judging the situation, I'm not saying Perry was right or wrong, but I never heard an actual concrete explanation. When Perry called it off at the last second it was such a bummer that messed Martyn's head up even more. . . .

MARTYN LE NOBLE: I walked back off the stage and sat there and said what the fuck? What just happened? Mike comes off the stage and he's crying and he goes, "I'm so sorry, that's so fucked up." I left. Although

I was really fucked up when I got there, I would still have been able to play. He could have dismissed me from off the stage. He could have walked over to me at the side, but it was in front of everyone.

"RELAPSE" (1997) THREE-MONTH TOUR

DAVE NAVARRO (to Alan di Perna in '96): *Personally, I don't want to be out on tour past the age of thirty.*

BRYAN RABIN: When Jane's re-formed in '97, Flea was standing in for Eric. I had really emotional feelings. I didn't want to see something once great that I'd come of age watching . . . now old, tired, and stupid. I needn't have worried for a second. Perry still was able to stir a cauldron and whip up this incredible frenzy. When you go see this band, you never feel like, oh, I'm in the Park Plaza or I'm in the Forum. You completely get transported, time stands till, and you don't want it to end.

PERRY FARRELL: I only did it because I thought it would be fun. Before this is not viable anymore, I wanted to do it one more time, have a good time with some friends and let it be that, but I'm already drained. I'm already starting to feel worn down, my words are not coming as quickly as I wish they would.[133]

STEPHEN PERKINS: Dave and Flea started hanging out with us and helping out with Porno after Pete was diagnosed with testicular cancer shortly after *Good God's Urge* was finished. Knock on wood, he survived and he's doing great. It all started when we did a song together ("Hard Charger") for the Howard Stern movie *Private Parts*.

JANE BAINTER: Eric and Perry tried to reconcile. They went to lunch to talk about it, but they just weren't able to work it out. I think it's a total mutual lack of toleration, like: "I already understand what you're all about and I'm not going to deal with it anymore. Can't. Won't."

ERIC AVERY: I just didn't want to drag the old whore out and dress her up again.

PERRY FARRELL: We weren't friends. I felt I was working very hard, not being appreciated, and uh . . . I wanna go and do my thing and I wanna be able to express myself and I don't want to have to play games with people to do that.[134] I wish he would have just said let's play some more. That would have made me so happy. If I was wrong, then that's a drag and I should be ashamed of myself. But then again, if he was wrong, he should be ashamed of himself. We could have been playing these songs together, and I don't know if he's going to have a situation like that again in his lifetime, but I've sized it up and surmised that this could be the great blessing that I've been given in my life so I should not throw it out the window. He should have hung in there.

(The worst part was that it showed that I was part of a group of people that couldn't get along. In the Jewish religion, all debts are forgiven. I thought it would be great to say, "Whatever happened in the past, let's just forget about it. Let's start over. We had a past together. We had a success together. Let's go off and, for the people, have a great time, and have them have a great time.")[135]

ERIC AVERY: Perry called [to ask me to rejoin] and I said I'd think about it. So we got together for lunch. I was looking at it more as an opportunity to heal the rift on a personal level. I wanted to say, "Let's each agree to just go our separate way as friends." It was going that way until he asked me if I wanted to come back and when I said no he just flipped out. He was just so angry. And I said, "I'm really sorry it's going this way, Perry. I'd hoped that we could part as friends today." And he said, "We were *never* friends!"

PERRY FARRELL: He knew very well why I was asking him to lunch—to invite him back to play and tour with us again. He could have said politely, you know, it's not going to happen. He could have saved me the heartache of winding my hopes up and then embarrassing me at the end of the meal by saying no. He could have just been upfront and said no, and I would have accepted it, but it was Eric's mind game to see me squirm. That's kind of the wrong time to say to a guy, "Hey, I know I just crushed you, but let's be *friends*." Ever see a cop beat the crap out of a guy and when he's putting him in the car he says, "Watch your head?" *Fuck you.*

CASEY NICCOLI: Perry never even apologized, which might have gone a long way. . . .

MARTYN LE NOBLE: I was doing a reunion show with Porno for Pyros for the Tibetan Freedom Concert right before the Relapse Tour. They were already working on the Jane's reunion from behind the scenes. A few people in Perry's organization came up to me and said, "Congratulations, you're going to be in Jane's Addiction." I was like, "Really? I am?" But I never heard about it again so I went back to Atlanta where I was living at that time and Flea ended up doing that tour, which in retrospect was probably a good thing because I was newly clean.

STEPHEN PERKINS: We just decided, "Let's do Jane's Addiction with Flea."

FLEA: Stephen called to ask me to play. I said, "Hold on, let me check my schedule." About two milliseconds later I came back and said, "Okay."[136]

PERRY FARRELL: We'd been old, old friends with Flea. I remember running into him at parties, seeing him and always admiring him. I went through Stephen to make the connection, cause I figured to get to a bass player's heart, you go through a drummer. Just like the way to a man's heart is through his stomach.

FLEA: They asked me [to play bass on the Relapse Tour]. I tried to be as faithful as possible to what Eric did. I really wanted to honor that. I didn't want to interject my own personality into it at all. It was like being asked to play in some great epic band [like] the Jimi Hendrix Experience . . . or Led Zeppelin or Joy Division. . . .

JOHNNY NAVARRO: Dave was straight when he entered the Peppers and straight at the end of the Peppers, although there was a relapse toward the end. He stepped out of the Peppers and relapsed again during the first Jane's reunion tour in '97.

ADAM SCHNEIDER: Relapse was an aptly named tour.

DAN NAVARRO: The first reunion with Flea was a very, very tough time for me. Dave was not in great shape. I was extremely angry that he'd thrown away six years of sobriety. I was absolutely petrified for him and he wasn't very communicative and I didn't see him for a year after that. It was heartbreaking. I was afraid of losing him. None of his family knew where he was headed.

BRYAN RABIN: During the reform in '97, Nancy Berry was having these incredible, unbelievable parties. Ken Berry's wife from Virgin Records. What I read about Led Zeppelin and Keith Moon at The "Riot Hyatt" [iconic Sunset Strip hotel] in the 70s, that's what these parties were like. Nancy was at a fever pitch. They lived in this huge house in Bel-Air and they would send all their neighbors to this hotel so's they could rock all night full blast.

FLEA: There was some severe, crazy decadence going on.

PERRY FARRELL: The problem that a lot of people have with me is that I'm having a good time. It's not even that they disapprove of what I do, it's just that I'm doing it, and they're not.[137]

BRYAN RABIN: It was the after-party for some event I can't remember and every rock star on the planet of every generation was there. Jagger, Janet Jackson, Courtney Love, Marilyn Manson, the Pumpkins, Dave Navarro, Trent Reznor. Every star of the mid- to late 90s was there. I was thinking, this is insanity, there's so many drugs up here, so much booze, somebody's going to die. These parties would start late and they were just so reckless. I'd be astounded—and I'm in the business of throwing extravagant parties myself—my mouth would be hanging open watching obscene amounts of money pissed away on these things. . . .

DAVE NAVARRO: I had an amazing time. I have very little memory of it.

TWIGGY RAMIREZ: One time Dave and I went to the Playboy Mansion. It was my first time there. We literally walked straight through the party, went into the bathroom and I did a couple of lines of coke. Dave tied off his arm with one of my dreadlocks and began to shoot up his drugs. We looked at each other—our skin was crawling—and we just ran out of the place because we were too paranoid, too creeped out by the people there, and this awful reptilian girl somehow slithered into the limo with us before we knew what was happening. When we got home she took a big crap in Dave's toilet, but the stool wouldn't flush down and she wouldn't fess up to pooping in the bowl no matter how much Dave tortured her about it . . . he made her feel this deep excremental shame, he was calling her The Pooper for the rest of the night.

BRYAN RABIN: We were sitting in some hut around the pool and these little makeout areas. The starlet Monet Mazur at the time was with Dave. Marilyn Manson. Maybe Rose McGowan was there, too, but definitely the Manson crew, Twiggy and Manson. About seven of us sitting around partying. It was late, around 3:30, 4 A.M. Dave is wearing ladies intimates with this draggy, Maribou feather kind of shock walker situation and there's Marilyn in full Alice Cooper drag. Two straight spooks facing each other off at four in the morning—the one straight guy is wearing a cape and fangs and the other straight guy is in a Maribou feather nightie. Dave was so loaded I just couldn't resist it. I convinced him to blow Manson so he got down on his knees.

TWIGGY RAMIREZ: That story has been told so many times that I don't know what's real and what's fake anymore. I think it was probably something that was just said as kidding around and the story and the mythology of the whole thing just took over. It was really nothing more than a friendly thing.

BRYAN RABIN: After a while, it was like, OK, OK . . . a joke is a joke, right? Finally, it all became so ridiculous I just lost it. I went off on Dave, "You came from such a vibrant, creative scene at the beginning . . . dude, I *idolized* you . . . why do you become such a sick, pathetic caricature? What the fuck is *wrong* with you?" I was like, "Dude, you're in your thirties . . . and you're trolloping around in women's panties and Maribou at four o'clock in the morning, still taking crazy amounts of drugs, trying to jack off a fading rockstar in public?" I took a picture with Monet's camera. Somebody stole the print she had made up. That photograph was floating around Hollywood.

MARILYN MANSON: I [was] in a Los Angeles hotel room trying to keep Jane's Addiction guitarist, Dave Navarro, from giving me a blow job as we sniffed drugs together. Dave ended up in the room of my bassist, Twiggy Ramirez, who had ordered two expensive prostitutes and was busy fucking them to the beat of ZZ Top's *Eliminator*.[138]

TWIGGY RAMIREZ: When Dave fell off the wagon and was partying again I was goin' at it full throttle, too. I was living at the Argyle and he brought some girls over and we were listening to ZZ Top's *Eliminator* really loud and having sex with these terrible girls. Maybe that's where this story comes from.

PERRY FARRELL: The '97 tour was one of the greatest I've ever been a part of. I disappeared a lot because I would be getting high. It was my whole life. We had an amazing group of dancers, among them was my future wife, who I met for the first time. And the antics, the wild times we had onstage and off, you can't buy times like that.

FLEA: It started off being absolutely incredible . . . some of the best feelings and shows and energy that I've ever felt in my life . . . complete power. But it ended up being sporadic, then terrible. Because of drugs, it became a complete fucking mess. The focus got diluted. People still liked it, but I just knew what it could be because I knew what it was in the beginning of that tour and it was a mighty, mighty thing. It could be that my perspective isn't good. I don't know. Other people thought it was cosmic genius.

PERRY FARRELL: Flea would say [years later] damn you guys, if you wouldn't have been so wasted, you would have been so great, but I thought it was amazing.

CHRIS CUFFARO: During the Relapse tour stop in Vegas, there was all sorts of drama going on. I remember going to Dave's room and I think Slash was there. Dave was back to that horrible old negative drug energy, not a lot of smiles. I was, like, here we go again. I hated the feeling I got of seeing him like that. Dave on drugs and Dave off of drugs, it's two different people, and when he's off them he's the nicest, sweetest guy with the biggest heart. I always tell people, "Don't let the looks deceive you. Behind the tats, the crazy makeup, the outlandish costumes, and the good looks is this geeky little insecure guy!"

PERRY FARRELL: *Three Days.* Watch the movie, it will tell you a lot.

LEVITICUS 25:9–25:11
The Laws of Jubilee

Circa 1997–99

PERRY FARRELL: Aaron Chason and I have been trippy friends since '91. I worked on *Gift* with him. Then he disappeared and resurfaced, having graduated from yeshiva, which is Talmudic studies. In 1999, he came to me proclaiming Jubilee, which is a fifty-year cycle where we are encouraged to free slaves and bring people together through massive parties and gatherings. Aaron figured I was the guy for the mission and so he set out to teach me about Jubilee. We went on to study Torah and Kabbalah. I'd also gotten heavily into electronic music and computer software and had written a solo album, and wanted to go out and proclaim freedom. I needed the best band I could think of to do a tour, and that was Jane's Addiction. So we got back together [in 2001], and we ended up raising money and freeing about 8,000 people out of Sudan. When the hour of Jubilee struck in 2000 that's what brought the band back together to record.

STEPHEN PERKINS: We raised $120K on the Jubilee tour and took it into Sudan and freed slaves, actually bought slaves, $4K a slave. Used Jane's money and did something, and I feel like we can do it again. Let's do something for the environment.

LEVITICUS 18:22

PERRY FARRELL (in 2003): The Hasidic community does not give consent to homosexuality.

PERRY FARRELL (to Yoko Ono in 1996): I would like to head toward Venus. I would like to be privileged to live there. Which doesn't mean I'd be material. If you could resonate at the unconditional love vibration, you would be able to live amongst the Venusians. And the Venusians could have these beautiful orgies that include having sex with men and women and children and animals. Anything your heart desired. Of course, you can never abuse anything. But there would be these tremendous orgies.[139]

PERRY FARRELL [to Mat Snow in *Q* magazine, 1991]: I like tripping up machismo. I like intermingling the macho and the feminine. I don't know why. I like hitting certain sensations with people, and one of the heaviest sensations is forcing people to feel sexually about things they keep blocking out—even murder. I think that's why people are pissed off at me. Maybe this comes from doing acid, but I believe everything is so relative, so cyclical, that I can argue any point on any side for hours and feel comfortable about it.[140]

PERRY FARRELL [from the *Ritual* booklet, 1990]: I'd like to see men love and romance instead of macho, which is so fake and phony. Nobody should feel ashamed or dumb, but feel love and honesty, bisexuality, homosexuality, heterosexuality, anything.

PERRY FARRELL [to *Q* magazine in 1991]: I don't see anything good coming out of suppression.[141]

RABBI YOSEF LANGER: If you're only inclined to have relationships with men [homosexuality is an abomination, according to Leviticus 18:22] and nothing else works for you, then yes, you have to be celibate.

PERRY FARRELL: He's my rabbi, I love him. We met him on tour in '97. Used to be Bill Graham's rabbi. He's a cat who drives a Harley Davidson with a sidecar through San Francisco. [Somebody] you can sit down and talk with, he doesn't judge you. I can guarantee you that if you went up and told him that you were gay, he'd sit down and have a drink with you.

PAUL V.: That's the problem with any religion. If you want to be spiritual or be attached to a religion and you're not homophobic, it's really hard to be the guy who goes to these institutions, "I want to change this retarded thinking, this bogus misinterpretation of virtue you've been spreading for thousands of years." Apparently Perry doesn't seem willing or capable anymore of upholding any of his stated beliefs from the 90s in his current approach to "enlightened spirituality."

PERRY FARRELL: Look, I can't defend all the actions of this rabbi. This guy is a good guy, and he's a San Francisco Rabbi Hasidic willing to sit and talk with anybody one to one, but at the same time . . . and, by the way, he's the head of the Hasidic community, so that means he's no rogue rabbi . . . he has responsibilities to the Hasidic community . . . and the Hasidic community does not give consent to homosexuality.

PAUL V.: Try telling the leaders of these big religious sects, like Christianity, Judaism, and even Islam: "Hey, you're all damned hypocrites, the whole bunch of you . . . no matter how cool and pure and virtuous you all think you are, you're still nurturing and upholding prejudice as a standard, and prejudice breeds nothing but hatred . . . this in the name of your almighty God of all-knowing goodness and justice?"

ENTER: DJ PERETZ, KING OF PURIMPALOOZA

ANDREW WALLENSTEIN (journalist, contributor to *The Forward*): At the Sabbath meal, conversation turned to the impending holiday. I asked the young rabbi across the table how the Bay Area community planned to celebrate. He said, "You've heard of Lollapalooza? We've got Purimpalooza . . . a scaled-down version with a Jewish flavor." He proudly ticked off the names of the scheduled acts, including Mozaik, DJ Mars and DJ Peretz.[142]

DJ PERETZ: I love electronic music. I started DJ-ing six years ago at my studio in Venice Beach. I would throw parties and hang out with ravers and young people who were writing electronic music. Serious young digital producers. They just kind of talked me through the process and the lifestyle. It's a whole other world that was at one time underground then surfaced in a big way and has recently sunk back down into the underground. But it's not going to go away just as surely as alternative music never went away.

ANDREW WALLENSTEIN: The rabbi described Perry Farrell's transformation from rock 'n' roll rebel to ba'al teshuva, a Jew who has returned to the faith. Perry [apparently] got caught up in the trendy kabbala movement sweeping Los Angeles and had changed his name to Peretz. This rabbi said he'd recently hung out with Perry at his home in Venice, where they wrapped tefillin and learned together.[143]

PERRY FARRELL (to Dean Kuipers in '98): You're not talking to a guy who has always felt a connection with Israel. I didn't like Jews. I didn't like being Jewish. I was bummed. I didn't practice Judaism, which I don't think is the most important thing anyway. Music is the definitive form of religion. Music and mathematics everybody understands equally. The beauty of the Jews, I saw as I got older, is in the brilliance of their metaphysics. It's a beautiful system. I think they're incredible people. But I think everyone's incredible. I would like to see everyone dancing.[144]

ANDREW WALLENSTEIN: Purimpalooza was held at the Great American Music Hall in downtown San Francisco. Hundreds of Jews of all denominations were there, some in costume. Sweat and marijuana permeated the air. Mozaik was an eight-person band in loopy costumes who looked like a white version of George Clinton's P-Funk All-Stars. Dancing veered between religious and secular; we were kicking our feet out in a circle one moment, undulating to trance music the next. It was difficult to distinguish whether the many long-bearded men in attendance were charedi or hippie, or both; one man had dyed parts of his facial hair purple for the holiday, but his gartel, the black band worn by some religious Jews, indicated he was clearly the former. Wavy Gravy, the iconic Grateful Dead associate, emceed in a star-spangled jester outfit, holding a plastic fish on the end of a leash; gamely acting the part of King Ahasuerus in a silly skit that told the story of Purim.[145]

DJ PERETZ: When I started DJ'ing it was overwhelming and the fuckups were the most embarrassing moments of my life. It's no easy thing. Aside from honing your technique, which can take a long time, you have your taste. You're the selector and oh my gosh, a great selector can be not that great of a mixer, but his collection can be so amazing. I'm hoping that I can continue to develop my DJ-ing. It's progressive, tech house, and I've been known to bust out drum 'n' bass or some badass jungle.

ANDREW WALLENSTEIN: Finally DJ Peretz took to the stage wearing a wide-brimmed hat and a Nehru jacket and proceeded to play perhaps the lousiest music of the evening, a watered-down trance music with little of the passionate intensity of his past rock recordings. The Jewish content of his new material consisted of his mewling Hebrew words over a trippy beat. I was only able to make out one word: "eeshah," which means *woman*.[146]

JOSH RICHMAN: Perry got heavily into his heritage as a Jew. We often speak or sing at the Seder we both go to every year at Guy Oseary's house where Perry sings "Daiyenu." Perry's made all these pilgrimages to Israel and stuff. He's definitely not the secular guy. There's your Hasidic Orthodox Jews who are just as secular as anyone else, and there's like three or four different versions of it. I think Perry follows a more open-minded thing but he also does some very hard-core Judaic things. He wraps tefillin, and he's very heavily involved in that process in his life and his children have these really beautiful Hebrew names.

PERRY FARRELL: Any Jew will say yes for Israel because it's where we come from. It's our families' background and it's our turf. A good rabbi would also say that it's a democratic society and all are welcome. We would never think to take anybody off the land as long as people living on the land had respect for the land. If you want to be a Christian or a Palestinian or a Buddhist, you can live on the land as long as you're not disrespecting the people. There's borders that are in Torah and we can all read them together. They're strict borders. The [Zionist] expansionism issue is very debatable. Read the Bible and it will tell you the borders of Israel. It's very clear where the border is. Go back to the Torah, which is the oldest known deed of that land that there is. We're not supposed to expand into other people's turf. Jews don't want to go up into Europe. Jews are not a better race of anybody. There's a certain quotient of them that are rotten. Just like anybody. Nobody escapes it.

STRAYS (2002–03)

PERRY FARRELL: Hopefully I'll get my money back this time. We worked collectively. We went out and did a bunch of shows to get the money . . . and pooled it.

STEPHEN PERKINS: It all started [around March or April 2002] with Bob Ezrin producing a Porno for Pyros track for the movie *Dark Blues* . . . an incredible song called "Streets on Fire" which was just epic. That segued into the *Strays* project.

PERRY FARRELL: Working with Bob Ezrin on *Strays* meant a lot because I knew that Dave loved Pink Floyd's *The Wall*, which Ezrin produced. Dave learned *The Wall* [as a kid]. He can play the whole album note for note. I knew he'd instantly have a lot of respect for him.

Cover of *Strays*.

MARTYN LE NOBLE: I was finally clean and joined Jane's Addiction and I played Coachella with them, we did an arena tour around the U.S. I had an agreement till the end of the year—and then they decided to make a record. We went into the studio, I was not getting paid upfront. I was recording, I was doing the shows, I was writing. I cowrote a bunch of the songs. Finally, we came to an agreement on how much they owed me and what kind of percentage and all this business stuff, which is important when you have kids and when you have a history with these people with finances. I was supposed to get paid retroactively because I had already been recording for three months.

PERRY FARRELL: We started recording on our own collective dime, and of course if you're recording with your own money soon enough you'll need more of it because you start to run dry. We booked other shows, other tours, played other festivals. We finally got to some places we had never gotten to, like Japan; we played the Big Day Out festival and went to Europe to play the big open-air festivals, like Reading. . . .

BOB EZRIN (musician, record producer): My job on *Strays* was to bring a sort of commonality to the process and make everyone think it was a group effort again and not just a bunch of solo projects trying to be strung together.

MARTYN LE NOBLE: I recorded pretty much the whole *Strays* record. And then Perry erased it. He suddenly fired me on the spot in Japan when we still had a whole flight back to the U.S. That's the last time I talked to him.

DAVE JERDEN: [new Jane's Addiction member] Chris Chaney is an amazing bass player. Chris Chaney played with Alanis Morrisette and now Eric is playing with her. They kind of switched spots.[147]

MARTYN LE NOBLE: Bob Ezrin didn't really understand Jane's Addiction musically. I remember arguing with him, "Like man, have you listened to *Ritual*?" He goes, "Frankly, I can't get through it. I think it sounds horrible. I'm going to make this a real rock band instead of an art rock band." Well, he succeeded. He took all the magic out of it. He made a rock record. The most magical moments on the Jane's Addiction records are the quiet little adventures to the left, and, of course Eric's magic bass. Eric Avery is the Man.

DANIEL ASH: Frankly, the quieter, those more soulful ballads, the slower numbers with less hard rock bombast were always my favorite moments of Jane's Addiction's music. . . .

REBECCA AVERY: When *Strays* came out I was sure now the world's really going to know how much the band needed Eric's creative input. Of course, I'm his sister, and, of course, I'm extremely biased, but it seemed that soul was sort of missing from that music, that undercurrent, that feeling, rhythm.

PAUL V.: I thought *Strays* was a really good record. I really liked it and I feel if that record was made by a new band that had no history, it probably would have been much bigger, but it was held up to the scrutiny of *Ritual* and *Nothing's Shocking*. There were some really good songs that could have been bigger hits, like "The Price I Pay," "Superhero." Compared to everything else out there I thought it was a contender. Thank God, it wasn't another fucking rap/rock record like Limp Bizkit or Linkin Park. I was glad that it was a really sonic, wet, big rock record, which there's not that many of these days.

MARTYN LE NOBLE: We went to Japan and played the Fiji Festival and did interviews where Perry had me answer questions about the future of Jane's Addiction. After the show Perry looked pissed off so I asked him, "Perry is there anything wrong? Is there anything I can do to help?" He said, "Yeah, as a matter of fact there is, it's just not working out with you, you're fired. Everything you play sounds like shit. There's nothing but feedback coming from your side of the stage." It was just ridiculous because I'm a bass player. There's no such thing as feedback coming from a bass amp. He goes, "Nothing you come up with we like. You're a horrible bass player!"

CHRIS CHANEY (Martyn's replacement): Martyn Le Noble is a great bass player, one of the best there is. I've heard everything he did on the Porno records and I think he's great, an extremely accomplished, creative player.

MARTYN LE NOBLE: I was stunned. I felt like somebody had punched me in the gut. Never saw it coming. I don't even know if he knew he was going to fire me. Up until he got the last glass of wine, I don't think he really knew what he was going to do. He had a bad show and it was everyone else's fault. He wanted to kill the keyboard player. During the show he was like "I want to kill that fucker." And I was like, "Why?" We got into a little scuffle over that. The next person was me.

CHRIS CHANEY: I get called to do a lot of rock records, and some pop stuff. I did records with Carly Simon, I did something with Chrissie Hynde and the Pretenders, a Celine Dion single even. It's not always totally where I'm coming from, but I'm a pretty diverse player who gets called in to play the bass. I did Andrew W.K.'s record. I did the last two Rob Zombie records, The Goo Goo Dolls, Monster Magnet. I did a record for Tommy Lee's Methods of Mayhem—that's where I first met Perk. I did the record, and we needed a drummer to play live cuz Tommy's the front guy. Perkins wanted to do it and Tom's like, "Man, Perkins? Dude, that's awesome!" One day Perk called me out of the

Millenial family man Perry moderating at home.
(John Eder)

blue and said, "Can you come do these shows in Europe with Jane's?"
And, "We're going to do some recording."

MARTYN LE NOBLE: Perry and Bob (Ezrin) replaced all my bass parts on
Strays. Perry was saying everything I played sounded like shit, but then
they had the new guy pretty much play exactly my parts, maybe a couple
of little changes, so I guess they couldn't have been that shitty. I went
bankrupt overnight because they hadn't been paying me. They were paying a guitar tech $1,500 a week and paying me $3,000 a month.

PERRY FARRELL: I'm not a guy who believes in 100 percent abstinence
unless you want to give a blessing. I've offered up certain chemicals as a
sacrifice, but that's mysticism. I still drink and smoke [marijuana]. But I
moderate. I would never be drunk when I have to take care of my kid.

MARTYN LE NOBLE: I was like, "I have *two* kids, I've been writing, recording, touring in good faith, and now you fire me, how dare you?" I never
got the retroactive money they'd promised. I had to give up my house, I
couldn't pay child support so my daughter and ex-wife had to move to
the East Coast and I never even got a phone call from the guy ever.

BOB EZRIN: Let's say they [were] pretty well drug-free [during the *Strays*
sessions].

CARMEN AND DAVE

"Carmen Electra's Aerobic Striptease teaches how to perform a lap dance. Strippers have the best bodies; they dance all night. If you take some of those moves, combine it with some fitness, you'll boost your self-confidence, feel sexy, and get an amazing workout."

FROM CARMEN'S DVD SERIES

DAVE NAVARRO [to Alan di Perna in '96]: I don't feel like selling myself. I'm not really into that. It's one thing to be in this band; it's like a huge machine. But when it comes down to my own personal feelings, I don't want to try and turn a buck on that.[148]

BRYAN RABIN: Carmen and Dave sent out a wedding announcement with the two of them lying naked next to a headstone that said, "till death do us part" . . . they got married on camera as the finale to an MTV reality show.

CARMEN ELECTRA: Life is not worth living unless there's a camera around.

JOHNNY NAVARRO: Brandt Mayfield was cutting my hair at his shop one day and he goes, "Johnny, Carmen Electra wants to meet your cousin." I go, "Really?" He goes, "Yeah, I cut her hair and she mentioned she thought Dave Navarro was really hot. I said, 'Really, I know his cousin.' She said, 'Can you set something up?' He goes to me, 'She's really sweet, really nice, really down to earth. You'd be surprised. Kind of like Dave himself.'" I called Dave and said, "Carmen Electra wants to meet you." He's like, "Dude, I don't think so . . . Carmen Electra? Too weird. I don't see it happening." At the time Carmen and Rodman were constantly in the media glare. A month goes by—my hair grows really fast—I go see Brandt again. I'm like, "Sorry to be the bearer . . . he's kind of just not into it, dude. Doesn't think it's much of a fit and he's coming out of something else anyway. I don't think so." Another month goes. Time for another trim. Brandt says, "Dude, Carmen really, really wants to meet your cousin. I'm telling you she's really sweet. I'm never wrong about these things. She's not the way she seems in public when you get close." I felt she was aggressively pursuing Dave rather than Brandt acting on his own persistence. I told Dave, "Brandt says she's really cool and I trust his opinion. He's totally convinced you'll make a good couple. You guys should at least meet."

Dave's like, "Dude, remember when we heard about Shannon Doherty calling her agent to tell Eddie Vedder's manager that she wanted to meet him?" I'm like, "Yeah?" He goes, "Remember how we thought that was kind of creepy? Shannon doesn't know Eddie Vedder from a fucking airport stranger. All she knows is what she sees on TV and videos and she uses her Hollywood power to arrange a date. That's kind of creepy, dude. All this chick knows [about me] is what she sees on TV. Sorry, it's just not gonna happen." So I go in again to see Brandt and give him the final, definitive no. More time passes—we're at like nine months now—and Brandt does it *again!* He goes, "Dude, whatever . . . I know you said Dave's not into it but Carmen still wants to meet him." I went back again, "Dave, Carmen's not letting go of this, she really wants to fucking meet you." He said, "I know, dude, I just heard this from another set of friends that are friends of hers. What do I fucking do? What would we even talk about?" I go, "Dude, people that look at you and your fucking boas and shit and dressing up like a chick in gowns and things, and doing drugs and doing what you do, is that really you?" He's like, "True, I'm not really what I look like, am I?"

Two weeks later, me and this other dude and Dave are playing poker and there's a call on his cell phone and he's like, "Dude, it's a fucking friend of Carmen's right now and they're all together and they want me to come down and meet her. Should I go?" "Fuck yes, what's wrong with you?" Cool as fucking Christmas, he's like, "You know what, I'm a little busy right now, how about tomorrow night at 9:00 at Jones, I'll come say hi." Like that, so fucking cold, ice cold. After he gets off the phone we're like high-fiving and shit, "Yes! This is the *shit!*" He went and met her the next night with five of her friends at Jones and they've been together ever since. That was four years ago [as of spring 2005].

They went to see *Requiem for a Dream,* not really the best first date choice of a film. They got really fast and furious and hot and heavy right away. They have this incredible relationship. He can say anything around her, do anything around her.

They'd been together about a year when Carmen called me wanting to know what was the absolute best birthday gift she could get him. I was like this and that and this and she was like, "I was thinking a Grand National." She's thinking like a dope '85–'87 Buick, and I'm shooting way down here, like a fucking cashmere sweater! I thought, fuck, this woman is playing for keeps. They had this great party for him at the Standard, they're getting ready to go home, we're all standing there and she goes, "Here, baby," and the valet hands him the keys and they roll out this fucking National. The look on his face and I knew they were going to get married.

DAVE NAVARRO: I'm looking forward to starting a family, having a child, having a stable home. I really hope so with Carmen. She has been an amazing, grounding element in my life, and is probably the most honest and caring person I've ever been with. Her public perception versus the way she is at home is such a night and day thing. She brings all-positive energy into my life, and I've changed spiritually as a result of our relationship.

JOHNNY NAVARRO: Dave relapsed again during 2002 and almost died. Dave and Carmen came to my family's Thanksgiving gathering—he was completely loaded and after they leave they're all looking at me for some fucking explanation. As ice cold as this sounds right now, I had to say. "You have to come to terms with the fact that he might not make it this time. Dave might not make it back, Dave might *die*." No one wants to hear that. Somebody had to warn them that catastrophe was looking imminent. Our family went through hell. Dave has a knack of really going off the deep end. He went so far out this time even I couldn't deal with him and I'd always been able to deal with him, no matter how crazy things got. This time, I don't even know this guy.

BRYAN RABIN: Dave Navarro is a gentleman absolutely devoted to Carmen. I think that their adulation of each other is probably what they're both most concerned about right now, the creation of their image and the creation of who they are to the public. They're so deeply in love with the way they look to each other. The most narcissistic couple I've seen in my life. They're both insanely beautiful. It's a rock 'n' roll fairy tale. She's the ultimate rock babe. He's the ultimate rock star archetype. She's larger than life, and contrary to public opinion, she is sharp as a tack, a very smart girl. And Dave's a very smart guy.

DAVE NAVARRO: I'm totally cynical and self-centered. I don't care about burning children in Africa. I care about how my hair looks.[149]

JOHNNY NAVARRO: Carmen had had it after a couple of months of Dave's using. Nobody knew what to do. Finally, she gives him the ultimatum, "I stood by you for a lot of this, but if you don't get your fucking shit together, I'm leavin' you. I mean it." No one had ever given Dave an ultimatum. He was like this panicky fucking child running around. He called me up and said, "Dude, I want to get clean, take me to treatment."

PERRY FARRELL: Life for some people is like a bad NA meeting that never stops. It's never been my way. I mean, god bless people, if they need help they should go get help. I like to get off the subject because if you talk about coke with me too much it only makes me want to do it all the more.

JOHNNY NAVARRO: I picked Dave up on New Year's Eve [2002–2003], checked him in to Brockman, but first we made a little stop. Halfway there he remembers he left some dope in his house. He goes, "Dude, I've got to do something." I go, "No deals, David!" He said, "If I leave that there, I won't stay clean." I go, "Fine, but if we go back, you have to stay at Brockman for one solid week." He goes, "OK" so we go back and he does his fucking last fix and then I finally get him checked in. He stayed twenty-eight days. He came out and that's it, he's stuck ever since.

DAVE NAVARRO: Carmen stuck by me through some really major experiences and I'm really grateful that I met her.

JOHNNY NAVARRO: Dave also got on meds, anti-depressants, and that changed his life. It's hard to imagine that in all these years, no one had thought to simply prescribe anti-depressants for the guy.

MIKE STEWART: David's everywhere now. You can't turn on a TV channel without seeing him.

PERRY AND ETTY

PERRY FARRELL: My wife [Etty] says, "People are more interested in the terrible things of your life than the things that brought you joy or have done well for you." There's so many amazing things in my personal life, my wife and my child, but unfortunately they're maybe not as interesting to people that are just focused on shit. We have the best time. We're a happening family. I want to mention Etty because I love her and it bugs her that she's a good thing in my life and people aren't really fixated on her. But I guess that's human nature. I tell her my ambitions now are focused on the environment and what I can do to turn the world toward hydrogen energy or alternative fuels—bigger, more adult things. My father got to see me perform a few times before he passed away. I used to whip my cock out all the time and it was always like, "Fuck the world, that's how it goes." So one night, there's my dad, and it's the first time he's gonna see me and I'm thinking, "Am I gonna shy away from this now or am I gonna just do my thing?" And I said, "Man, I gotta do it." So out goes my cock and I'm rockin' out and I put on a really energetic performance, and after I get offstage, I see my dad come flying at me with a towel and he put it around me because I was sopping wet. He wasn't trying to hide my nakedness. He was putting the towel around me because he didn't want me to catch cold. But I've changed. I don't think people would want to see me whip my dick out anymore. . . .

DAVE NAVARRO (website posting): Sometimes things just don't work out. [Jane's Addiction] has broken up and rejoined roughly four times over the years. Perhaps that should shed some light as to where we are now. We really don't know. We do know that we really gave it everything we had this time and made a really great record after many years of silence.

STEPHEN PERKINS: Playing music with friends always came first . . . and after nearly twenty years people's perspectives and values change. Since splitting with Jane's, Dave and I have rediscovered and reconsolidated our childhood friendship, and we're playing together again and writing songs every day with Steve Isaacs. I spent six years with Jane's and six with Porno for Pyros. I spent a lot of time working with Perry . . . all I hope and pray for is that our legacy will be decided by the songs we wrote and sang together with joy and that the sound and soul of the music we created together will live on . . . long after all of us are gone. . . .

ACKNOWLEDGMENTS

This book's text was birthed in early '03 when New York playwright-rock journalist-comedy spiel writer-author Marc Spitz (my collaborator on previous West Coast glam-punk spew) approached me about an assignment to assemble an oral history of Jane's Addiction for a cover story for *Spin*, where he labors as a senior editorial staffer and columnist.

I am therefore forever indebted to Spitz and his formidable Supreme Team colleagues at *Spin:* Sia Michel, Charles Aaron, Lisa Corson, Caryn Ganz and Jeanann Pannasch, with help by Anna Maria Andriotis, Andy Downing, and Amanda Petrusich. They helped shape the earliest version of this text, which originally ran in August 2003.

My eternal groveling thanks are also due the following pop music and culture reporters/editors/publishers from whom I heisted previously published materials. You're the glue that helps hold this book together once it passed from being an authorized project. I owe you all dins 'n' drinks (for two) when in L.A. at a cool C-list restaurant of your choice. To whoever I screw up and omit, you get a fancy dessert out of it, too, and as many drinks as you want.

Laurence Livermore and Al Kowaleski *(Flipside)*, Barney Hoskins (www.rocksbackpages.com), Sonny Harris (www.xiola.org), Dean Kuipers *(Spin, L.A. Times)*, Alan di Perna *(Guitar World)*, Bruce S. L. Duff *(BAM)*, Steve Appleford *(Rolling Stone, L.A. Times)*, Jay Babcock *(L.A. Weekly, Arthur)*, Simon Reynolds *(Melody Maker* [U.K.], *New York Times)*, Mat Snow *(Q)*, Neil Strauss *(Regan Books, New York Times)*, Bruce Kalberg *(No Mag)*, Bill Crandall *(BAM, Rolling Stone)*, Andrew Wallenstein *(The Forward, Hollywood Reporter)*, Dave Navarro (Regan Books), Karen Schoemer *(Newsweek)*, Roy Trakin *(BAM, HITS* magazines), Joe Gore *(Guitar Player* magazine), Steve Hochman *(L.A. Times)*, Jeff Spurrier *(L.A. Times)*, Dee McLaughlin (www.virginmega.com), Mike Ross *(Edmonton Sun)*, Brian Warner/Marilyn Manson (Regan Books), Darby *(Ben Is Dead)*, Leon Bing *(L.A. Weekly)*.

My chief concern was assembling a rock bio that's entertaining as well as informative. Dave: I kept the ransacking of your book down to a legal minimum. I needed your pearls of wisdom to keep the story bumpin' along. So dude, in return, let me now shamelessly plug your book, as required by your publisher:

Don't Try This at Home (New York: ReganBooks/Harper Collins, 2004). And here's the ISBN, 0-06-039368-8, also required by your publisher. Peace. Out.

APRIL 2005

NOTES

1. Steve Appleford, "Get Happy! Perry Farrell Finds Nirvana on the Way to Lollapalooza '95 and the New LP," *Rolling Stone*, 8.24.95.

2. Jay Babcock, "Perry Farrell's Musical Mystery Tour: The Hedonist at 42," *L.A. Weekly* cover 9.7.01.

3. Mat Snow, "Jane's Addiction," *Q* magazine, 6.95.

4. Ibid.

5. Bruce Kalberg, *No Mag* (defunct artzine), circa Fall 1984.

6. Babcock.

7. Bill Crandall, "Jane's Addiction's *SNL* Appearance Will Mark the Band's Largest Ever Audience," *BAM*, #522, 11.21.97.

8. Excerpted from Dave Navarro and Neil Strauss, *Don't Try This at Home* (New York: Regan Books/HarperCollins, 2004).

9. Marc Spitz, "Jane's Addiction: The Dance of Decadence. 18 Years of Crazy Sex, Hard Drugs, Lollapalooza, Drama & Visionary Music," *Spin* cover, 8.03, pp 68–84.

10. Ibid.

11. Ibid.

12. Ibid.

13. Ibid.

14. Navarro and Strauss.

15. Ibid.

16. Ibid.

17. Alan di Perna, "Anarchy in the USA," *Guitar World,* circa 11.91.

18. Navarro and Strauss.

19. Joe Gore, "Inside the Peppermill," *Guitar Player,* 4.95.

20. Navarro and Strauss.

21. Karen Schoemer, "The New Allure of Heroin," *Newsweek*, 8.26.96.

22. Ibid.

23. Navarro and Strauss.

24. Gore.

25. Navarro and Strauss.

26. Alan di Perna, "Beyond Addiction," *Guitar World*, 2.94.

27. Spitz.

28. Roy Trakin, "Jane's Addiction: Addiction by Subtraction," *BAM*, #347, 11.30.90. Profile and interview.

29. Di Perna, "Beyond Addiction."

30. Snow.

31. Ibid.

32. Ibid.

33. Babcock.

34. Bruce "Screamin' Lord" Duff, "In Deep with Jane's Addiction. Rad Rockers Make Big Splash," *Music Connection* magazine cover, 5.18.87, pp. 14–15.

35. Ibid.

36. Lawrence Livermore and Al Kowaleski, *Flipside* fanzine #52 Spring 1987. Excerpted in its entirety by consent.

37. Di Perna, "Beyond Addiction."

38. Ibid.

39. Livermore and Kowaleski.

40. Spitz.

41. Ibid.

42. Ibid.

43. Ibid.

44. Ibid.

45. Steve Hochman and Jeff Spurrier, "Renaissance After Hours," *L.A. Times* Calendar Section, 4.5.87, pp 64–65.

46. Spitz.

47. Schoemer.

48. Ibid.

49. Trakin.

50. Dean Kuipers, "Cashing In," *Spin,* 6.91.

51. Ibid.

52. Snow.

53. Trakin.

54. Duff.

55. Alan di Perna, "Red Hot & Bothered," *Guitar World*, 3.96.

56. Babcock.

57. Ibid.

58. Spitz.

59. Ibid.

60. Ibid.

61. Ibid.

62. Ibid.

63. Ibid.

64. Navarro and Strauss.

65. Snow.

66. Spitz.

67. Ibid.

68. Snow.

69. Kuipers.

70. Spitz.

71. Ibid.

72. Marilyn Manson and Neil Strauss, *The Long Hard Road from Hell* (New York: ReganBooks/HarperCollins, 1998).

73. Spitz.

74. Di Perna, "Red Hot & Bothered."

75. Spitz.

76. Ibid.

77. Ibid.

78. Ibid.

79. Navarro and Strauss.

80. Ibid.

81. Spitz.

82. Jennifer Brannon, excerpted from *Ben Is Dead* (defunct fanzine; see www.benisdead.com).

83. Excerpted from *Ben Is Dead* fanzine.

84. Spitz.

85. Ibid.

86. Kuipers.

87. Spitz.

88. Snow.

89. "In Brief," *Rolling Stone*, circa 1990.

90. Spitz.

91. Snow.

92. Trakin.

93. Spitz.

94. Alan di Perna, "Shock Exchange," *Guitar World*, 11.97.

95. Spitz.

96. Ibid.

97. Simon Reynolds, "Jane's Addiction and Lollapalooza: A Woodstock for the Lost Generation," *New York Times*, 8.4.91.

98. Di Perna, "Red Hot & Bothered."

99. Spitz.

100. Di Perna, "Red Hot & Bothered."

101. "Yoko Ono & Perry Farrell Talk About Fame," *Mondo 2000* magazine #16, ca. 1996, pp. 90–97. With extra special thanks to RU Sirius, Heide Foley, and Yoko Ono.

102. Mike Ross, "Rejoining the Cult. Legendary Band Together Again, Promoting Strong Comeback Album," *Edmonton Sun,* 10.13.01.

103. Dee McLaughlin, "Exclusive Interview. The Cult: Still a Force to Be Reckoned With," www.virginmega.com 8.8.01.

104. Spitz.
105. Kuipers.
106. Reynolds.
107. Spitz.
108. Ibid.
109. Trakin.
110. Spitz.
111. Di Perna, "Red Hot & Bothered."
112. Spitz.
113. Di Perna, "Red Hot & Bothered."
114. Sirius, Foley, and Ono.
115. Spitz.
116. Ibid.
117. Ibid.
118. Ibid.
119. Ibid.
120. Ibid.
121. Ibid.
122. Ibid.
123. Ibid.
124. Di Perna, "Red Hot & Bothered."
125. Navarro and Straus.
126. Di Perna, "Red Hot & Bothered."
127. Ibid.
128. Ibid.
129. Ibid.
130. Navarro and Strauss.
131. Sirius, Foley, and Ono.
132. Spitz.
133. Crandall.
134. Babcock.
135. Crandall.
136. Di Perna, "Red Hot & Bothered."
137. Reynolds.
138. Manson and Strauss.
139. Sirius, Foley, and Ono.
140. Snow.
141. Ibid.

142. Andrew Wallenstein, "Jane's Addiction Frontman Discovers His Roots," *Forward* magazine, 3.19.99.
143. Ibid.
144. Kuipers.
145. Wallenstein.
146. Ibid.
147. Spitz.
148. Di Perna, "Red Hot & Bothered."
149. Navarro and Strauss.

INDEX